Charles College, Catonsville, Maryland, the Catholic University of America, Harvard University and the University of Washington; he has taught at St. Edward's Seminary in Seattle, and at historic St. Mary's Seminary in Baltimore. His pastoral experience in many fields includes service in peace and war with the Navy and Marine Corps. He is presently Catholic chaplain at the U. S. Navy Postgraduate School in Monterey, California.

"Reverend Dr. Edward Cronan has made a very important contribution in this work to sound and constructive thought about basic religious and social problems. He has brought a brilliant mind to the service of Thomism in its task of applying old truth to the relief of modern intellectual confusion. He deserves special recognition for *The Dignity of the Human Person* because it is both simple and profound."—Dr. Ignatius Smith, Dean, School of Philosophy, The Catholic University of America.

"At a time when the enemies of our country from without and critics from within are prone to question basic concepts with respect to the dignity of man, it is a pleasure for me to commend Chaplain Cronan's book to thoughtful readers. It is a succinct and clear effort to emphasize the importance of man's dignity in the light of God's image. Its careful reading will be a rewarding experience for those of us in the Armed Forces who will recognize its profound implications." —Rear Admiral Edward B. Harp, Jr., Chief of Chaplains, United States Navy.

The Dignity of the Human Person

Nihil Obstat:

IGNATIUS SMITH, O.P.,
CENSOR DEPUTATUS

Imprimatur:

MOST REV. PATRICK A. O'BOYLE,
ARCHBISHOP OF WASHINGTON.
APRIL 18, 1950.

THE
DIGNITY OF THE
HUMAN PERSON

by

Edward P. Cronan

With a Foreword by

HIS EMINENCE FRANCIS CARDINAL SPELLMAN

PHILOSOPHICAL LIBRARY
NEW YORK

To
Dr. Ignatius Smith, O.P.

Foreword

AN age which has seen in swift and shocking succession the incredible horrors of Belsen and Dachau, the brutal mass-killings in Katyn Forest and the devilish brainwashing of millions by their Communist captors, can afford to linger long and reflectively over this volume by Father Edward P. Cronan. Its theme, "The Dignity of the Human Person," could scarcely be stressed at a more opportune time. For no century has witnessed a more widespread, more cunning or more relentless and ruthless attack against those twin citadels of human personality—the mind and the will—than this century which is ours.

The beginnings of that attack were not in our times, but we have seen the latest ravages and they haunt our waking moments and even torment us in our sleep. Man, once acclaimed as little less than the angels, now, in a large part of the world, wears only the pitiful look of the hunted animal. Deprived of his freedoms, stripped of his rights, harried and hounded in his private and personal life, he can no longer feel safe within his own home. He is subjected to an enslavement of personality, so total, so complete, as to be unequalled in any period of history. It is the culmination of that vain and pretentious humanism which attempted to seal man off from God and make the creature, instead of the Creator, the measure of all things.

Father Cronan's book offers a correction to that false humanism which would isolate man from the Source of his existence, the Source of his rights. It helps us to identify, to understand and to evaluate the true basis of human dignity.

This book with its carefully and closely reasoned exposition of the dignity of man merits attentive reading and study because of its essential importance and its urgency in our troubled times.

✠ F. CARDINAL SPELLMAN

Contents

Contents

ABBREVIATIONS

Summa Theologica . . .	I, q. 1, a. 1, ad 1 (or) S.T., I, q. 1, a. 1, ad 1.
Summa Contra Gentiles . .	*C.G.*, I, c. 1.
In IV Libros Sententiarum .	I *Sent.*, d. 1, a. 1.
Commentaria in Aristolis .	I *Meta.*, I *Eth., De Anima, Polit.*
De Regimine Principum . .	*De Reg. Princp.*
De Veritate	*De Ver.*
De Potentia	*De Pot.*
Compendium Theologiae .	*Comp. Theol.*
Lectura super Johannem .	*In Evang. Joan.*
Super Primam Epistolam Pauli	*I ad Cor.*
De Genesi ad Litteram . .	*De Gen. ad Lit.*
De Diversis Quaestionibus .	*De Diver. Quaest.*
De Trinitate	*De Trin.*
Sermones	*Serm.*

Introduction

OURS is the world of "The Bomb." Yet by itself, a bomb is no hurt nor harm nor help. Danger is born only from those who bomb. So this book evaluates not the product, but the producers. One hopes it is more in line with full facts and actual human nature and life than some dramatic *Weltanschauungen* which have been alluring men toward the "solution" of existing crises by theories validly holding on to life only as fantasies and fads. The angle of vision in this book and the depth of digging do not make the easiest reading. We think the topic is *the* central question today. But there is only one way of handling a deep truth: *deeply*.

The treatment will seem to many perhaps one-sided. The original sources used are almost exclusively Thomistic. This adherence shows no intention, and we hope offers no evidence, of that taboo, "authoritarianism." Investigation has convinced us that no other sources, particularly and regrettably contemporary thinkers, have treated this current problem in so thorough and satisfying a manner. Too much current writing in this connection has been only a psychological study of a modern mood. Or it grew too rhetorical for the clear and solid thinking which alone can lead to any solution of today's personal and social crisis. By now it should have been burned into our "progressive" minds that we need learn little new; we need to remind ourselves of what men once knew and we have forgotten too often for our own comfort.

This analysis intends to point out the natural and permanent dignity of a human person. Its full aim is to show that the final *raison d'être* of that worth, is rooted in man's image-

relation to his God. The actual measuring of specific aims and
activities in life against this standard of the constituted dignity of man, is the onus we believe, of other fields. We purpose only to draw the profile lines of his bare status. Therein
we offer for all those same human affairs and decisions, an
intrinsic and invariable, and therefore a primary and valid,
standard of measurement.

This treatment never intends to be any analysis of *completed* man as he actually and historically is when re-created
and elevated by the redemptive power of God. Our profile is
not untrue, but simply what is in men as the natural core of
them. The use of "image" is in no sense meant to be synonymous with that concept when used by theologians of a Person
of the Trinity, a field beyond philosophy, nor of man himself
in any supernatural condition. What we do say of man however, is in all cases still the *human* truth in him, still existentially real, the nature-nucleus of all he is.

Such a particular study of man is a critical necessity today.
"The question of the value of a human person is never a
'mere abstraction,' fit only to entertain philosophers. It is the
standard of measure for how men shall treat other men, and
as such *it is vital.*"[1] Ignorance of this proper picture of man,
or a distorted view of it, has caused policies and decisions in
current human affairs too often treasonable to man's person,
and tragic for his life. The gropings of sociologists and dip-
lomats too clearly evidence no *point de parti* of abiding worth,
nor measure nor goal which would give them the force of
direction or at least an equilibrium to stand the test of shift-
ing passions and viewpoints, or the resilience to abide against
discouragement and time. Some dark days one cannot decide
whether the present civilization is treating animals as men
or men as animals, either by an obvious exploitation or that
more subtle and camouflaged philanthropy or social welfare
or progress whose heart and technique are still impersonal.
Human persons ought to be the focus of world attention. But

1. Francis Sheed, *Communism and Man*, p. 137 and *passim*. For a most interesting, and magnificently carried out study of human spirits as they now
evolve "the American Dream," confer *Fortune*, "The Permanent Revolution,"
February, 1951.

none must seem an unfeeling bone of contention. Too many
key men act in men's affairs with a pathetic lack of *human*
intelligence. Or they handle humans as if they were subhuman units, a treatment identifying them with dogs, in wars
growing "colder" daily and more freezing to men's spirits.
Today's crisis is not of oil; it is human and personal. Facing
it, one must advertise for all men again, the "uselessness of
making a monkey out of man."

Stale repetition of "the dignity of man" seems a political
commonplace, and useless to repeat again. ". . . yet Western
culture is dying wherever it has been forgotten; for the
rational nature of man is the only conceivable foundation
for a rational system of ethics. Morality is essentially nor-
mality; for a rational being to behave without reason or
against it, is to behave not exactly as a beast, but as a beastly
man, which is worse: for it is proper that a beast act as a
beast, that is, according to its nature, but totally unfitting for
a man . . . because that means complete oblivion of his
own nature and hence final destruction. . . ."[2]

No digging for evidence of this is necessary today. Evidence slaps our face daily. So many competent authorities
have pointed it out so sharply that we do no more than allude
to the condition in passing. The tale of our times is already
told, and well. Our task is to remake the "myth of man" into
something real and create for him again the possibility of new
times. We are convinced that a clear accounting of man's
proper value, without the ancient mistake of exaggeration,
needs a sharp and *positive* picture of the position and worth
of the human person who is supreme in creation and the sole
visible image of his Creator. We cannot continue shouting
"the dignity of man" without knowledgeable bases or explanation or conviction. We must see what it rests on, and
therefore what kind of living can be lived, and what hopes we
may have, in a world where war has made life cold and man
impersonal and confused.

Men must, even in atomic times, regain for the atom split-
ters some unity of tensions, some stability of posture and

2. Etienne Gilson, *Unity of Philosophical Experience*, pp. 272–274.

stance between the undignified error of unbalancing all creation into a totally anthropocentric universe, and that crass
contradiction of evidence which would make impersonal or-
ganizations or mechanical marvels the subhuman centers
for a human world. As long as things are, they must be what
they are. And so men must learn to act. And so men must act
toward other men as they are and as they with inescapable
functioning are made to be—created copies of their Creator.

The Dignity of the Human Person

CHAPTER ONE

Object of Evaluation

THE most valuable item in the universe is man: he alone is the image of his Creator. He alone has divinity for his destiny. This truth and the conviction of its necessary application to life on life's Wednesdays and Thursdays, to life's traffic in our Western world and life's nakedness in the East, we think is an emergency topic today. But here it is useless to leap in *medias res*. The only satisfactory rediscovery of a lost fact and vision cannot be an easy hunt nor a "popularized" and tabloid and *ersatz* sketch of human roots and bases. Almost the essence of current confusion is that too many have tried too long the immediate and expedient, both as a procedure for movements and a measuring rod for evaluations. For a time most hurried in history, and problems so practical they ache, despite all the pressing tension someone must insist upon ultimates of value. Men must be made to be concerned with basic principles and terms as the only practical diagnostic standards and value-remedy. Men must know person and personality, dignity and goodness and perfection, participation and likeness, and the surest principles for applying such ultimate standards to the value-object, who is today's MAN, man still alive, but fearfully and briefly living with his destined futures already forgotten. This then we must know: *what* man is, how much he can be, and whether future and glory is possibly in him at all.

PERSON. It is extremely confusing today to try to distinguish the different connotations behind the common interchange in usage of the two words "person" and "personality." Although rarely used by the Schoolmen, the word "personality" then signified only the "*forma*," the pattern according to which the individual was made a "person."[1] But by now the word has accumulated a distinct psychological meaning, and it is much clearer usage to exclude "personality" from the metaphysical investigation of "person" and exclude "person" from the psychological determination of "personality." Both are necessary for the complete picture of the existing and operating human being, but signify distinct realities, however intimately related and unified in one center of attribution.

The etymology of the word "person" is only of antiquarian interest in most respects and is easily found in many printed sources, encyclopedic and otherwise.[2] But one conclusion from its etymology must be kept in mind: the beginnings of its use clearly show that it was then, and has continued to be, a term labeling not so much the nature of something as the dignity consequent upon its nature, much the same as one uses it still today in common speech in the phrase, "a real person" or in the derivative word "personage." The point is that philosophy borrowed it because, though one species of creature had much in common with others, it had such sole superiority that it required a "special name."[3] It indicated a unique dignity *of being* as it still does, while personality really points to the originality or uniqueness *of function* manifested by that personal being.

Scholastic philosophy has made no pretense of changing the definition of Boethius for person: "An individual substance of a rational nature."[4] Even when he breaks up the definition into its elements, Aquinas holds to the same essentials: substance, rational nature, individuation.[5] But since

---

1. *Summa Theologica*, I, q. 39, a. 3, ad 4.
2. James H. Hoban, *The Philosophy of Personality in the Thomistic Synthesis and in Contemporary Non-Scholastic Thought*. Washington: Catholic University of America Press, 1939, p. 25 ff.
Sister Joan Wolfe, *The Problem of Solidarism in St. Thomas*. Washington: Catholic University of America Press, 1938, p. 188–223.
3. I, q. 29, a. 1, c.; q. 29, a. 3, ad 2; I *Sent*. d. 23, q 1, a. 1.
4. Boethius: *De Duabus Naturis*, cap. 3 (PL 64, 1343).
5. I *Sent.*, d. 25, q. 1, a. 1.

many modern writers, non-scholastic as well as scholastic, have befogged the issue with explanations perhaps less philosophical than rhetorical, it is a far from useless repetition to clarify the meanings and relations of some of the components of that original and tested definition: nature, individuation and individuality, subsistence, and the consequent implications of independence and autonomy.

NATURE AND PERSON. A brief reminder of what has always been meant by "nature," will immediately lead one to see the relation of nature to person.[6] Personal individuation is not found in the notion of essence or nature, which defines only the species. Essence being "that by which a thing is what it is," must also be "that by which something acts" and in this way is called "nature." This consideration of essence under the nature-aspect is most fitting when talking of a person[7] where the concern is not the species finally, but the existent individual. Person is "*he who has* being," and nature is "that *by which* he has."[8] Humanity is a nature, and one human man is the person. Nature in this case, will be the clue to the specifying difference of man, and so the reason for his "special name" because it is *by* his nature that a person *is* a person, yet different from other subsistent substances.

INDIVIDUATION. Nature, *as such*, is but a universal, an essence; we can trace it as existing only in individuals, and the problem has always been: what makes individuals, individual? The understanding of this is important to the present topic, because the subject whose dignity we consider is supremely individual. Although the answer given by Thomas and the Thomists is perhaps not completely satisfactory, it has been needlessly complicated, both because the word used (*principium*) is not focused enough for clear ideas, and because there is some confusion between what is meant by "individuation" and what is today ordinarily meant by "indi-

6. It surely is not equated with "substance" among scholastics, as done by Mullin in *Essence and Operation*, Catholic University of America Press, 1941, p. 9. Nor yet unrelated, as Wolfe (*op. cit.*) accepts from Berdyaev.
7. I, q. 29, a. 1, ad 4; II *Phys.*, 192, b14; cf. *C.G.*, I, c. 21.
8. III, q. 17, a. 2, c.; and ad 1.

viduality."⁹ One must restrict individuation to only a numerical distinction, still a kind of repetitious monotony. "Individuality" is not only independence in existence, but an originality in unique degree, and currently is descriptive of all those habitual functionings which make an individual unique in his psychological personality. In this instance, we are now speaking only of an "individual," that is, a being divided off from all other beings, and not itself divisible into others. Individuation seems to be a question of matter and its division, and the attempted answer of Thomism is based both on the determined potentials of matter and its attribute of extension. But the crux of the question is in the word "principle." It must not here be identified with that which causally actualizes. Matter does not bring individuals into existence, or effect being. With the problem of individuation, when we speak of matter as a "principle," we speak of it more as a *sine qua non* condition, an *occasion* necessary for numerical distinction of individuals. Even then, it is necessary to keep clear the scholastic theory that it is not a mass of matter *in se* they are speaking of, but *the relation* of original matter-potential to activating essence. This means that in the case of man, though the life-principle needs matter-principle to make itself actually existent as an individual, matter does not give existence but is given it. Life is acquired, an individuated existence is attained, *in* a body, but not *from it*.¹⁰

9. Lengthier consideration of all modern psychologists mean by "individuality" (vide next section) and particularly all that Thomists mean by "matter" in their discussion, might have led Maritain not to claim St. Thomas as source for his theory on "individual and person."

10. This question is so tenuous and so often misunderstood, with such strange consequences for personal unity and value and social theories, that the clearest brief summaries of the Thomistic position are quoted, since they reduce matter to its proper and inferior level and show they never meant to point to actual matter or even prime matter as the causal source of an individual. This theory is particularly important now for a civilization which has got *engrossed* in matter.

. . . materia . . . necessario erit primum principium esse incommunicabilis. *De Princip. Individ.*, c. 3.

. . . anima non individuatur per materiam, ex qua sit, sed secundum habitudinem ad materiam, in qua est. *De Anima*, 6, ad 13; cf. *C.G.* II, c. 81.

Hoc autem esse terminatem, quamvis acquiratur animae in corpore, non

The individuated unit is not traceable causally to matter. It *needs* matter to exist as an individual; it exists *through* matter; but matter does not *cause* it.[11] The whole point and importance of this question here, is not just that our day has exaggerated the position and importance of matter, but given even this individual existence too exclusive a place in the question of "person," and run the danger of making "persons" out of dogs and trees. Even if one makes the body (in its ultimate source in "prime matter," not in an actual existent matter-mass) only the *conditio sine qua non* of individuation, and makes the soul the proximate cause under the Creator, but then still places the essence of person *only* in the subsistence of the composite, he still must find a specific difference for person in his rationality of soul, although obviously subsistence is necessary for *personal* reason. Matter enables rational nature to find a fit individual existence and be a person.

SUBSISTENCE. This makes the individual existential: the actualization of a nature into existence so that it is then an independent existing substance. Subsistence explains how the individual can exist independently and yet not exist essentially. Thomism teaches that if the existence which a particular created nature receives is to be incommunicable (as it supremely is in persons), belonging to one alone and unable to actualize another nature at the same time, it is

---

tamen ex corpore, nec per dependentiam ad corpus. I *Sent.*, d. 8, q. 5, a. 2, ad 6.

Notandum est quod principium individuationis animae humanae est ordo transcendentalis ad hoc corpus. Individuatio animae non pendet a corpore causaliter, sed quasi occasionaliter. Multiplicatio corporum est occasio in fieri animarum. Ordo transcendentalis ad hoc corpus est principium intrinsicum individuationis animae . . . hoc vero non est causa proprie dicta, sed conditio individuationis animae intellectivae necessaria, qua conditione desinente, desint individuatio. John of St. Thomas, *De Generatione*, q. 2; cf. *S.T.*, I, q. 29.

Gilson treats this question completely and clearly and gives true Thomistic doctrine in his *The Spirit of Medieval Philosophy*, p. 190 ff. He sees that: ". . . matter is precisely a principle and nothing else . . . the original and individual differences of each concrete being . . . are made possible by matter, but proceed from its form, which alone gives actuality . . . (cf. also, p. 465 ff.).

11. Jean Rosenberg, *The Principle of Individuation*. Catholic University of America Press, 1950.

necessary that this nature have been made "transferable" from an essence into an existing essence, by a power of separate actualization into existence. The nature of man, for instance, is complete with the union of body and soul, and then subsistence gives to that complete individual nature the power of appropriate existence independently to itself, if and when existence is offered to it by a Creator. And by that very actualizing power, once made actual in existence, subsistence makes that being incommunicable, one whose existence "is mine, and mine alone." This is important for the theme of the value of the human person, not only because person must be of an individual and independent existence, but because person *subsists* with a more excellent subsistence, and therefore got the "special name" of person. Just here many have leaned slightly askew in tracing the *rationale* of person, since they have made subsistence the sole essence of person, whereas Aquinas not only insists upon rationality too, but places its existential superiority to a *superior* manner of subsistence, not only incommunicable, but *dominating its own actions* and selecting them freely, by means of its reasoning power.[12] The union of body and soul effects a perfected existence which rationality makes a *personal* existence, distinguished from other subsistent composites who lack it. It is not the independent existence, but the reasoning nature which explains a person's mastery of operation and unique ability to be perfective of his own existing and operation to the extent of his own free choice.[13]

PERSONALITY. We shall contend later that not only does a distinctive dignity reside statically as it were, in the human person, but that such dignity is increased by the proper hu-

12. The subtleties and complexities of this subsistence problem, and the disagreements about it, and the complications added by the Incarnation, are well known. There is a complete and careful treatment in J. Gredt, *Elementa Philosophiae* (Friburg, 1937, vol. 2, p. 27 ff.). Explanation of the terms *suppositum* and *hypostasis* seem unnecessary here. For further reference, cf. *S.T.*, I, q. 29, a. 2, ad 1; III, q. 2, a. 2, c. Gilson, *op. cit.*, p. 200 ff.

13. III, q. 2, a. 3, c. Obviously, subsistence belonging to *this* nature, is necessary for person; without it, no "complete" nature is yet "person." Both are essential.

man functioning of that person's powers. This operational person, called "personality," is in some way the extension and increase of the person and can further perfect his mode of existence. So this dynamic side of person needs to be briefly defined to give a full picture of a living person. When one speaks of personality, it were better if he did not mean "what makes a person, a person" but meant all that patterned manifestation of the individual person and his powers which set him off from other individualities. Here particularly, metaphysical individuation should not be identified with this psychological "individuality," because that would be to miss the whole point of the more than numerical uniqueness of each individuality, and therefore miss perhaps the importance and possible destiny-level of *each* person who is dynamically evolving toward greater perfection. It is not just the numerically distinct unit who is the focal point of the universe, but this dynamically unique individuality. "Die Nature scheint Alles auf Individualität angelegt zu haben." (Goethe)

". . . the term individuality is first used to signify separateness and uniqueness of each human being. But mere separateness and uniqueness are not the psychologists' chief concern. Wasps and mice, trees and stones possess this elementary distinction. In addition . . . a human being displays a psychological individuality, an amazingly complex organization comprising his distinctive habits of thought, and his own peculiar philosophy of life. It is *the total manifold psycho-physical individuality which is personality.*"[14]

This question is intricate because it treats of the complex organizational activity of individuals who are themselves of infinite variety, and the modern preference for exclusively mathematical, statistical, and microscopic techniques, has tended to put the problem on the one level at which perhaps personality can least be analyzed and evaluated as anything

14. Gordon Allport, *Personality, a Psychological Interpretation.* Henry Holt, New York, 1937, p. 24. This is the most rounded and sensible study we have been able to find among modern psychologists, where too much of the writing has been to record measurements of what was too little defined before measuring.

far different from the "free" and almost personalized Heisenberg particles. At any rate, they all make it clear today that "personality" as universally accepted, is *not* a metaphysical concept, or reality in the meaning of substance, not saying *what* a man is, nor even *by what* he is, but *how* he is *such*, like the distinction between the old *quid* and *qualis*. Personality is an empirical concept. One might say that the "metaphysical person" is the foundation of the "empiriological person," the latter the operative manifestation of the former. Person is a permanent, static, immobile reality, incapable of greater or less; but empirically, as a personality, it is changing, dynamic, active, variable, significant of non-essential properties and differences which admit of constant development. Personality is to person as a perfecting process or a non-perfection is to an original power-datum. Since "person" is a word applied to but one kind of creature and equally to all of that species, it looks more to a species of individual than to one individual *as existing* in action and personal expansion. The latter aspect is the field of personality, which by observable data of his manner of operation, tells what kind of person, one person is.

Allport's definition of personality seems to us still the most satisfying:

"Personality is the dynamic organization within the individual, of those psychophysical systems that determine his unique adjustments to his environment."[15]

Those "psychophysical systems" mean the complex of habits, specific and general, all the attitudes, sentiments, dispositions, traits and groups of traits in a latent or active condition, including both mental and neural, patterned into a unified system. The word "determine" means that those systems of traits are not only passive receptives of extrinsic stimuli, but "determining tendencies" from within the individual which can select and control the very stimuli they react to. (One notices at once the similarity to the Schoolmen's potency and act theory.) So those systems then can "provoke" expres-

15. Allport, *op. cit.*, p. 44.

sive and adjustive acts, for which the external stimuli are the occasions or instruments. The individual himself then is the efficient cause of adjustment to environment, in large measure by a spontaneous and creative choosing activity of his own. Such a view is closely related to our thesis of the person as self-perfective, and autonomously so in great degree. Since personality is this resultant pattern of existence in an individual coming from the operation of all his own powers in their own autonomous creativity and in their reactions to all environmental influences, any explanation of "environment" should include *all* his relations. One must include not only the present and physical, but the accumulated and habitual experience of past psychical history, and the influence, through surrounding reflections, of the Creator, whose created personal images especially, are stimuli!

This definition takes care then, not only of all the causes and occasions of personality, and of its internal constitutive elements, but of its mysterious and binding integration into unity, that over-all oneness so observable in its diversity. It can be seen not only that personality takes in the whole personal activity, but that it is something distinct from and more than character; it is not only individualistic distinctiveness by reason of distinction of objects but by diverse manners of acting, mental, neural, and physical. It is some comprehensive attempt to express all we seem to mean by that total manifestation of the operating and existing individual person which is so woven into each person that we call it "personality." It is the person *who* acts, *by means of* his personality, *according to* his character. Character is measured by an end-pattern; personality is the color-picture of the total: material, end-value, process of development, and manner of operation.

If one gets some understanding of the intrinsic and extrinsic powers and influences which bring about the integrated or integrating whole of personality, he can see how intimately the principle of these operations is the person himself, and the operative personality is the blossoming of seed-powers within the person. These are often beyond observation and not traced back by many modern psychologists. But all seem now agreed that besides the immediately created spirituality, personality is basically and in a very appreciable measure the product of heredity, which transmits a neural-chemical combine into a temperament changed by the self as it develops, changed by innate endowment as individually given in inherent powers, and then by external influences of environment. Some reduce the "raw materials" of personality to three: physique, intelligence, and temperament, and these in themselves are never more than slightly altered by conditions subsequent to birth.[16] Here is that point of investigation where the scholastic principles of faculties and of potency and act or potential-energy and tendency, and its transferral into active operation, can take us beyond the observable and help to an understanding of these roots of personality. No modern has offered any explanation to take the place of these, and unless some such are used, the analysis never goes beyond the surface. Since person should not be equated with personality, the basis of the distinction will lie in the fact that existence, and its mode of action, are two really distinct actualities; therefore what they actualize must be distinct. The powers of a man, by which he operates, adhere to him and in him, but are not that which he is: operation is not in the genus of substance but flows from substances, in which there reside potentials which are the source-energies of operation. Since these energy-potentials determine the mode and limits of operation and are themselves determined by the disposition of the owning substance, then from observable actions, one can trace back through the patterns to an evaluation of the person himself.[17] As for the attempt to

16. Allport, *op. cit.*, p. 107. Allport is continually quoted not only because he seems most consonant with fact and philosophy, but because his work records and critically evaluates most of the other sources.

17. *De Anima*, a. 12; I–II, q. 55, a. 2, ad 1. It is interesting to notice that some modern psychologists are unconsciously approaching the theory of potency and actuality as they notice the strangely defined drives of natures. They speak of the tendency to completion of operation (i.e., to a specific "perfection") as a " 'conative perseveration' which can scarcely be denied: . . . the completion of the task itself has become a quasi-need with dynamic force of

categorize into primal drives, these inherent potentials in man which break out into operational personality, Allers is perhaps most successful when he suggests the primal and double driving power in humans; the will to power, and the will to community. The goal of the first is self-preservation and complete realization of self; of the latter, that further realization of self in others, called love. In speaking of these two deepseated nature-drives behind our varied potentials, Allers insists that there is always present a consideration of value and says that the old Aristotelian and Thomistic axiom that "every being tends toward the good," is justified by modern psychology.[18] This question of the springs of action ingrained in man, and of the directive force imposed upon them by their very nature and capabilities, and of man's conscious and rational choice of values before action, is of great importance for the study of personality and its development, because drive-potentials *must* operate, and they seek their completion in acts which will perfect personality and extend personal dignity. The understanding of this, while one observes the blindness to it in a mechanical, material, and impersonalized world, offers some insight into the roots of modern tensions and troubles, and hints at some of the solutions lying in man's own true natural operation.

And yet men with such common basic principles of operational life, are individually different. This must be taken into account because, despite the equal dignity residing in the substantial persons *qua* persons, there are differences in value

---

its own. . . ." Cf. I. Kendig, "Studies in Perseveration" (5 Parts), in *Jr. Psychol.* (1936), pp. 223–264.

Also Allport's statements: "Motives are always a kind of striving for some form of completion; they are *unresolved tensions,* and demand a 'closure' to activity under way . . . some things, as learning, never reach perfection, so lasting interests are permanent sources of discontent, and *from their incompleteness they derive forward impetus.*" *Op. cit.,* p. 205. Cf. also Allers' notation (in *Psychology of Character,* New York: Sheed and Ward, Ed. 1943. Tr. E. B. Strauss) about the concept of K. Bühler (*Die Krise der Psychologie,* Jena, 1928) who attaches great importance to a form of pleasure besides the conscious desire for satisfaction, an appetite he calls *Funktionslust,* or "pleasure in right function."

18. Allers, *op. cit.,* pp. 29–30. The whole work analyzes man from this dual viewpoint.

gained through development of personality, whose perfections accrue to the person who owns them, and to whom they must therefore be attributed. The scholastics have distinguished two bases of diversity in men: the different substantial and intrinsic perfections in soul and body, which is a metaphysical difference; and the resultant psychological differences arising from the diverse functional perfections of souls, as effected by varied collaborations with different bodily sense powers. The full working out of this doctrine is a thesis in itself, and scholastics are not all agreed upon it. We accept as reasonable the contention that there are between men not only functional and non-essential differences, but substantial differences. This traces a gradation in perfection among humans back to an original graded creation.[19] While nothing in the development of human persons is more important than the part played by the unique soul-powers, the functioning of the will and of the intellect is too broad a subject to be included here. The works already mentioned, and particularly the treatment of emotions and habits, and of the whole pattern of human makeup and operation of powers, set down in the *Summa Theologica,* both in I–II and II–II, make available a complete treatment, and give a much deeper understanding of these powers and neuro-psychic activity than modern treatments. They show what Allers has expressed very concisely and neatly: that man has in him in his rational side, and in the whole pyschosomatic tapestry of his personality, " 'value-potentials' . . . and can make them 'real,' can 'become what he is.' "[20] Other modern psychologists, too, are becoming aware of the part of implanted potentials, and

19. Cf.: II *Sent.*, d. 32; d. 21, a. 1, ad 2; I *Sent.*, d. 8, q. 5, a. 2, ad 6; I, q. 91, a. 3. Cf., Slavin, *op. cit.*, p. 80 ff. for a correct summary of the whole Thomistic position on this: ". . . one soul is more perfect than another by individual perfection because it is proportioned to a more perfect matter. . . . The soul has greater nobility because of its proportion to a better disposed body, which perfection it does not receive from the body or from its dependence on the body, but from Almighty God, Who shapes the soul He creates according to the body into which He infuses it. . . . When God intends to infuse a more perfect soul, He predisposes a more perfect body for it. . . ."
20. Allers, *op. cit.*, p. 59 ff.

their defined goals, and even of that final and total goal of the whole person[21] which has so much to do with personality integration. This integration of personality is a value-standard, and therefore important for the evaluation of personal dignity, because it grades the level of perfection achieved in the realization of personal existence-potentials, and therefore helps to measure personal worth. The forces against which it is achieved, and those with which it is attained, give an indication of how it is possible for a person to be extended through personality development, and Allport's idea of completed personality as a "balance of forces or tensions" is in line with the scholastic doctrine of the perfection of habits. The comparison of all this development to integration, with the Absolute Perfection which is God, is superbly synopsized by Allers:

"Man is not compounded of 'parts,' although he expresses himself on various levels and manifests various aspects. Such 'watertight-compartmentation,' and views that maintain that man is a summation of his parts, result from limited and discursive reasoning and from the practical necessity of considering the aspects of man one by one and one after the other. In reality the human person is a collection of contradictory factors and antagonistic forces under great tension from all sides. That which in the divine Being, God's *Ipsum esse,* may be regarded as a tensionless unity, appears in His creation as a unity of tensions . . . 'unity of tensions' (Przywara's phrase) is in fact, the essential structure of human personal existence . . ."[22]

Allport too, speaking of the completely realized personality which is integrated, speaks of the perfect actualization of the mature personality in the balanced attainment of the goals of two drives which seem opposite in direction, the one being immersion in autonomous interests which are the opposite of egocentric, the "capacity to lose oneself in the pursuit of ob-

21. Allport, *op. cit.,* p. 219 ff. Noteworthy are his references to the statistical studies of C. Bühler, in *Der Menschliche Lebenslauf als Psychologisches Problem* where it was found that successful life-histories each evidenced a characteristic *Bestimmung* and intention, as did suicides evidence the opposite.

22. Allers, *op. cit.,* pp. 123–124.

jectives not primarily referred to the self," and the embracing
of which constitutes an "extension of the self"; and the second
being that peculiar detachment of the mature person from
these interests, in surveying and evaluating his own preten-
sions in relation to his abilities, a kind of "ego-centered" insight into himself, in order to escape immersion in "self."[23]
In all these operations, the few best modern psychologists
agree with the scholastic doctrine that the reasoning power
which distinguishes the person, is the guiding and governing
factor in integrating the personality into the more perfect
actualization of its innate potentials. This so "extends the
person-self" that personal dignity is increased thereby, because between operations and the operating person, as between soul and body activity, there is what Slavin has happily styled "simulaction," because operations *belong* to the
person, and as *he* instigates and governs them, he in turn is
influenced and developed by them.

These things have been brought up in order to emphasize
the perfectibility of personality, which belongs to the person
and must be attributed to his credit. The evidence of that
perfectibility as achieved on different levels is a further
evaluation standard for the dignity of a person relative to his
own species of person. This perfectibility is beyond dispute
today,[24] and this dynamic aspect is only going to be further
proof that the original datum of person can be evaluated
higher than other substances, because such free and extensive perfectibility is no part of other individuals in the cosmos.
In fact, Allers has put it well when he says that the innate
and inescapable drive toward perfection or completion, which
is at the same time, an inherent power-potential for it, is the
very core energy of the whole fundamental movement we call
"life," which, *when completed* in the realization of those perfectible energies, *is* "perfected":

"Individual life . . . is nothing more than the *successive realization of all values inherent as potentialities.* The transformation of

23. Allport, *op. cit.*, p. 213 ff.
24. Allers, *op. cit.*, p. 17 ff., *et alibi;* Allport, *op. cit.*, p. 190 ff.

potentiality into act . . . is the essence and meaning of human life. I am convinced that the tension between what has been realized—granting the possibilities of a storehouse of values in the core of the person—that this *gradient of values* . . . provides the real motor power, the actual driving force by which the movement of life is maintained. When a man has ceaselessly realized all that there was of value-potentialities in the depths of his being, his life must come to a standstill. He must die. That is, I think, why so many saints die young . . . one says of such people that they were *früh vollendet*—'completed early.' "[25]

That is then, the human person and his perfectible personality, the whole operating unit we shall attempt to compare to other units of creation and then to the Creator, to evaluate according to what ultimate criteria the next chapter may find for dignity and goodness and perfection, and the immediate criterion of participation and image. Those standards may easily be applied to persons judging and evaluating causes by their effects, persons by their actions, "trees by their fruits."

25. Allers, *op. cit.*, p. 210.

CHAPTER TWO

Standards of Evaluation

SINCE this is a comparative study, whose field of comparison is the ordered universe and the reciprocal relations of its graded units, one must remember the essentials of "*relation*," that it is some link between two things, established by something identical in both.[1] And *order* is that relational arrangement we try to define by three essentials: the note of distinction between units, of prior and posterior relation, and that extrinsic common denominator used to relate the proportionated units on a common basis.[2] This study is investigating the proper arrangement of distinct creatures in the universe, under the common denominator of relative value. That is why we first hunt some absolute standard to be relative to, and through the explanation of terms now set forth, find that term whose definition shows it to be that absolute standard of dignity which can measure the relative.

DIGNITY. Dignity is a word for "worth," and a theory of dignity is a philosophy of value. Upon this topic, modern thinkers have written much that is characterized chiefly by an exaggerated relativism or subjectivism, which almost neutralizes the value of their very theories.[3] But in the Thomistic

---

1. I, q. 13, a. 7: ". . . secundum aliquid realiter conveniens utrique."

2. I *Sent.*, d. 20, q. 1, a. 3, ad 1; in *Physic.*, lib. 8, c. 3; in *Ethic*, lib. I, c. 1; *In Div. Nom.*, IV, 1; *De Pot.*, c. 7, q. 9 and q. 11; *S.T.*, I, q. 42, a. 3; II–II, a. 26, a. 1 (and Cajetan comm. hoc loco). Since the terms are fundamental to a relational and evaluational subject, understanding of "order," "absolute," and "relative" is essential. For full discussion of these questions, cf. *The Absolute and Relative in St. Thomas and Modern Philosophy*, Sister M. Camilla Cahill, Catholic University of America Press, 1939.

3. For brief survey of modern value theories, confer: Mullen, *Essence and Operation in St. Thomas and Modern Philosophies*, p. 58 ff.

synthesis, dignity or value is imbedded in substance, an objective reality distinct from, though related to, any subjective reaction to it. The honor due dignity does not lie in the object, but it is a reaction to some excellence in that object of honor.[4] Worth is rooted in the thing itself. Value points out something objectively existing in being, which is the object of an inescapable impulse of beings toward it. The mental judgment of dignity must be always a judgment founded on some objective reality for those who see the mind as an instrument of the real and not just of its own mentality: judgments of value *are* judgments of reality.[5] That is why it has always been recognized until recent times, that dignity or value is resident in an object, but constitutes for a subject a goal of natural drives springing from the intrinsic nature of beings, something which finally makes their source, also their goal. And yet it is true that the concept and reality of "value" or "worth" or "dignity," as such, is not in itself an ultimate. Objective though it be, it remains a term more expressive of the *relation* between object and subject, more connotive of the appreciation of what that value-something really is in itself. According to the Thomistic theory, that value-something, that dignity-basis in objects, which all beings honor and desire as "worth," is *goodness*.[6] Something is valuable in that it befits other natures and they have a natural drive toward it, and in all beings, that which causes this tendency is "goodness." It is goodness, existing in beings, which will explain dignity, its consequent.

GOODNESS. Objectively, goodness and being are one. But because we cannot grasp all that being means, they differ subjectively when we look at being as the basic attraction for everything. When we see that being lures all to it, we call it "goodness."[7] As such, being draws all things to it as their own goal of attainment or completion and its goodness then is the end-goal for all. Goodness is in all that is, substantial

4. I–II, q. 2, a. 2, c.; *C.G.*, III, c. 28.
5. Cf. Pierre Rousselot, *The Intellectualism of St. Thomas,* p. 9 ff.
6. III *Sent.*, d. 35, q. 1, a. 4.
7. I, q. 6, a. 3, c.; q. 5, a. 1, c.

and dependent being. Of course, the less limited a being, the less does it need superadded subsidiary being for perfectibility in operation, since that goodness is already attained in itself. And the more its goal of being is taken into itself, the more complete and therefore "good," is that being already. It is easily seen the direct bearing this may have on this thesis, since such a "better" being, with less limits, with a self-contained end, may be found only in man, who will then contain more goodness than others and more dignity.

The important point here, and really the essence of goodness, is that it is a relational aspect of being. Existent goodness, as we know it, is a reality entailing a two-fold relation: one to the field of force it creates for other existents, and another to some absolute above the more or less we meet in things. Because of this second relation, one must conclude that any evaluation of a created and therefore dependent reality such as person, can be made only in comparison with that good which is the all-inclusive reality. This is clear because what *has* some good, must derive it from that absolute which *is* goodness, the source of all else and the center of that field of force in being. This total focal point has tremendous significance, because it directs attention to the integrative and unified scale of relations among creatures in the cosmos, which finally find their source, and the balanced unity of their forces of attraction, in the same total good found partially but radically in all lesser beings and lesser goods.[8] It is because of this they have value, and value can then be equated with goodness, with the added implication of graded appreciation. And goodness is that very attraction which being exerts in itself, "that which all things aim at," because *it is,* and all must be pulled to be because they too *are.*[9] The whole truth of goodness lies there.

Yet, this definition of the good seems more descriptive of its effect than constitutive, and still has about it some odor of the *petitio principi.* What constitutes that desirableness of

8. Cf. Mullen, *op. cit.,* pp. 67–75. For full development, cf. *C.G.,* III, c. 22, with its sources and cross references.
9. Aristotle, I *Ethics,* I, 1, 1094a.

beings which we call goodness, in its essential and objective sense, is *perfection in being*. It is this perfection that pulls beings to beings and beings to being. Perfection makes the goodness of anything, and therefore everything, by very nature, is attracted to perfection, and anything is itself an attractive force in so far as it is perfect.[10] Goodness then is a term of perfection *and* relation. Its first relation we saw, is to absolute being, the totality of perfection and attraction. The other relation inevitably is in the field of attractive-force any relative being creates for other beings. There its perfection is a magnetism *perfective* of the attracted being in so far as it prompts or "magnetizes" the other being toward actualization into the greater actual perfection which the model-object has.[11] This essential goal-attraction radiating from being to being is the source of the principle that goodness "overflows itself," is "diffusive of itself," in the sense that being is *in itself* an attractive aura exciting all toward it as their ideal goal *to be*. This is the reason why all actual being is operative in some way, and why anything begins to be, since this magnetic aura is the force pulling an efficient cause into being an efficient cause, and producing being![12] The efficient cause is the influencing source of the beginning of something's perfection, but only the final cause or goal is the consummation and completion for the whole being. The efficient cause gives the *forma by which* a being expands toward final perfection, but only *in* its end-goal, the very reason for its existence, does that being attain perfection.[13] This "diffusion of itself" is not the effusion of the efficient cause, but is the creation by the perfected and attracting goal, of that disposition of attraction—for completion in the non-perfected. The end then, is the true measure of the whole goodness: an effect shares the goodness of the efficient cause only in likeness of form, but the perfect end indicates all the goodness something can be,

10. *C.G.*, I, c. 40; I, q. 5, a. 1.

11. *De Ver.*, q. 21, aa. 1 and 2: being as the goal of all beings constitutes therein, at the same time, the model to imitate, and so is not only good as a final cause, but as "formal."

12. I, q. 5, ad 1, and a. 4, ad 2; I *Sent.*, d. 34, q. 2.

13. *C.G.*, I, c. 40; III, c. 16.

because its attainment is the perfection to be swallowed whole by the whole being.[14] Goodness then, is simply actual being as it is essentially magnetic to a being, so that there is in all, a necessary attraction for it, which Thomistic philosophy calls an "appetency," a "universal tendency in all created things towards participated existence," a tendency identical with "every inclination of a being to its proper object."[15] That is why St. Thomas speaks of "convenientia" and "connaturalitas" and "coaptatio" in this connection. Something is attracted to being because it too *is*, and can more *be*, and so is inevitably drawn to more being as the near-vacuum to full air. Direction by God offers no violence. It is an attracted following of drives *within* nature, and toward a *like* nature.[16] So goodness is expressive of both that perfection of being *in se* and its perfectibility which is instigated by its attraction for being. Therefore, the ultimate worth of any reality such as a person, must be measured by its present perfection or possession of being, by its resultant perfectibility-potential, and by its closeness to that absolute perfection which is its essential and final and sole polarity. This is the dynamic basis of all properly *human* activity: *Agens agit simile sibi.*

But it must be measured too by the consequent to its attractive force, and that is its communicating ability. "Creation hungers, and creation receives." In causing being, efficient agents communicate goodness.[17] This is important to evaluation purposes because it is clear no possessing agent can communicate what he has not, and that he can communicate only in the measure he has.[18] The more good, the higher or more extensive the being of the agent source, the

14. *De Ver.*, q. 21, a. 1, ad 4; IV *Sent.*, d. 8, q. 1, a. 1, ad 1; *C.G.* I, c. 40; III, c. 6.

15. I, q. 78, a. 1, ad 3; *C.G.*, III, c. 16: "unumquodque autem si perfectione propria careat, in ipsum movetur." Cf. G. Gustafson, *The Theory of Natural Appetency*, p. 78 ff.; also, I. Smith, *Classification of Desires in St. Thomas*, p. 18 ff., and also Garrigou-Lagrange, "L'Attraction universelle" in *Philosophia Perennis* (Vol. II).

16. *De Ver.*, q. 22, a. 1; I–II, q. 8, a. 1; q. 40, a. 1, ad 3.

17. III, q. 1, a. 1, c.; IV *Sent.*, d. 46, q. 1, a. 1, c.

18. I, q. 19, a. 2.

greater communication.[19] This communication can pour out goodness in greater range[20] and bestow a higher type of being in so far as it can bestow, for instance, immaterial being, which is less limited and so is superior to material being; and it can give in a higher mode of communication in so far as a fuller being of a higher type, can communicate *freely*, and so communicate goodness not only by nature, but by conscious free will.[21] Finally, this communication of goodness, though it is perfective of and perfecting the recipient primarily, still reacts upon the communicating agent who is actualizing his faculties and so increasing being-goodness in himself, perfecting himself by bringing his powers into actual operation and so progressively transferring his own perfectibility into actual completion or perfection.[22] And since all this is increase in "perfection," it is clear that a full understanding of value and goodness depends upon understanding the real nature of that "perfection" which constitutes goodness objectively, and which can explain the relations brought about by perfection, explain *why* it is attractive, both with the perfectible and with the ultimate standard, absolute perfection. If behind dignity lies the good, which is perfection as an attractive force in being, then perfection will define dignity itself and we shall have found the final unassailable criterion for man's value.

PERFECTION. "Perfection" is a word for "complete." It has the meaning of "whole," "finished," "not lacking anything." Any mode of being is a perfection[23] but the emphasis of the word is upon the actual being, the completion or actualization which being finds in existence. The essential point is that perfection, in the Thomistic system, *defines* the actual ex-

19. I, q. 65, a. 3, c.; *C.G.*, III, c. 24; IV, c. 11.
20. *C.G.*, III, c. 24.
21. Cf. R. Garrigou-Lagrange, "The Fecundity of Being" in *Thomist*, II (1940). Cf. Sister Enid Smith, *Goodness of Being*, p. 91 ff., for interesting remarks on this fecundity of goodness of being in such fields as charity, and its perfective reaction upon the communicator.
22. I *Sent.*, d. 8, q. 3, a. 3; and I, q. 119, a. 2: ". . . est autem naturalis ordo, ut aliquid *gradatim* de potentia reducatur in actum . . . primum quodque est imperfectum et postea perficitur."
23. Garrigou-Lagrange, *God: His Existence and Nature*, vol. I, p. 309 ff.

istent, and is in fact its term of measurement: something is perfect just as far as it actually *is*.[24] Consequently, all created perfections finally hinge on fullness of actual being itself, on completeness in existence, because all perfections point to absolute existential perfection, complete, full-rounded existence with no lack and no further possibilities.[25] Insofar then as something actually exists, then to that extent is it *completed* in being, a measure identical with measure of perfection. The concept simply means that a thing *is*, means looking at being from the viewpoint of its actuality in existence. Because goodness is perfection and perfection is existential being, then *to be existing* is the primal perfection, the root constitution and explanation of the good, the ultimate significance of both concepts.[26] Then the absolute Perfection completely existing by essence, must be the source and measure of all partial existences which derive their being and existence, and measure their extent, against this total perfection of the whole.[27] Obviously, of the varying degrees of existence we observe, none of them *is* existence: "more" or "less" can be said only by measurement against a maximum. No being relatively existential therefore, can sufficiently explain itself, but must be finally explained by something beyond the relative: the fuller existence, or the completely full existence which contains all. This is existence itself essentially, who *IS*, and to whom are therefore necessarily related all existences, as the partial and potential to the totally actual.

Evidently here lies the final standard of value. Measured against this, we can see that something created will have value or dignity commensurate with perfection: he will be perfect in so far as he *is*, and simply because he is, and so will be *worth as much as he is*; the more something is, the better

---

24. I, q. 5, a. 1.
25. I, q. 4, a. 1, c., and ad 1; also a. 2, c; and I, q. 5, a. 3, c.
26. *C.G.*, I, c. 37: ". . . esse igitur in actu boni rationem constituit . . ."
27. *C.G.*, I, c. 31; I *Sent.*, d. 36, q. 2; *idem*, d. 35, *q.* 1, a. 1; I–II, q. 102, a. 1; *idem*, q. 106, a. 4; *Comp. Theol.*, c. 109; also I, q. 29, a. 3; I, q. 14, a. 6, c: "Propria autem natura uniuscuijusque consistit secundum quod per aliquem modum divinam perfectionem participat."

it is. Dignity is an existential value determined by estimating how much actual being something has, how completely one *is*.[28] Determining that, however, faces you with the problem of the one and the many. To bridge this gap between the essentially absolute one and the distinct many, one must give brief consideration to that method in logic and that process in reality which joins the two, because this relation is central to the explanation of our final aim, the measurement of man's dignity. And the full comprehension of the "image" in created perfections can best be understood only when it is seen to derive as a direct and necessary effect of that causal activity called participation.

PARTICIPATION. Participation is a word for "taking active part in." This process tries to explain how the one essential perfection is actually related to the many perfectibles. Being is verified in each relative existence, each in its own way and degree and each susceptible of more or less, because it *is*. Perfection in being is completion in actual existence, so something has perfection because it participates in existence, and in the measure it participates. Sharing in essential existence is the only way in which it can *be*. Clearly, created being can and does have existence only partially and not totally or essentially, because the proportioned limits of each nature determine the sharing, so that the less limited each existence is by its specific essence, the more it participates in that existence or perfection to which all that is must finally be traced, the illimitable whole.[29] Participation explains *how* beings become proportionately and intrinsically related to

28. Such ultimates deserve more space. For fuller treatment and bibliography, cf. J. B. Sullivan, *First Principles in Thought and Being*, Catholic University of America Press—1939; Sister M. Camilla Cahill, *Absolute and Relative in St. Thomas and Modern Philosophy*, Catholic University of America Press—1939; Sister Enid Smith, *Goodness of Being in Thomistic Philosophy and Contemp. Significance*, 1947; Gustaf J. Gustafson, *Theory of Natural Appetency in Thomas Aquinas*, Catholic University of America Press—1944; L. B. Geiger, O.P.: *La Participation*, Vrin, Paris, 1942, for comprehensive treatment of the following section in relation to these concepts; J. F. Anderson, *The Bond of Being, Essay on Analogy and Existence*, vide especially ch. 22, pp. 295–314.

29. I *Sent.*, d. 3, q. 1, a. 3; I, q. 4, a. 3.

absolute perfection, not just as inferior to superior in the
order of quality, but in the ontological causation behind the
order of perfection. Partial perfection means dependence in
being and must be traced to that independence in existence
from which it must causally originate and also be ordered as
to its perfect end.[30] Aquinas points out that in some way the
cause is in the effect, because the effect brought into being
by the cause, shares then in the being of the cause.[31] Efficient
and final causes are in the effect through their influencing
power: they excite and communicate activity; a formal cause
is intrinsically related to its effect, and communicates being,
because it puts into the effect the likeness of the cause either
according to what it was formed from, or toward which it is
formed. The last sense is called an exemplary cause, the
model after which the likeness is made.

Participation is the explanation of the receptive side of this
causal relation: the participation of limited being in that
being which is *a se* totally existing and causes all beings. The
end result of that producing cause is the likeness of its *forma*
in the thing produced, a copy necessarily there because relative beings participate with a limited sharing in essential and
complete existence. Nothing can attain actuality except by
sharing unlimited actuality proportionately, and what is
shared, is common to both.[32] Since total existence cannot be
"static," but essentially diffusive and communicative, finite
sharing of it is but absorbing the necessarily attractive emanations of infinite perfection-existence.[33] Participation then, is
being in a limited and proportionate state, what another is in
a greater or absolute state, and this necessarily means constituting a being by partial possession and in its own manner,

30. *De Anima*, a. 7; I, q. 42, a. 3; I *Sent.*, prol. The causal order is the Aristotelian emphasis, as its explanation by participation is Platonic.

31. I, q. 43, a. 3, c.: "Deus est in omnibus rebus per essentiam, potentiam,
atque praesentiam, *sicut causa in effectibus participantibus* . . ." I, q. 8,
a. 1; *De Pot.*, q. 3, a. 7.

32. I, q. 44, a. 1; a. 3, ad 2; *Quodl.*, 12, a. 5, c.; *C.G.*, I, c. 13; *In de Div.
Nom.*, c. 5, lect. 1; *De Pot.*, q. 3, a. 5, c.; *C.G.*, I, c. 40; and I, q. 75, a. 5,
ad 4: "omne participatum comparatur ad participans ut actus ejus. . . . Qua-
cumque forma creata per se subsistens ponatur, oportet quod participet esse."

33. Cf. Geiger, *op. cit.*, p. 240 ff.

in some likeness to another which possesses more of the same
existence, or has existence essentially and totally. Participation brings about the limited and inadequate imitation and
expression of superior existential perfection. Evidently, participation is in the participant, and it makes in the sharer a
likeness of the participated, not *e converso*. Participating
being receives the *forma* of the participated, either from the
very nature of the participated, or from that being-*forma*
existing originally in the intellect of the being participated
in,[34] an intelligible *forma* according to its nature. But the
extent to which multiple beings can partake of complete, illimitable existence depends upon the possibilities of participation itself, and then upon the limited potential of different
types of perfectible natures. Limited existents will differ by
the number of limited perfections they attain, by the superiority of any one perfection as a mode of existence, and
by the fullness of participation in any one or more: "there is
a kind of gradation among creatures, by which some manage
to share in more perfections, and more noble ones, and share
them even more fully."[35] And secondly, the extension and intensity of participation will be variously confined by the various finite capacities imposed upon different created beings
by their own limited natures, which will define their ability
to receive perfections in number, and kind, and intensity.
Each created species can share existence only in the manner and to the extent of its own nature, since it is each one's
nature which will determine the measure of its existence.[36]

34. I, q. 15, a. 1: "Agens autem non ageret propter formam nisi inquantum
similitudo formae est in ipso. Quod quidem contingit dupliciter. In quibus
enim agentibus praeexistit forma rei fiendae, *secundum esse naturale;* sicut
in his quae agunt per naturam; sicut homo generat hominem, ignis ignem. In
quibusdam vero, *secundum esse intelligibile;* sicut in his quae agunt per intellectum; sicut similitudo domus praeexistit in mente aedificatoris." Cf. also
C.G., II, c. 2.
35. I *Sent.,* d. 22, q. 1, a. 2: "In creaturis est quidam gradus secundum
quod quaedam quibusdam plures perfectiones et nobiliores a Deo consequuntur, et plenius participant." Participated perfections which involve in us,
imperfection, cannot be in God formally, of course, but only virtually.
36. I *Sent.,* d. 36, q. 2, a. 2; also d. 35, q. 1, a. 3; d. 8, q. 1, a. 2;
d. 17, q. 1, a. 1; and any number of *loci,* since this principle is basic in
Aquinas.

It is precisely this which makes the difference in the species of beings, and makes equality of species impossible: unequally determined natures allow only unequal participations in existential perfection, and therefore unequal perfections.[37]

The very word-meaning of "participation" makes evident the relation effected by this process activity. If that which emanates in the absolute and original, and that which is relative and anterior participates proportionately in the same reality, though in the manner only of its own nature, this divine perfection must be the exemplar of which all created perfections are the exemplifications. They must constitute a likeness of the original which has been communicated to them. The all-perfect is such a model in two ways: His ideas are intellectual exemplars of everything as the thing made must be first in the mind of the maker; and He is the communicating model in the likeness of the very nature, as good is the source and model of all goods.[38] As final and formal cause, they must push toward Him and in a measure, acquire Him; as efficient and formal cause, they share in Him who communicates His existential perfection to them in His likeness. He *is* totally what they *have* the partial likeness of because they *share* in it. The extent and mode differ; the identical perfection is one.[39] Perfection is the cause; caused participation is the method of "distribution," and limited images of the causing perfection are the created result. So the evidence and measure of perfection offered by goodness' image in a creature, is a valid proximate standard of that creature's value, a true indication of its share in total perfection.

LIKENESS. Likeness then is definitive of the end-result of participation. It is descriptive of a *fait accompli*, accomplished by that reciprocal process whereby out of the over-

---

37. *De Subst. Sep.*, c. 10.

38. I *Sent.*, d. 19, q. 5, a. 2; d. 8, a. 3; d. 43, q. 1, a. 1; d. 22, q. 1, a. 2; d. 42, q. 1, a. 2; *C.G.*, II, c. 2; *C.G.*, III, c. 18 and 19: . . . "Deus sit finis rerum . . . hoc solo modo quia ipse rebus acquiritur. Ex hoc autem quod acquirunt divinam bonitatem res creatae, similes Deo constituuntur. Si igitur res omnes in Deum sicut in ultimam finem, tendunt ut ipsius bonitatem consequantur, sequitur quod ultima rerum finis sit assimilari Deo."

39. I, q. 6, a. 4; cf. Geiger, *op. cit.*, p. 240, for extensive treatment of this.

flowing total He is, God communicates perfections in limited ways, and limited creatures participate in his unlimited existence, which is perfection, which is goodness. Therefore, any progress toward the proper perfection of its own nature, is at once a sharpening of the divine image because it is greater sharing in total perfection. The more something shares a common thing, the more is it like.[40] It is this likeness then which validly stamps and measures any creature in its grade of perfection. Obviously, it cannot be *ad aequalitatem* when measuring against an absolute which it can only partially share: the part is never the whole, and in this case, the whole being infinite and simple, the manner of sharing must itself be totally different from the manner of possession by the whole.[41]

Likeness, or similarity, or resemblance, whether it is only in an appearance, or in operation, or in nature itself, or in existence, is some degree of sameness, something of a cause repeated in an effect, a repetition which constitutes an echo therein of the cause. Evidently there are degrees of likeness, like diminishing echoes, and it is in the terms of this that the Thomistic system evaluates the caused creatures of the universe, especially the human person, in order to estimate each one's degree of participation in perfection, the consequent position and dignity of each, and the ordered integration of the whole creation toward that cause and source it must dimly reflect, more or less vaguely imitate, and finally acquire.[42]

In tracing the kind of entity a likeness is, Thomas starts with the principle that every effect is like its cause, either in its mere existence, since it shares in the same existence and being, or in existence, nature and properties. Since a likeness

40. *C.G.*, III, c. 21.

41. *In de Div. Nom.*, c. 1, lect. 1; II *Sent.*, d. 17, q. 1, a. 1.

42. For Thomistic definitions and distinctions regarding "similitudo," cf.: I *Sent.*, d. 3, q. 2, a. 1; q. 3, a. 1; d. 38, q. 1; *De Ver.*, q. 10, a. 7; *C.G.*, II, c. 2; c. 46; *In Epist. I ad Cor.*, Sec. 2; *S.T.*, I, q. 4, a. 3; q. 45, a. 7; and particularly for man, the *locus classicus*: I, q. 93 *in toto*, where the thesis of *imago Dei* is fully worked out and the source in Augustine's *De Trinitate* is clearly shown.

is some kind of unity of form in the similar things, one must be the cause of the other, or both effects of one cause. Since some things are patently more similar than others, it is evident there are grades of similarity according to whether things are similar by the transient and external influence of efficient causality only, or similar intrinsically through formal cause, or by formal cause which is of the specific nature, or all this and in mode of being too. Since the causal agent must act according to the mode of its own nature, it must stamp some likeness of itself in the nature of the effect it brings into being according to its form. This need not bring about wholly the same nature or the same manner of existence, but at least in some way and degree, must impress something of the causer upon the caused which came from it and acquired its existence from it. That formal likeness can be only generic, or specific too, or in the same mode also.[43] That likeness which reflects only causality without being some copy of the nature of the cause, is so much more remote than an image of the nature of the cause in form, that Aquinas distinguishes the two by different names, calling the lesser, only a "tracing" of the cause, and the greater likeness an "image":

. . . every effect somehow or other re-presents its cause, but in various ways. For a certain effect reflects only the causality of its cause, but not its nature, as smoke represents fire; and such a representation you call the likeness of a trace; and a trace shows only the influence of something transient, not what kind of thing it is. On the other hand, a certain kind of effect represents its cause enough to be a likeness of its nature, as the produced fire does the producing fire . . . and this is the likeness of an image.[44]

To that likeness which he calls only a "trace," Aquinas gives three components: some resemblance, an imperfection of resemblance, and the extrinsic causal influence by which one can trace the original cause as cause or at best the likeness of generic form, though not specific nature.[45] The image,

43. I, q. 4, a. 3: "Dicendum quod . . . similitudo attendatur secundum . . . communicationem in forma. . . ."
44. I, q. 45, a. 7, c.
45. I *Sent.*, d. 3, q. 2, a. 1, solut.

however, being a closer resemblance, one of formal causality also and so reflecting the specific nature or the essential properties of the nature, then includes in its likeness, the specific difference of that nature.[46] This is why we speak of a close likeness as "the very *image* of" and why we tend to use figures like "mirroring" although some contend this is ambiguous.[47] The image then is a species of the general term "likeness," the highest type of a likeness, adding to likeness in general the closer and sharper and more complete and clear note as found in the idea of "copy" or "imitation." Any image is a likeness, but not every likeness is an image.[48] And yet, since "likeness" is generic, it is also used to express a greater or less in an image, to express a perfection of image.[49] But the image then, as image, exhibits two essentials: *specific* likeness of nature; and consequently, a clear indication of its kind of origin. A "trace" indicates a cause, but the image exhibits what kind of being the cause is.[50] The perfect image will attain equality of nature, while the imperfect will not be itself constituted wholly in that nature it reflects, only partially and differently so.

However, when one deals with the image of infinite perfection, the case is somewhat different, because the likeness can be an image, but cannot be in any sense a quasi-repetition of His nature, however it reflects that nature. Here the image is not in the same sense specific, but only analogical to His "eminent degree" of perfection, since we deal with existential being and nature which is outside and beyond

46. I, q. 93, a. 2, c.: . . . "non quaelibet similitudo ei etiamsi sit expressa ex altero, sufficit ad rationem imaginis. Si enim similitudo sit secundum genus tantum, vel aliquid accidens commune, non propter hoc dicetur aliquid esse ad imaginem alterius . . . *requiritur ad rationem imaginis quod sit similitudo secundum speciem*, sicut imago regis est in filio suo; vel ad minus secundum aliquod accidens proprium speciei et praecipue secundum figuram, sicut hominis imago dicitur esse in cupro. . . . Manifestum est autem quod similitudo speciei attenditur secundum ultimam differentiam." . . . Cf. II *Sent.*, a. 16, q. 1, a. 1.
47. Allers: "Microcosmus," in *Traditio*, No. II (1944), p. 324. Cf. *De Ver.*, q. 10, a. 7, c.
48. Augustine: *De Div. Quest.*, q. 74; PL 40, 85.
49. I, q. 93, a. 9, c.
50. *In Epist. I ad Cor.*, sect. 2.

genus and species.[51] How anything created and limited by nature, can image the unlimited nature of perfection has been explained by the analogy of participation in proportion. This created nature is the image of the causing nature but only partially, and only in the manner possible to the caused nature, which is not the same as the cause's mode of existence, which is total and essential and simple. But some created natures *can* be an image by showing specifically, although partially, the definite essential properties of the divine nature not shown by other creatures. And in that special image we can find the immediate value-basis of the human person, because the original it is the image of, is the absolute perfection—value, the ultimate standard. In this image then, we have what is needed: an available, observable, objective and valid value-measure for man. Final and complete and true value is God, and man is of value in the measure he is God-*like,* in the measure his nature, and therefore his existence and powers and operation, are the copy of the divine nature. From the "traces" of divine perfection in creation, one can "trace back" the power and causality of God. From an image, one can see reflected what kind of person He is, and if a creature so images, he can do so only in the degree he *shares* that nature in his own manner and proportion. Therefore the quality of the image will indicate the "quantity" of that creature's share in the original perfection and be a true measure of his value or dignity, which is existential perfection.

PROCESS OF EVALUATION. The previous explanations of the standards of evaluation already indicate the process of measurement of human value. The more extensive the operational powers the less limitation in mode of existence and the more superior the being, because the greater likeness to and participation in absolute existential perfection. The degree of actuality in operation can be judged by extension in number and variety and by modes which indicate less limitation in their nature, as the degree of immateriality evidences less limitation than materiality.

51. I, q. 4, a. 3.

As something acts, so is it, and actors then can be graded equally by their actions. The more superior the act, the more superior the one who acts,[52] since everything must operate and even exist only in the measure of its own nature's capacities. In measuring the perfection of the nature then, one includes not only the actualizations already in existence and operation, but the potentials, which themselves are actual potentials and indicate the perfectibles which are measurements of potential perfection. And the already actualized variety in existence and operation helps to chart a gradient, because that realized level indicates levels of potential.[53] Obviously then, with regard to the human person, the center of attribution, all operations and powers must be accredited to him as natural to him. This means also that those perfections and perfectibles found natural and personal cannot be successfully opposed without essentially lessening or changing a nature, a transfer manifestly impossible.[54] Something can be only what it is and never what it is not; therefore nature must be accommodated to, not accommodate.

Evidently then, the evaluation of man's dignity can be done by application of these found standards, in a manner entirely realistic and scientific: accepting only data that *are* and concluding from them, only what *must then be*.

RÉSUMÉ. The concept of person has been delineated from the concept of personality as substance from accident in order to clarify the distinction between the person *who* is and the powers he *has* and can develop. It has been insisted upon that it is rationality which is the specific difference in the human creature which entitles him to the name of "person" and that it is his rational power above all which has importance in his personality development. In order then to be able to evaluate the dignity of that rational person, the concept of dignity has been traced through goodness and perfec-

52. *C.G.*, II, c. 21. These principles can be found on almost any page of St. Thomas, and are obvious enough to be beyond and sans need of demonstration.
53. I, q. 54, a. 3, c.: "cum enim potentia dicatur ad actum, oportet quod secundum diversitatem actuum sit diversitatem potentiarum."
54. *C.G.*, II, c. 15; II *Sent.*, d. 9, q. 1, a. 3.

tion until it was seen to be equated with completeness in being, and itself relative to absolute being, which was then shown to be the necessary final criterion for the evaluation of men. And then, in order to relate men to that final standard, the concepts of participation and likeness were investigated, and shown to be the reflections in human persons of the absolute perfection of God, and hence the immediately valid standards of measurement of human dignity according to perfection. Rationality makes the person, and rationality is a perfection of being, reflecting by image in man the infinite perfection which is the criterion of value and dignity.

CHAPTER THREE

Evaluation—Man and Creation: Its Perfection

IT is not within the province of this study or the scope of its treatment, to give an exposition of the Thomistic philosophy of creation and the proofs for its necessity. That thesis takes its start from the inevitable implications of the whole analogy of being and the theory of causality. The immaterial part of man particularly is shown to demand a beginning beyond and above matter, and it is argued that true creation, *"ex nihilo, nullo supposito,"* of man, and in final analysis, of all being, must be traced to being itself, which is inclusive of all that participates in it, absolutely self-sufficient and essentially existent. The thesis is not only that what is evidently participated and dependent being demands a source, but that all being must finally be traced to an emanation from that being itself which is self-existent. And that is what is meant by Creator and creation, not a question of the observable genesis and development of species, but of the original efficient cause of all. All that we see which is, and once was not, must originally have come from what IS by essence and always is, have come from it by efficient causality, by true creation *ex nihilo* in the absolute sense. That is why everything must be traced to the true Creator and why, in some degree and varying measure, all that is which has come to be, not only gives by its manner of existence the clue to the manner of its becoming and the kind of source from which it comes, but images its original cause.[1]

1. For development of the thesis of creation, cf. I, qq. 44–46; q. 65; q. 90, a. 2, c.; q. 91, a. 2; q. 118, a. 2; *C.G.*, II, c. 85; II *Sent.*, d. 1, q. 1, a. 4;

The relation of man to the rest of creation shows that he possesses more actual existence and perfection, and therefore a *greater likeness* to his Creator than the rest of the visible and ordered creation. The many finite and modified substances of creatures show they are from some ultimate principle, and their species show the idea of their maker as the form of a house shows the conception of its maker; their ordered relation shows the intelligence and love of the one producing them. Of all these, however, man shows himself superior in the perfection of his nature and the dignity of his goal.[2]

SCALE OF SUPERIORITY. This human person we are evaluating, lives in a universe whose creatures are patently multiple, varied, and graded in a manifest order. There is no need to belabor the issue of order in creation any more than the very concept of creation: the "scientific" chaos-and-chance theory and the postulates which refused to recognize a hierarchy in nature, were short-lived and have passed.[3] Of

---

De Ver., q. 27, a. 3, ad 9; *De Pot.*, q. 3, a. 9; *Comp. Theol.*, cc. 93–94; Gredt, *Elementa Philosophiae Aristotelico-Thomisticae*, vol. 2, pp. 158–163; Garrigou-Lagrange, *God: Existence and Nature*, Vol. 1. Confer also the previous section on "Participation."

2. I, q. 93, a. 6; *C.G.*, III, c. 111.

3. A. N. Whitehead, *Science and the Modern World*, p. 5. "There can be no living science unless there is a widespread instinctive conviction in the existence of an order of things, and in particular, of an Order of Nature."

Vannevar Bush, *Modern Arms and Free Men* (Simon and Schuster, 1949), quoted in *Life*, Dec. 5, 1949, pp. 89–100: "The world is split into two camps . . . on the one hand those who believe in freedom and the dignity of man, and on the other hand, those who believe in a supreme conquering state to which all men would be slaves . . . (to the latter) the law of fang and beak is the only law . . . nothing admirable in man except his will to survive and dominate by force or cunning. . . .

Fatalism is no longer a mere negation; it becomes now an active philosophy based on an interpretation of science as utter materialism. . . . Yet the whole affair is a ghastly fallacy. Science has been misread. Science does not exclude faith . . . (Note: Bush's "faith" is equivalent to "philosophical reasoning.")

Science does not teach a harsh materialism. It does not teach anything beyond its boundaries . . . it studies how the cosmos is assembled and how it moves. But it does not examine how the cosmos first appeared to be reasoned about . . . it is silent as to whether there was a great purpose in creation of the cosmos . . . those things are forever beyond its ken . . . it studies the functioning of the brain of man. But it does not define consciousness or

this ascending superiority in nature, through increasing extensiveness and a complexity of ways of existing, of operative living and generation, we have empirical knowledge, as we have of how the variant grades of perfection and their inequalities fit so well into the unified and ordered whole. "Out of two concepts—imitation and imperfection—springs a third . . . instead of a vast monotony, creation will exhibit a manifold of existences, rank upon rank of quality, grade after grade of activity . . . evolution and system and plan. The very failure of the finite is wrought to a new success; out of the imperfect imitation emerges the perfection of order."[4] Today all this is once again admitted and "scientism" is being smothered by the certainty that such an arrangement as this demands an absolute existence and a total, simple perfection as its source and measure. Diversity cannot be denied, but continuity can be preserved; creation's unity can be seen very reasonably from the viewpoint of a common source, and explained by analogous participation.

The concept of hierarchy in creation, and the use of the principle of analogy, allow for an explanation of creatures by a Creator transcendent to them and yet intrinsically related to them. If creatures are the varied participations in and the consequent likenesses of their Creator, then such an analogy can explain not only creation itself, but the architectonics of the varied universe. Similitude will give a sufficient reason for a creature's determined essence in the very fact of a similitude determined by its sharing the original in its proper measure. In this way, it can be seen that being is one, though many distinct beings compose a finite system of images of that in-

tell us why there is a being on earth who can reason as to why he is here. . . .

The entire company of men of goodwill believes . . . in human freedom . . . believes in the dignity of man . . . believes there is something in free creativeness of individuals worth preserving in the world . . . believes there is such a thing as truth—not the mere accepted convention . . . in absolute truth . . . a possible destiny for man higher than the mere struggle for existence."

Cf. also: A. Carrell, *Man the Unknown;* LeConte du Nouys, *Human Destiny;* Edw. O'Connor, *Potentiality and Energy;* and Joseph Marling, *Order of Nature.*

4. Edw. Pace, "World-Copy," in *Catholic University Bulletin,* 1899, p. 211.

finite in varying degrees of similitude. So unification of the
whole is achieved through the relative and participated perfections we observe in their reciprocal structural and operational cooperations, all converging finally in the absolute,
the original they remain distinct from, but which all share in
and which all reflect with multiple and variant fidelity. Since
the Creator is Himself "existence by His essence" it must be
that created existence be His proper effect and a shared resemblance of the same existence, so that each creature will
be like Him in the measure it *has* that existence, which *is* His.
He is transcendent to all, yet is *in* all, and intimately in them,
by very being. It was in the vision of all this that Pascal called
creatures but "veils covering God." Obviously, this is far
from the viewpoint of pantheism, because it remembers that
the Creator is total existence by essence, and the creature
very limited existence by participation.[5] The relation is transcendental, above genus and species, but real. It is from the
necessary logical and ontological effect of the concept of
analogy that the scholastics insisted upon the concept of imitation, the effect of participation. This becomes the expression of the relation of all to the Creator, the supreme law by
which our world is related to its God. It is the universal principle upon which is found the relation of the various orders
and species of reality. It links the subjective and the objective
even in our thinking, as it binds the whole external universe
harmoniously and really to God, as in God Himself, we see it
in turn as the source and motive and mode of activity to
which the universe owes its being.[6] This view allows for the
universe as it is, not only in ordered levels but something
more than motionless, as it is obvious that the graduated

---

5. *De Pot.*, q. 9, a. 3; I, q. 8, a. 1, c.; *C.G.*, II, c. 22; I, q. 4, a. 3; Pascal,
Pensées, Ed. Brunschvicq, p. 215. Cf. R. Allers, "Microcosm" in *Traditio,* II
(44), 401: "To the medieval conception, discontinuity is a main feature of
reality. The modern mind is focused mainly on continuity. Some continuity
had to be recognized by the Schoolmen. They solved the problem by applying
the principle of analogy and by the notion of an intermediary being, or rather
by the idea that the highest being in one order somehow participates in the
nature of the next higher level. . . ."
    6. Cf. Pace, *op. cit.,* pp. 211–212.

creation is not something petrified in an inert or static condition, but a creation teeming with further creative change.

Things exist in operation, and the Thomistic view of the universe is as we see it daily: dynamic and progressive.[7] Beings are, and because they are, they move toward more being and achieve in the actualizations of their potentials, more perfection. Different levels of existence are observable in their widening circles of operation and rising rungs of perfection, a dynamic of existence like a spinning top. And at the same time, apparently opposite to their centrifugal movement, their multiplicity and increasing operative complexity is drawn back again to the center of their inverted vortex above, so that despite a permanently preserved distinctness all created beings and operations seem ultimately being drawn into a kind of fused-union with the original and final simplicity which is the Creator. The full meaning of creation then, as a dynamic structure and as a process is comprehended only when it is seen that creation gives not only existent being to creatures, but by that same act, bestows something of its own desire to further communicate, pouring out its own power of creativity upon creatures themselves, by which they are doubly like their Creator.[8] God's creating has made every creature a little god itself, in that through its own potentials, it further actualizes new forms by bringing more beings into actuality and "filling up" the stature and content and reflections of creation toward a multiple and completed representation of the model ideas in the mind of a Creator Himself, totally one, simple, and infinite. He has communicated in innumerable created shares, not only His being and

7. Alb. Mag., *Lib. II De Causis et Processu Universitatis*, tract IV, c. 14, an interesting section which repeats the theme of Augustine, is parallel to Bonaventure much more than Aristotle, and gives further evidence of the broad influences upon Thomas' thought which is so much more related to Augustine and Plato in much of this view of creation and its dignity. Albert speaks of all receiving divine life and light being poured into them, and becoming "potens, appetens, et aliquo modo, apprehendens esse divinum . . . in quibusdam non nisi naturaliter sunt, in quibusdam autem vegetabiliter, in aliis vero sensibiliter, in quibusdam rationabiliter. . . ."

8. *De Pot.*, q. 3, a. 15, ad 14; *C.G.*, II, c. 43.

existence, but such a being as is inevitably also creative in them.[9]

This participation of creatures in the Creator is the necessary dual communication of that absolute goodness which is itself communicative completeness in actuality, and which, though what it creates is never equal to or worthy of its cause, must share the cause's form which is both the final aim of its creation and the original cause of its likeness. Since this cause is the totally perfect agent, He achieves His intended likeness perfectly, in a multiple and varied gradation of creatures which reflect His goodness not only in graduated levels of beings and extending complexities of operations, but in their communicated and participated creative ability to produce the same themselves. In this way, creatures become both the likenesses and the efficacious cooperators of their Creator, an efficacy which makes themselves better likenesses, and gives them the most certain mark of their divine origin. Their activity is a constant effort to further assimilation to God, imitating His being in its very fecundity, so that their own causal and creative activity is the likeness and analogue of His infinitely fecund actuality.[10] Since He is infinite He cannot communicate Himself completely, but communicates both Himself and His very power of communicating, as far as possible within the limits of created essences and different natures. Out of that inexhaustible goodness

9. *De Pot.*, q. 2, a. 1, c.; *C.G.*, III, c. 20; *De Pot.*, q. 3, a. 16, ad 5. *Gilson epitomizes* the Thomistic view notably well here: (*op. cit.*, p. 349). Son efficacité ne s'épuise pas dans las poussée qui fait sortir les êtres de Dieu. En même temps que les creatures réçoivent un mouvement qui les pose dans un être rélativement indépendant et exterieur à celui du Createur, elles en réçoivent un second qui les ramene vers leur point de départ et tend à les fair remonter aussi près que possible de leur première source." Cf. *idem*, p. 260, ". . . un universe qui n'est voulu par Dieu qu'à titre de ressemblance divine, ne sera jamais trop efficace, il ne se réalisera jamais trop completement, il ne tendra jamais trop fortement à sa propre perfection pour reproduire . . . l'image de son divine model; 'unumquodque tendens in suam perfectionem, tendit in divinam similitudinem': (cf. *C.G.*, III, c. 21) principle d'une inépuisable fecondite . . . puisqu'il régle la morale humaine en même temps que la métaphysique de la nature."

10. *C.G.*, II, c. 45; III, cc. 21 and 22; cf. Gilson's expression, *op. cit.*, p. 259 ff.

which is without need, He wills to communicate Himself of His very nature, to the extent that the active beings He creates be themselves also communicators in goodness, and double sharers, as it were, in absolute goodness, so as to be doubly a likeness of Him.[11]

Since such absolute good is infinitely abundant, and created natures must be finite and limited, creation overflows with diversity, each created type reflecting a different facet of the creative infinity, some sharing more of its essential and total goodness, and so showing a greater likeness to it, some showing less, but none sufficient in its limitations, to represent the inexhaustible communicating source in that whole perfection which is complete but simple actuality. "Each individual thing holds its place in the scale of being by a positive determination and a negative. Whatever it contains of reality, of property, of function, or efficiency, is positive, and is therefore in its degree, the semblance of God. But inasmuch as it is wanting in the fullness of being and limited in the range of its powers, its value is marked by a negative sign. . . . The lowest elements of the world are made in His likeness but the likeness goes not beyond existence and action. Higher up in the curve, life appears—an inward abiding energy like His own—but unconscious. Consciousness itself, a distant reflection of His knowledge, lacks in the realm of mere sentient beings, the crowning value of intelligence and will. Human reason, closer approximation still of the original Mind, is circumscribed . . . Throughout the universe, imitation and limitation are variables—the one is the function of the other."[12] Each imitates, but because each is limited, what one lacks another must supply, so His existing is exhibited in many forms and variant ways.[13] Some are, some live, some feel, some know, each higher type superior in complexity and spontaneity and immanence of activity, in greater likeness of His total immanence; some types more extensive and varied in operation because they need more powers to accom-

11. I, q. 47, a. 1, c.; *C.G.*, III, c. 21 and c. 70; *De Ver.*, q. 5, a. 8; *De Pot.*, q. 2, a. 1, c.
12. Pace, *op. cit.*, p. 211.
13. I, q. 47, a. 1, c.

plish their greater participation and the closer likeness to Him which goodness intended in them.[14] Some are less limited then in nature than others, less subject to change, and so closer likenesses of the simple and immutable original which they reflect like pieces broken off. By this plan and process, we see the perfection of the one universe ending in a unified pattern only through the multiplication of superiorities in each succeeding grade of creation, the resemblance to their maker increasing throughout the increasing complexities of higher and higher forms of life.[15]

It is because of this manifest gradation in existence that the term "life" is an analogical term. Beings differ in essence, and so they differ in the vital motion of existence and life; the more being there is, the more existence. Moreover, it is an essential characteristic of vital activity to be from within and as more of this immanent kind of vitality is seen, the higher in being is the nature, and the more does it reflect God.[16] Such a God-like quality is not too difficult to determine, since one can distinguish three elements in vital activity: a determining principle, the execution of motion, and the functional result. Grades of life are distinguishable in proportion to their measure of these. And the ascending spiral

14. *De Ver.*, q. 22, a. 2, ad 3.

15. I, q. 3, a. 7, ad 2; cf. *C.G.*, II, chapts. 39–45; III, c. 69. Because it is a much more original statement and put clearly and beautifully, one of Augustine's words on this should be read. Cf. *De Diversis Quaest.*, Q. 51, No. 2; (PL 40, 32). (And note q. 51, No. 3, where first we meet the concept of resemblance to God based on upright posture!) "Multi enim modis dici res possunt similes Deo: aliae secundum virtutem et sapientiam factae, quia in ipso est virtus et sapientia non facta; aliae in quantum solum vivunt, quia ille summe et primitus vivit; aliae in quantum sunt, quia ille summe et primitus est. Et ideo quae tantummodo sunt, nec tamen vivunt aut sapiunt, non perfecte sed exigue sunt ad similitudinem ejus; quia et ipsa bona sunt in ordine suo, cum sit ille super omnia bonus, a quo omnia bona procedunt. Omnia vero quae vivunt et non sapiunt, paulo amplius participant similitudinem . . . Jam porro quae sapiunt, ita illi similitudine sunt proxima, ut, in creaturis nihil sit propinquus. Quod enim participat sapientiae, et vivit et est. . . . Quare cum homo possit particeps esse sapientiae, secundum hominem, secundum ipsum ita est ad imaginem, ut nulla natura interposita formetur; et ideo nihil sit Deo conjunctus. Et sapit enim, et vivit, et est: qua creatura nihil est melius."

16. I, q. 18, a. 3; *C.G.*, IV, c. 11.

of beings ends in that species which most exhibits these essentials and so most participates in and reflects in itself, its source which is total being and completely actual existence, life itself essentially.[17]

The understanding of that source of creation, which is unalloyed actuality and activity, is necessary for the understanding of creation not only in its origin but in its end. The static order of being, and particularly the dynamic order of existence and operation, cannot be coherently explained without the understanding of the effect of creation's final cause upon creation, its incitement to completion within each order, its direction of all classes to the proper completion-result of their natures and powers in imitation of His activity, into the further perfected and perfective likenesses of His own perfection. This goodness is the attractive final cause acting upon beings and their natural appetency, so that they *must* "struggle" to preserve their existence and maintain themselves, to repel the onslaughts of disintegration and the forces warring against their continuance in being. It is the inevitable activity-likeness shown in this *nisus* for self-maintenance which is the reflection of Him Who is *ipsum esse subsistens,* so that the whole basic "world-evolving process" is a process of growing like God. This "straining" after absolute goodness which pulls beings toward its own completeness results in more and more perfect forms of existence continually coming into actual being. The modern concept of universe "flowering" from below is only counterpart to the scholastic concept of its "flowing" from above. The full picture demands both aspects. Forms "emerge" as new manifestations of the power which governs the course of nature, but it is the creature, not the original Creator, who gains through this, as it becomes more actual and less remote in likeness of Him who IS and who therefore is essentially and totally perfect and good.[18] All individual movement in existence exhibits progress from the incomplete but potential to

17. I *Sent.*, d. 36, q. 2, a. 2; cf. Geiger, *La Participation*, p. 229.
18. Cf. Pace, "Assimilari Deo," *op. cit.*, p. 350, where this theme is beautifully stated.

the complete and actual, from the imperfect toward the perfect. From its source-perfection, each thing has got an affinity in being to Being, imbibed a thirst to perfection beyond its present state, each unit manifesting its nature-thrust toward self-realization and toward a consequent harmony of correlation, cooperation, and subordination into the solidarity and inclusive perfection of the whole universe.[19] As perfection in the order of being brings on necessarily perfection in operation, these two coalesce into the perfection-value of the entire active unit, the capacity of any creature making possible what the end incites it to, so that it can "become what it is"; and the final perfection of the whole universe is achieved upon the completed actualizations of all its diverse types until it can reach that perfected likeness of its Maker which was intended and for which dynamic potentials were given.[20]

This final and inciting goal which explains the order, and the graded perfections, and the divinity-reflections in the dynamic universe, is that same source-goodness which first communicated creation's energy-potentials to it and is now its attractive model-aim, the final cause which is diffusive of itself and intimately within all beings who share Being. The fact and influence of such finality is in things inescapably, because it is rooted in Being itself and in participated beings, a law of reality which must cause increasing actuality and resemblance. Each being *is*, and is good, both by force of its first principle which is exemplary, effective, and final, and also because the likeness of divine goodness inheres in it and is the basis of that connaturality which institutes the further pull and movement to a greater likeness.[21] That natural drive within each is its own intrinsic energy-source of change, the "intentional factor" in nature which is the basis of its perfectibility. And its consequent process of perfecting is evi-

19. Cf. J. O'Mahoney, *The Desire of God*, p. 78 ff., for a more popularized and rhetorical statement of some of these themes, but withal a correctly Thomistic one.

20. I, q. 73, a. 1, c.

21. I, q. 6, a. 4, c.; I, q. 65, a. 2, ad 1; cf. Gustafson, *op. cit.*, p. 60; vide *supra*, Ch. I.

dence in turn, of the natural perfective capacities which make that dynamism possible.[22] This explains how dynamic direction to completion within each sphere, and a constantly maintained order between levels of perfection progressing toward the correlated perfection of the universe, responds to the force of the final cause, each grade contributing its own limited and shared likeness to the more extensive likeness of the whole universe.[23]

From this aspect, Nature can be looked upon with a view which perhaps identifies the outlook of both the medieval schoolman and our day's physicist: it is a set of forces controlling and guiding the universe, where any unit's operations are efficacious within its own predetermined limits, and often seem to possess a kind of "freedom" or plasticity of operation within those limits, even though rigidly governed in existence and operation by their own intrinsic principles.[24] This attraction-aspect of final causality explains not only the variation and dynamism, but the gradation, the subordination, and the superiorities of the creatures of the universe, as long as one uses the concept in conjunction with the analogy of proportionately participated being. To each its own; but each to another also. Even among creatures totally material and unaware, each has its share in actual perfections and in perfectible capacities, and a place in the perfecting of the whole, where each not only contributes its own increasing perfected likeness to the whole, but in reciprocal action with others, increases theirs. Each level is inevitably pulled toward that perfection of its own capacities whose very movement is a likeness itself of the *Actus Purus*. And that dynamism to completion is by nature fitted to mortise with the levels above and below. Each grade is planned and directed intrinsically toward others, each finding its immediate end in the perfecting of a higher level by the support of and the very inclusion of its own perfections in that superior species. This gradation of the reciprocal dynamism of parts, with their multiplied

22. Arist., *Physics*, II, 1, 192b, 22; *S.T.*, I, q. 94, a. 1, ad 4.
23. I *Metaphys.*, lect. 1, princip.; I, q. 6, a. 1, ad 2; I, q. 44, a. 4, ad 3; and on this topic, cf. Gustafson and Marling, *opera citata, passim.*
24. I–II, q. 109, a. 1.

perfections of species in creation, is a growing likeness in
each part, and perfective of the resemblance of the whole
universe, for such a process is more perfective of a resemblance than it is of individual accidentals within each species.[25]

Finally, all creatures move in another order, a movement
ad extra, beyond the universe, toward that Maker so immanent in things made,[26] yet so infinitely transcendent to them,
one with them and yet infinitely beyond them, toward
whom they reach.[27] In these senses, the phrase "expanding
universe" had a more than astronomical sense and was a
scientific expression of the perfective dynamism philosophers
insisted upon long ago, a concept that explained not only by
natural capacities, but by the reciprocal action between
complete actuality which attracts what is connatural to it in
being, and the derivative and relative existents attracted,
who thereby directed their own completion in operation, and
also the perfection of the multiple whole, whose being and
actuality and goodness and consequent resemblance to its
Creator becomes a very process-image of Him, continually extending its likeness to that total existence-energy which is
for them both creative and communicative source, and final
attracting force. So incessantly is woven and expanded that
dynamic order which is the actualization and likeness of the
optimum universi.[28]

25. I, q. 21, a. 1, c., and ad 3; *C.G.,* II, c. 93.
26. I, q. 8, a. 3: "in omnibus ille est per potentiam inquantum omnia ejus
potestati subduntur, est per praesentiam in omnibus in quantum omnia nuda
sunt et aperta oculis ejus; est in omnibus per essentiam, inquantum adest omnibus ut causa essenti."
27. *C.G.,* I, c. 78; II, c. 93; nothing in this treatment of the mysterious
and marvelous likeness of creation, especially man, to God, is intended to
convey any impression that one should forget the analogy of being enough to
receive any implication that there is any resemblance approaching an *adae-
quatio.* Obviously, such is impossible. Cf. *De Pot.,* q. 3, a. 16, ad 7: ". . .
Licet sit quaedam similitudinem creaturae ad Deum, non tamen est adae-
quatio. . . ." And *idem,* q. 3, a. 15, ad 19: ". . . creatura assimilatur condi-
tiones . . . (sed) *Alio* enim *modo* esse sit in Deo et in creatura, et similiter
bonitas. Unde licet a primo bono sint omnia bona, et a primo ente sint omnia
entia, non tamen a summo bono sunt omnia summe bona, nec ab ente necessario sunt omnia per necessitatem."
28. Cf. Pace, "Assimilari Deo," *op. cit.,* pp. 353–354.

This substantial order of likeness, and that dynamic and varied perfecting of the universe into further likeness in the whole, is observable in its process and easily concluded in its meanings and implications. It can be attributed only to the substantial goodness of the communicating Creator, the cause and *forma* of goodness, which originated creation and which is the same attracting goodness toward which creatures must move and in which they find their completed end. Each is limited by its nature, some more than others, in an ascending spiral of superiorities which culminates in the one grade which alone is even an end in itself, which contains and yet surpasses all the others whom it makes use of in completing itself, a species differentiated in superiority by an immateriality evidenced in the presence and operation of a will and a mind, powers which operate in a superior manner and with a unique directness toward their supreme perfection-goal, a goal far beyond other creatures'. This species is the peak of creation's perfections, and the masterpiece of divine likeness in a unique way because he not only includes the rest, but adds intelligent awareness of them all, in common with the Creator Himself. He has existence, self-maintenance, causal activity as others; he, besides, can *know* God, and the maximum image is reached as his god-like intelligence functions upon the God it is like.[29]

SYNTHESIS OF PERFECTIONS. This most perfected species is actualized in the individual human person, who is then most like his God: *quanto perfectior—tanto Deo similior*.[30] But this planned supreme niche for man in creation is the more obvious and marvelous when he is seen to be not only superior to all else in complexity and immanence of vital activity, but when one sees that he is, in his person, a summation of all lower created elements. Their very composition is included in his so that he comprises the rest in this individual unit. This has always struck men, this touching of the higher order by the lower, this use of and very inclusion of the lower within the higher until one reaches the least limited

29. *C.G.*, I, c. 56; c. 46.
30. II *Sent.*, d. 16, q. 1, a. 2.

and most actual species above whom nothing else is visible.[31]
The Schoolmen and the thinkers before them, saw man, because of his compounded nature, as the final horizon of material creation and the dividing line between this visible
world of creatures, and higher pure spirits who have no ad-
mixture of matter. Since man contains both in himself, he
joins all creatures in himself. The recognition of his inclusion
of all levels of existence within himself in his four vital functions is commonplace and classical; "he has existence in common with stones, life with plants, sensation with animals, intelligence with angels."[32] This is the famous view of man as
the *microcosm*, that species and that individual within this
species, who contains all the rest of creation.[33] He is native to
them: he himself contains them in his nature. In this way, he
duplicates in himself the rest of the external and *macroscopic*
universe, and because of this is inevitably called a *microcosmus*. The clarity with which the Aristotelian and Thomistic
philosophies pointed out *how* man not only duplicated but
contained the *major mundus*, saved those systems from pantheism and the "world-soul" of Plato. Man contains all the
elements of the larger world, and he can contain the very
forms of all else within him, but in a manner of actuality different from their own, in the "intelligible being" of his understanding. It is in this manner that he is the superior and final
summation of all else, that he "assimilates" all else, a position
of not only being "like," but *taking into* himself the likenesses
of others so that they are "part of him"; and he becomes, by
his own assimilating nature, also all the others which he surpasses not only by specific differences, but an identifying inclusion of them all in himself. Man's own individual body

31. *C.G.*, II, c. 68. Aquinas is taking over the thoughts and phrases of Denis
Areop. in *De Div. Nom.*, c. 8; and *Lib. de Causis*, I, 8.

32. Greg. Mag., *Hom. In Evang.*, XXIX; PL 76, 1214a. This is probably
the *locus classicus* for this famous concept. Cf. I, q. 96, a. 2, c., et alibi.

33. Confer the summation of this whole view by Allers, "Microcosmus,"
op. cit., pp. 319–350. "Man alone integrates within himself the constituents
of reality . . . he occupies an absolutely unique position by containing the
whole world on a minor scale."

I, q. 91, a. 1, c.: ". . . omnes creaturae mundi quodammodo inveniuntur
in eo."

is as it were, a pocket-size model of the whole material universe, to which he adds, besides all other elements, the very forms of all other natures by the progressive assimilation of them in his mind. The lower in the universe is *taken into* the higher, and man can take all into himself, can with thought "draw all things unto himself," and so extend his person by the inclusion of all within him, so that in a way he equals and he *is* all.[34] Obviously, that which includes all else in some way is superior to any one in the things he contains, participates immeasurably more in actuality, and is therefore a far greater likeness of the Creator, an *all-inclusive* likeness of all created features. It is not only that man stands at the peak of creatures, but much more: it is a cumulative peak, including all forms of being below it and then adding its own, imitating the Creator as well as they do in the way they do, and surpassing them cumulatively and specifically by the specific difference of his intelligence, a new and uniquely immanent activity.[35]

The specific difference man adds to the perfection of the creation he sums up is immateriality, which resides in his spirituality, his soul, his intelligence. Only the human species is distinguished by this non-material component.[36] Such a part of man makes his dignity distinct even in its manner of origin. As happens in no other species, such a spiritual soul must be the direct and immediate creation of God in each instance. It needs no argument to outline the impossibility of man's spiritual element being transmuted from some matter, and therefore none to conclude that each must be individually

34. Cf. Aristotle's original πῶς ἅπαντα concept, and Aquinas' whole development of this in I, q. 75 ff., and *In De Anima*. The specific treatment of man's superiority because of his mind, we take up in the next section.

35. I *Sent.*, d. 36, q. 2, a. 2; Geiger, *op. cit.*, p. 229; Maritain, *Existence and the Existent*, pp. 67–68.

36. This element in man he has in common with angelic creatures and in this he is the true *microcosmus* of creation. It is not our object at all to delineate the nature of simple immateriality or prove its presence in man. For the object of this study, such are *data* and so treated, as will be the universal character of his thinking and the detailed proof later of the universal-object of his will. Our object is to point out the significance-value of these things relative to all else.

brought into being *ex nihilo*.[37] That in which he surpasses the
rest of creation is so completely a different non-material element that the very manner of its being brought into being
emphasizes the first instance of all his dignity, in that it demands an individual and separate act of creation for each individual soul, the personal and personalizing touch of the
Creator, marking him at once above all others. This puts the
human individual, not only above other species, but places
this *individual person*, for the first instance in creation, in a
position of dignity residing in him alone, as one individual
not subordinate to and dependent upon his species. By this
he becomes, alone in creation, more important than his
species. Because he is individually made by the Creator, and
by this rooted in two worlds, his individuality is unique. And
because this part of man is not material and so not partitive
and corruptible, he alone is distinguished by a nature which
demands permanence in existence. By very being-content
alone, without further operation, this would place his value
above all others. In this permanence of existence, clearly he
is uniquely a likeness of God, far more than he is as the cumulative likeness of the rest by his bodily composition. This is
an existence unlike any inferior life, and as the existing of
that soul informing his body becomes operative, the root
vital activity itself immediately manifests its superiority;
alone among things made, the spiritual human *is aware*, and
in his awareness controls his own life and acts with far
greater immanence of being in his self-contained existence.
Among living things, plant life shows some execution of vital
motion from within, but no awareness of its functional result
nor therefore any self-determining principle; they are determined externally in activity, toward a predetermined end.
Animals have vital activity in execution *ab intrinseco*, and
even a life principle inherent in their own nature, which
knows some particulars when present, but they have no
vision of the functional result and no such controlling intrinsic
principle that is able to see an end and decide upon means to
reach it. In all creation only man has this, the completely

37. I, q. 90, a. 3, and a. 11.

immanent vital activity, which not only executes motion but determines himself to it in full awareness of and free choice of his functional results and total end.

Spiritual man's inclusion of material elements in his being further perfects his position because in him their very material being and activity is elevated. They now exist by virtue of a higher principle of life than their proper one in their own natures; matter in man exists by an immaterial and spiritual principle which is *his* proper spiritual principle. This binding of all material elements in him gives them a new power and meaning through such intimate relations, so that purely animal functions in man differ from such in other animals, and man raises the lower forms to a higher form of existence in himself. The human person is above matter in virtue of his spiritual controlling side, but he is not separate from matter. His superiority which is partially attained and exercised *through* matter, lifts that matter belonging to his person and enlivened by his spiritual vitality to a stage above its proper level, because the level of existence and value follows the existing nature, and here matter is joined to and activated by a life-principle far nobler than its own.[38]

God has made living creatures in a greater likeness than inanimate beings: a likeness not only of His being and existence, but made them *agents*, in a similitude of His creative causality itself.[39] And since the Creator has communicated much more being and more existence and potentials to the human person, and since in this species alone is the individual most important, that individual is himself more communicative and in his own being he unifies all other elements into a greater perfection of unity which leads those varied elements, in man, into a greater likeness to the simple One whom all creation reflects in innumerable fragments of varying brilliance. And his operative existence, in its greater participation in goodness, is also more communicative of being, of furthering actualizing of himself and others. Even

38. I, q. 55, a. 2; III, q. 2, ad 2; *De Pot.*, q. 3, a. 11; Gilson, *op. cit.*, p. 301; Smith, "Human Social Life," *New Scholasticism*, p. 288.
39. *C.G.*, III, c. 21.

in the least nature, there is seen some kind of communicative activity within limits, but not at all in the same degree as with man. Chemical affinities are a relationship, a "hidden sympathy." Organisms are more communicative: they assimilate others and change substances; plants aspire to and do assimilate environment and at the same time enrich their environs with fertility. So the species there collaborate with each other, condition each other in a reciprocal but measured communication of being. Animals assimilate better, with sense perception putting them in conscious communication with their environment, helping the animal to "depart from himself." Then however, the rational animal communicates in a far superior degree, gives himself consciously, and gives in the highest mode of free communicating, using not only capacities peculiar to him alone, but all those below him which he contains in himself.[40] There are varying degrees of perfection according to the different levels of existence, all sharing and communicating good; but that species which can lean to goodness itself, and partakes much more of communicated goodness, indicates by perfectible capacities and existent operations, that it possesses much greater being and value than the lower creatures who manifest their communicative power in narrow particular operations and particular goods only. In the human species there is operative superiority both in manner of activity and in multiplicity of operations flowing from greater potentials to greater ends and more and greater goods.[41]

This communicative goodness which flows from man more than others is particularly noticeable in his transcending his own species in his generating offspring. He preserves his species without having species-preservation as the primary

40. *C.G.*, III, c. 22.
41. Gilson, *op. cit.*, p. 281: ". . . les choses inférieures à l'homme peuvent prétendre à quelques perfections particulières; elles exercent donc un petit nombre d'opérations d'ailleurs fixes et determinées. L'homme, au contraire, peut acquerir un bien universal et parfait . . . nous le voyons situé au dernier rang des êtres, . . . il est donc convenable que l'âme humaine acquière son bien propre au moyen d'une multitude d'opérations qui supposent une certaine diversité de puissances."

goal of his being, as have all others. This distinction of Thomism is the result of the clarification of human nature by Christianity and is all the more interesting because it developed from an Aristotelian system what was never envisioned by that pre-Christian system. The very consequences resultant in the Aristotelian system worked out in the Christianized system, to the advantage of the individual instead of the species. Then it was seen that this human individual, with the immortal spirit and destiny, is the principle intention of nature because he alone is incorruptible. This is what invested the human individual with the dignity of the permanent being, the indestructible person, the sole original source of rational activity responsibly deciding his own future destiny, and holding an eminence seemingly more Creator-like than creature-like.[42] Man does preserve his species by his corporal functions, but the composite unit-person is, alone in creation, above his species; his chemical and biological functions he orders to the specific good; but because of his spiritual functions he also commands the service of the species. Just as his body ministers to his soul, so does man through his body also minister to his race, but the race in turn in this instance must minister to this individually important and unique human person who is spiritual and permanent as an individual and so above his species.[43]

This production of others of his species which man accomplishes as do lower species, evidences his further worth as it does theirs, in their communication of being or goodness. It is more actuality and more perfection to cause other being, than just to be, without producing. Production of being is the imitating of God in the creative action of causing other beings, a further likeness in one's own productive operation,

---

42. Gilson, *Spirit of Medieval Philosophy;* cf. p. 203 ff.
43. I, q. 98, a. 1. Note: It is this dual *function* of the one indivisible person which allows us to distinguish really distinct functions, but not to force a distinction between the "individual" and the "person" since there is unity there, one center of attribution only, one informing principle through which the corporal now works as well as the spiritual. For further treatment of this dual functional relation in society, and a critique of the opposite theory, cf. Ferguson, *op. cit.,* p. 135 ff.

and further sharing his communicative goodness. The causing of other beings is *fuller* being in the cause, a fuller share in godliness. In all creation there is this evidence of divine likeness insofar as it is "creative" or self-generative.[44] In man's case, not only does he evidence superior being in his greater potentiality to generate, and to imitate the overflowing goodness of God by the very operation of generation, but does it in greater likeness to God, because even his bodily generation is now activated by a spiritual principle, and further superior to other creatures' generating because he accomplishes it with awareness and freedom, and then, because it generates a human individual, in which generating, a person generates inclusively all lower forms of corporal being. Moreover, the human person being what he is, his generation means the unique dignity of being a cooperative act with an immediate and direct act of the Creator upon the individual being generated. The human person alone, in generating, is instrumental in bringing into being another spiritual individual. In fact, the human individual does in some way help "create," that is, develop the human spirit in another: one individual is the direct instrumental cause of the increasing actualization of another soul by its instilling of thoughts, sentiments, character-values, and such spiritual perfections, so that, in some developmental way, they hand on the seed of the spiritual principle too, and in their generating achieve a process and a result generically above other generations which unconsciously and inevitably work to the preservation of their species beyond the corruptible units of it, and remain within the bonds of the material. The human generates *through* matter, and does produce matter superbly, in the complex inclusiveness of all elements such as no other creature does,

44. I, q. 103, a. 6. Cf. Arist., *De Anima*, II, c. 4, 415b, a magnificent statement for a pre-Christian thinker: "for any living thing that has reached its normal development the most natural act is the production of another like itself . . . in order that, as far as nature allows, it may partake in the eternal and the divine . . . this is the goal toward which all things strive . . . Since no living thing is able to partake in what is eternal and divine by uninterrupted continuance . . . it tries to achieve that end in the only way possible to it. . . ." Cf. also *C.G.*, III, c. 21.

but the person is the means of materially generating originally, and psychologically generating later, another individual who is more than matter and above his species. Here
there is much, much communicative power and actualized
perfection, so a much greater share in divine being and existence and likeness to divinity, much beyond anything else
we know, much closer to that creative perfection which is
not only potent, but omnipotent. The more unifying and
extensive of self anything is, the more perfect it is itself. God
is this completely and no creature approaches man's likeness
to Him in this way,[45] either in embracing other elements or in
the production of abundance in being.

Finally, with respect to the universe itself, man is not only
its showpiece, and not only its model in miniature, but his
perfective actuality is perfective of that universe, both by
what he is in himself and what influence he has upon it. In
summing up all else in himself, he gives all else unity and
direction. He *completes* the universe and brings it to focus,
making one out of its widespread parts. He surpasses, yet he
includes all others, and in so doing, unifies all others.

Man fittingly brings all others back to their first principle
and "closes the perfect round of things" by his integrating of
all creatures and elements in his own inclusive perfection.
He expresses the representation of God by material things in
a formal and personal way, a way which seems necessary to
adequately reflect a personal Creator. "This is why man is so
crucial for the purpose of the universe; it is he who turns the
material praise of nature into the formal love and adoration
of a person. For this rational man not only stands at the peak
of the universe; but he also epitomizes it."[46] He is the ter-
minus, the peak, the epitome, the summation of the universe,
and not only in the cumulative sense but the sense of completion, that he adds to it what it lacked in its reflection of its
Creator: immateriality, supreme individuality, intelligence,
and the continued generation of his own perfect kind. He is
"lord of the world" because he is himself a "world within a

45. I, q. 57, a. 2.
46. *C.G.*, IV, c. 55; Cox, *A Thomistic Analysis of Social Order*, p. 6.

world," that in which every element finds itself superiorly represented and elevated, and through whom every element becomes "aware" of its end, and in whom lower creation reaches finally a higher end than due to its own nature. He becomes then a kind of apotheosis for matter which he "divinizes" by inclusion and commanding intelligence.

And this supreme individual who synthesizes and surpasses the universe, then perfects it by completing it, and insures continued actualization of his perfective supremacy by adding to it reproductions of the same supremities, at the same time he is progressively perfecting himself retroactively. Because his operations further actualize himself through the use of the other species of creation, he preserves them by his awareness of mind, in their own natures, and in their position in the total arrangement. He even dynamically images within himself that very arrangement of the macroscopic arrangement and operational order, as the lower elements of his own system collaborate with and are subject to his higher elements, as all find a necessary part to play within him as they do correlatively in the larger universe, as all contribute to unity from their own multiplicity and accomplish within man himself the integration of the outer universe, to which man adds the awareness of purpose and arrangement and relative values. In him therefore, as the mode of existence and operation of the whole unaware creation is elevated to a higher level, he is further perfecting himself through them also, as they are through him. All that they share of absolute perfection in their many species, he contains in one individual. In this *minor mundus* he reflects all their likeness and enriches them with his own.[47] Through their likenesses in him he perfects himself, and in so doing, elevates them also, in him, to achieve a superior similarity to their Creator. The root principle of this dynamic perfecting

47. The collective whole of the universe obviously contains *"more being"* and so is more perfect *by extension*. But as containing the highest quality of being, including all other created qualities in a measure, *intensively* speaking, a human person is more perfect than anything else, and as a permanent perfection, more perfect than all the rest of the non-human universe. Cf. I, q. 93.

of all else, as the principle of his own perfection and perfectibility, lies in his immaterial side, his peculiarly superior likeness in his intelligence, that rationality which made "person"
a new name among creatures, a label properly and uniquely
belonging only to rational man.

SUPERIORITY OF MIND. Reason is the key to man. All the
superiorities observable in the human person are traceable to
the possession of that one root power which is his specific
difference: rationality. By this he surpasses the rest of creation not only in his specific power, but because through it he
elevates those lower powers which he has in common with
lower creatures, completes the universe, and perfects himself. Of the four levels of existence, this is the topmost. One
simply *is*, another level has the capacity only for material
nourishment and growth and generation, another is a sens-
ing and self-moving level, and the last is the intelligent level
which is aware of all and breaks into the immaterial world.
When this is joined with the material in man and is matter's
life principle, intelligence elevates even matter to a higher
mode of existence and operation for it now operates as nowhere else, by the power of a spiritual force, as God operates.[48] Other substances exist independently, even have a
degree of awareness of external objects, but it is *this*, the
power of reason, which distinguishes the human from all of
them and their blind or seemingly quasi-autonomous operations. The human person's reasoning power is the dominant
feature of the entire universe, and nothing like it is found
through a telescope or under a microscope, evident as this is
to the very minds having that power which can recognize
its own presence in creation. Man is superior as seen above,

48. I, q. 18, a. 2, ad 1; I, q. 80, a. 1, c.; I–II, q. 31, a. 7, c. The kernel of
the whole Thomistic position on this value-position then, is concisely stated
by Lenz, (*op. cit.*, p. 146) and instances the abiding scholastic interpretation
of the same: ". . . die Vernunftigkeit und Geistigkeit der Natur, die die
Person vom blossen suppositum unterscheidet, zugleich auch die Würde der
Person begrundet." Note. The rather repetitious insistence upon this seems
over-emphasized only if one forgets the obvious tendency of men to forget
this fact, and the extreme conclusions one must reach, even touching besti-
ality, consequent upon persons existing and operating without the use of the
one power which makes them persons!

because he contains all other elements in himself, but much more superior because in his nature alone, something superbly new is added to creation. "Man possesses on one hand, the full perfection of animal nature, and therefore he enjoys at least as much as the rest of the animal race the fruition of the things of the body. But animality, however perfect, is far from being the whole of humanity and is indeed humanity's humble handmaid, made to serve and obey. It is the mind, or the reason, which is the chief thing in us who are human beings. It is this which makes a human being human, and distinguishes him essentially and *completely* from the brute . . ."[49] The real import then of this added superiority is that it is not just the "best of a kind" but a different kind of thing, a new, immaterial, spiritual power climaxing creation, uniquely perfective of the rest of the universe, a power which, aided by its very perfecting relation with the rest, is in turn perfective even more of man himself. The human person alone can see creation as the Creator sees it, can "read His meanings and follow His example."[50] This is a perfection completing the universe's likeness to its Maker, representing that aspect of Him which nothing else reflects at all.

It is important to see that man's position as such a unique perfection and likeness is a *planned* superiority. From the divine arrangement which allocates perfection to created things according to their best measure, it was a consequence that some creatures would be intellectual, established at the very pinnacle of things. All creation is a likeness of its Creator, true, but God being what He intelligently is, creation was not *enough* likeness. Such similarity we can find in nature in two ways: either in the proper existence of a nature, and/or in cognition. For His purpose then, that the likeness of Himself would be perfectly in things in all possible ways, it was necessary that divine goodness would communicate itself to things into likenesses constituted not only by existing in a proper natural existence, but in that other mode of existence

49. Leo XIII, "Rerum Novarum," from text in *Social Wellsprings* (Ed., Husslein), p. 170.
50. Cf. Pace, *op. cit.*, p. 214 ff.

like the Creator's own, a likeness existent in a knowing nature, in his intelligence. It is because of this superior and potentially unlimited intellectual spirituality that he *consummates* the rest of creation in being, existence, and operation, and is the ultimate in excellence.[51] Thomism considers this immaterial element in man not only superior to the rest of creation which is only material, but as the necessary culmination to the perfection of that universe which the Creator wills to be a complete likeness (*secundum quid,* manifestly). The divine intellect is the source of creation and contains creation in His intellect. Therefore the perfected likeness of Him in creation could be completed only by having, in *some* creature at least, that intellectuality which would be a reflection of His own, a superior manner of existing, and operatively perfective of others' modes of existence in its natural ability to "contain" the others in its own existence, multiplying them, as it were, existentially, and extending itself existentially, in all of them. In this, man alone integrates the universe, and in that operational perfection only further magnifies the prestige he would have already held, by being the only creature of his spiritual kind in the world.[52]

This is a predominant and extremely important point in the Thomistic viewpoint of man, his actively central and integrating relation to all creatures by intelligence. He is not just *superior to* them, but superior because of a *ruling relation to* them, and they become superior to themselves *in him.*

51. *Comp. Theol.*, c. 148; I, q. 76, a. 1, c.; *C.G.*, II, c. 46.: ". . . necesse fuit ad creaturarum perfectionem quod aliquae creaturae essent intelligentes . . . in quibus secundum esse intelligibile forma divini intellectus exprimatur."
52. Cf. Lenz, *op. cit.*, p. 153 ff.: "Solche intellektuelle Naturen sind ihm ein notwendiger integrierender Bestandteil des Universums. Weil Gott selbst Intellekt ist und durch seinen Intellekt die Dinge geschaffen hat, musste das Universum wenigstens in einem Teile den gottlichen Intellekt nachbilden, es musste intellektuelle Naturen geben, die nicht bloss ihrer Natur nach Gott nachahmten, sondern auch durch ihre Tatigkeit weise ihrem Ursprung glichen . . . So stehen sie als hohere Ganzheiten mit Personwurde im Universum, das in ihnen kulminiert, sie sind in summo rerum vertice constitutae. . . . Weil der Mensch teil hat an dem Lichte des gottlichen Intellekts, nimmt er auch teil an der besonders bevorzugten Stellung der intellektuellen Substanzen im Universum."

Because of his intellectually containing them, he brings them
into clear focus, as it were, before their Creator. This is why
he completes or perfects the universe because in his rational
soul he possesses what the rest of creatures lack in likeness to
the nature of their Creator. He enables the universe then, to
attain to the likeness of its effective cause in a way which indicates the nature of that cause as they do not. His intellect
is the only creation directly reflecting the principle of creation, divine intellect. It is because of this uniqueness that
we can see the analogical application of the word "person"
even to God Himself then, as the similar summit of dignity
in His substantial intellect.[53] As a consequence of his rationality, man "rounds out" the universe with regard to the
likeness of these created effects to their cause. An effect is
supremely perfect when it *completely* circles back to its principle. Therefore, so that the universe of creatures might attain its final perfection, it is necessary for creatures to return to their principle. But each and every creature can
circle back to its principle only in the measure that they bear
the likeness of their principle according to their existence and
nature in which they possess a certain perfection, as all effects
are particularly perfect when they are like their agent cause
in a supreme degree. Therefore since the intellect of God is
the principle of the production of creatures, it was necessary
for the perfection of creatures that some creatures be intelligent. Moreover, since an agent acts according to its own
nature, the likeness in the effect is according to that nature.
The causing nature, however, is received in the effect sometimes according to the same mode of existing in which it exists in the agent, and sometimes according to another manner of existing. The first kind of likeness is clearly more
perfect. The perfection of creatures consists in a likeness to
God, as the perfection of any effect is a likeness to its agent
cause. But the total perfection of the universe requires not
only the second likeness to God, but also the first, as far as
possible. But the model according to which God makes a

53. I, q. 29, a. 3, ad 2; Augustine, *City of God*, Bk. XII, c. 13. Cf. Gilson,
Thomisme, p. 283.

creature, is an intelligible form in Him. It is necessary therefore for the total perfection of the universe that there be some creatures in whom the form of the divine intellect would be expressed in an intelligible species too. So one species, according to its own nature, was made intellectual according to the model of divine nature itself.

Man's unique superiority to other creatures is seen in his intellectual operation with regard to other existents, since he is cognitively related to them as God is related to them. God fully comprehends and embraces all creatures in Himself. True, this is represented in corporal creatures, but by another manner, in that a superior body is always found embracing and containing in its elements the elements of a lower, but this is by an extension of quantity, a material way. Since God contains all creatures in a simple manner and not by extension of quantity, it was necessary, so creatures would not lack an imitation of God *in His manner* of containing, that intelligent creatures be made, so some creatures could contain bodies not by an extension of quantity, but like God, *simpliciter*, in an intelligible mode.[54] So one type of creature is far superior to others in the importance of his position of completion among creatures, and further superior in the very unique nature of that specific difference which enables him to complete the perfection of the universe. His likeness is not only superior but unique. The human person alone among creatures can, like God, "contain" in himself the natures of the other creatures and also the very order of nature as it is arranged in all its multiple individuals. He can even parallel that order in himself in the arrangement of intelligible beings in his mind according to their naturally-existent arrangement in the world. And he models this too by his dominance over and ordering of the material compounds in his own composition, where he brings actions into being, and invests his material actions with a super-material dignity, because they become in him "created" and governed now as God creates and

54. This whole exposition of man's cognitive relation to creatures, and his consequent greater likeness, his unique likeness to the Creator, and so his position of supreme dignity in completing the universe, can be found most completely in *C.G.*, II, c. 46.

governs, by a spiritual intelligence. He can, under the guiding
rule of his immaterial faculty, parallel and duplicate that uni-
verse-arrangement in his whole person, as his knowing and
his willing establish such an order among his own corporal
elements of body. By the power of intelligence, and his godlike arrangement of all things in intelligible being within
him, he can preserve such a parallel of intended order in the
external universe, in the physical, moral, and personal orders,
even among the intelligence and wills of others like himself.
The rest of creation can only witness this by blind following.
But human persons can recognize that order and contain the
natures comprising both its elements and their ordered relations, contain them, as God does, in an intelligible being,
immanent in his personal self. He not only includes, but
through reason, he *expresses* the universe and its coordinated
likeness, *in* himself, *for* the rest, *to* God.[55] He can follow the
universal dynamic order consciously, and further it by rational foresight, in himself, and through others, and thus not
only possess a superior nature, but perfect his inferiors by
the operation of his own natural superiority which sublimates
them in a higher mode.

Intellectual nature is far superior then to any other, not
only as the immaterial is superior to the material, because the
spiritual by nature is not limited as is the material to the possession of one essence, but superior by a kind of capability
of infinity, in being able to become all natures by intelligible
inclusion of them in himself. This is what makes man such a
supreme agent in act, because he alone communicates *ad
extra* so intimately and awarely and comprehensively, and
yet he alone can turn back upon himself and his knowing,
and be aware even of his awareness.[56] This power is intimate
to him as no material power can be, a power therefore and an
immanence possessed by no other. Inanimate beings communicate nothing except by the external reciprocal action of
one upon another; animate beings like plants, communicate
from within in a way, but terminate externally, as sensitive

55. I–II, q. 94, a. 4, ad 3.
56. *C.G.,* IV, c. 11.

beings begin externally the flow of communication and end internally, actualizing the inner faculties of imagination and memory. But the intelligent species can be. *both the source and term* of its vital emanations: it may depend for its original stimulus upon external beings for actualization, but its mental generation exists by, for, and in, its internal intelligence itself. (Only divinity is higher, which begets a mental Word consubstantial with itself.)

This is not only significant of a higher existence and operation but perfective of its own superiority, inasmuch as, where other activity is more perfective of objects external to itself, intelligent activity most perfects itself.[57]

A person can "become all things" by taking all natures into himself intelligibly and entwining himself in all natures, identifying himself with all reality as God does, by intelligible inclusion. By so doing he accomplishes the incredible increase of his own actualization, not only by the actualization of his own powers, but through that very actualization, by the assimilation of all other actualities and perfections into his own existent being.[58] This gives a kind of relatively infinite extension or extensibility to his own person, a spiritual, intelligent, and unlimited capacity-power toward perfect actualization in the special powers proper to him alone, and in the intelligible actualizations of all else contained by him within himself. By this spiritual ability he can also immaterially enfold within himself, not only the natures of material things which he so "divinizes," but things which in their own proper existence are immaterial and external to him in reality, the non-corporal and therefore more valuable existents, even the obscure knowledge of which is of more value and makes the knower more valued, than certitude about corporal things.[59] Material substances participate in one type of being, or in one way; he can share in all, and therefore can share in the highest immaterial types of being other than his own, so that even beyond the *extensive* superiority of includ-

57. Aristotle, *De Anima*, III, 431b; *C.G.*, III, c. 112.
58. *De Anima*, lect. 1.
59. *De Anima*, lect. 1.

ing all material being intelligibly in his intellect, he is *intensively* superior by intellect in that he can include there types of immaterial beings themselves superior to the material. His proper intelligent function is to contain intelligibly not just the sensible appearances of those substantial and accidental beings but being *in se.* And above all, he can not only know participated beings, but being itself, abstracted from any limited particular, being the unparticipated. It is in this completion of others, and this containing of others, even of being, that man is not only existentially perfect and immensely superior, but always dynamically so because this is an activity which makes him operationally superior and is in turn perfective of *him* in his actualized person.

There is a double perfection in all things: one that a thing subsists in itself, the other in that it is ordered to other things. Each of these perfections in material things is terminated and finite because it has one determined nature by which it is only in one species, and determined natural powers therefore to only certain things. It has inclinations and order proportioned only to its own nature. But in each of these perfections immaterial things have a kind of infinity since in a certain way they can become all things, having a likeness of all either in actuality or potentiality, and this is cognition. And they have a kind of consequent capacity for infinity in the inclinations and direction of their rational will. In all these ways rationality perfects the knower himself.[60] Non-knowing creatures can possess but one essence and so cannot perfect themselves as can knowing creatures, which can possess many essences intelligibly as the likeness of a thing known is *in* the knower. The knower then is much less limited, much more capable of expansion and extension of his substantial and actual self.[61] It must be remarked that not only is the material prevented by materially-limited nature from perfecting itself in the possession of other natures, but the perfections of another nature are lacking to it. Only in one creature is the perfection proper to one creature found in another, as the

60. III *Sent.*, d. 27, q. 1, a. 4; I, q. 7, a. 2, ad 2.
61. I, q. 14, a. 1, c.

perfections of something known exist intelligibly in the knower. In this way it is possible for an intelligent creature to exist and include in his own existence the perfections of the whole universe.[62]

This then is the human person's superiority by his unique intelligence: he surpasses all and he includes all he surpasses; he can contain beings other than those material, and while by this he perfects the universe, at the same time his intellectual operations perfect the perfecter himself as no non-intelligent activity does. He alone is like the Creator in this way, a unique likeness in himself and further superior because he is the completing likeness for the universe, and such a dynamic intelligent likeness that he can further perfect himself as only *knowing* can, by an "expansion" of spiritual being.

SUPREMACY OF WILL AND FREE WILL. Rationality must have its own natural tendencies, and in the measure it is superior in knowing to all other creatures, so it is superior in its inclinations. Since the human person is capable of knowing everything, even being itself within the limits of his created essence, and since to know being is to know it is good, he is capable of desiring the universal he knows, of reaching for goodness itself. His rationality immediately means that his rational appetite inclines to universal good, goodness without limits and far above the capacities of lower creatures who, because they are limited by material nature, incline only to a limited good. Man surpasses everything else here in the inclination he naturally has, and in his consciousness of that inclination, and in his free manner of reaching for it in particular instances, as in the extent of what he reaches for and is pulled to.[63] Here too, the human person also includes what

---

62. *De Ver.*, q. 2, a. 2.

63. P. A. Rohner, article in *Divus Thomas* (1933), "Natur und Person in der Ethik," p. 58: "Die Person kann vernünftig denken, kann Zwercke vorziehen und nachsetzen, kann die Mittel frei auswahlen, weil in der menschlichen Person eine Edelnatur liegt deren tiefstes Wesen, Liebe zum Guten in allem ist. Die Liebe zum Guten erhebt die Person über alles das, was nicht das Gute in Person ist. Die *Liebe zum Guten ist der Grund alles Fortschrittes des Menschen* und der Menschheit. (Italics ours.) Die Liebe zum Guten ist die formale Bedingung der Möglichkeit der menschlichen Rangordnung der Werte."

he surpasses. He too has the limited natural attractions of lower creatures since such limitation must be contained in his unlimited capacity. All that is, is inclined to the good, though in different ways. Some are attracted only by an unconscious disposition of nature without any knowledge of it, as are inanimate creatures. Some other creatures feel the pull of goodness with what is, in some manner and measure, *recognition* of that good as an object. This is because of the "knowing" of their senses and estimative sense about a particular object which is "good" for their pleasure or pain. But to know the very nature of the good which attracts, belongs only to the creature who has the ability to understand, and only such a creature is attracted toward goodness directly and perfectly: he is attracted to unlimited goodness itself, he knows what it is that attracts him, and although he *must* move to it, he can consciously and freely move toward it in his choice of means.[64] Clearly this creature then is attracted toward universal good and can obtain it. This fact remains clear not only from experience but as a conclusion from metaphysics and logic, without constantly interjecting the qualification of the limitations of man's essence, limitations still metaphysically existent in spiritual beings. He is different from others as the banqueteer from the scavenger of crusts.

Each creature is attracted by that good which fits its nature, and each can reach therefore, only that same good. The

64. I, q. 59, a. 1, c.: Because of a current discussion to be dealt with more later, St. Thomas' own words should be seen in this instance. I, q. 77, a. 2, c.: ". . . res quae sunt infra hominem, quaedam particularia bona consequuntur; et ideo quasdam paucas et determinatas operationes habent et virtutes. Homo autem *potest consequi universalem et perfectam bonitatem,* quia potest adipisci beatitudinem. Est tamen in ultimo gradu, secundum naturam, eorum quibus competit beatitudo; et ideo multis et diversis operationibus et virtutibus indiget anima humana."

Idem, ad 1.: ". . . in hoc ipso magis ad similitudinem Dei accedit anima intellectiva quam creaturae inferiores quod perfectam bonitatem consequi potest, *licet per multa* et diversa. . . ."

C.G., III, c. 22: "Considerandum autem quod unumquodque, *inquantum participat similitudinem divinae bonitatis,* quae *est objectum* voluntatis ejus *intantum participat* de similitudine divinae voluntatis, per quam res producuntur in esse et conservantur. Superiora autem divinae bonitatis similitudinem participant simplicius et universalius . . . inferiora vero particularius et magis divisim."

human person alone has a nature partly spiritual and capable of the universal. Therefore he alone has will, and an attraction to universal good which is not only natural and inescapable, but rational and aware. He is superior to others because he still has all the particular inclinations they have; he surpasses them further because he has far greater inclinations and possibilities than they have. He more than surpasses them, he is uniquely different, because his radically different spiritual principle is attracted to goodness itself, and rationally so. He is pulled toward good in the preservation of his existence, as are all existents; along with living and generating existents, he too moves to the preservation of the generated extensions of his own existence and being, in his progeny. But he also moves himself to good in a way proper only to him, as the only creature whose nature is spiritual and consequently capable of consciously appreciating total goodness, as God does. Because of this universal attraction, even some particular goods are peculiar to his appetite alone, because only a rational person can feel the attraction of sacrifice, for instance, or justice, or any good so directly and intelligibly representative of divine goodness.[65] He wants far more than any other creature, *and he knows it. He is different*: everything in life pleases him. If all he has is good, all he has not yet is good too, and he is restless until it is got.

That this superior universality of the human person's desire is so, and that therefore his intimate and close and peculiar likeness to the Creator is a fact, that all this is supremely and valuably and inevitably natural to him alone, is clear from individual experience and all human history.[66] He must have an "infinite capacity for good" whose desires evidently

65. I–II, q. 94, a. 2.
66. It is scarcely our place and purpose here to elaborate this fully. We accept the experiential fact as *datum*, intending only to indicate its significance. For a treatment of this which is complete and famous for its psychological insight, Cf.: I, q. 14, a. 1; q. 81, a. 3; I–II, qq. 2–3; q. 87, a. 7, ad 2; Supp. q. 41, a. 1, ad 1. Cf. Enid Smith, *The Goodness of Being*, and Gilson, *Spirit of Medieval Philosophy*, especially pp. 272–275, where he shows an ability very rare today, to be at once lyrical and philosophical: "Disgust with each particular good is but the reverse side of our thirst for the total good; weariness is but the presentiment of the *infinite gulf that lies between the thing loved and the thing within love's capacity.*"

are infinite, and constantly unsatisfied by either the quality or quantity of particular, limited goods. The significant point here is the extreme superiority of man's will to the good over that of all other creatures. In any evaluation of the position of the human person among creatures, the magnitude of this difference must be appreciated. The superior distinction of man in this respect does not flow from his possession of some more or less greater degree of capacity, but rather lies in the fact that not even the sum of particular goods could satisfy him. His spiritual capacity makes his desires and potentials for goods not only of greater extent, but of such greater extent that they are different in kind, as the limited differs from the unlimited and the universal is contrary to the particular. Neither by quantity nor nature can material goods complete rational man. Their inability to satisfy him is a kind of negative imitation of their total inadequacy in the fact of God's goodness. Their lack is not just the result of any quantitative deficiency, because their very sum total leaves him incomplete and unsatisfied. Their lack is *qualitative*. They lack the character of completeness and finality which alone can fit the rational and spiritual capacities of human persons, and so they cannot possibly complete the desires of a spiritual appetite, any more than they could the original whose imitation man is. Then too, from a less negative viewpoint the superiority of his conscious and free movement toward such a good must be appreciated if one wishes to evaluate properly this extreme superiority of the human person. He alone knows and appreciates and freely moves to the same good that the Creator does, in which progress he is not only a superior participant, but the unique likeness of Him who *is* the all whom man alone, by nature, must want.

The more observable side of man's superiority of will is a consequence of his rational appetite to universal good. Because he is not limited to any particular nature in his understanding nor therefore any particular good in his desires, he can choose between them. We are all conscious of the freedom we possess in this choosing. The human person is not bound by nature to one type of action or operation or choice of object, as are other creatures. While man enfolds in himself and therefore is united to and understands the rest of creation, he surpasses it in his use of the very elements which he and they have in common: he has *command decision* over his actions: he is master of himself and his powers of operation, having the power of choice to act or not. This is not just a kind of subsistence as an existence independent of other substances, yet rigidly controlled and directed to one particular function for one particular and limited good; this is that "more excellent manner" of existence which necessitates a "special name." This is a uniquely autonomous existence in possession of all elements within him and the free use of them, the free *central control* of being and operation in himself, the free disposition of his powers. Where others are more acted upon than acting, he commands his own spontaneity as a master agent.[67] Although he *finally* owes his excellence to that source and end of his being and of the superlative powers given to attain that end, his operative dignity flowing from that first intention, he observably achieves and consciously continues to increase and demonstrate that dignity in the self-dominant operative living through which he shows himself master of his own actions. He alone in creation is so autonomous, because he alone is the "master of the acts which lead toward his end." Obviously, this is a far higher mode of living and this the only instance of such in creation.[68] This is the inevitable consequence of his spiritual rationality, the necessary corollary to his universal understanding and desires. He not only can see and plan, but he can choose means to an end and therefore dominate possibilities now present to him and also those of the future, allowing himself exten-

(margin note: we cannot violate this)

---

67. *C.G.*, II, c. 47; cf. Maritain, *Scholasticism and Politics*, p. 63 ff.

68. I, q. 29, a. 1, c. and *De Pot.*, q. 9, a. 1, ad 3: "Hoc autem quod est *per se agere excellentiori modo* convenit substantiis rationalis naturae quam aliis. Nam solae substantiae rationales habent dominium sui actus; ita quod in eis est agere et non agere, aliae vero substantiae magis aguntur quam agant. . . ." Note. It is not our aim to demonstrate the *presence* of free will, only to point out its uniqueness and therefore its significance for the value of man in creation.

sive "play" in movement both within himself and in the operation of his own powers, and in the use by those powers of external goods and of all goods, material and immaterial. Man can not only choose among actions and goods to be used, these fruits of the earth, but can possess all as his field of choice and so can "possess the earth."[69]

The effects of his free choice put him in a pre-eminent position among creatures. By this ability he can freely choose to communicate being and goodness. In this he is supremely like the Creator because he acts in the same rational free way, and in so doing pours out goodness, actualizing more beings and perfecting others. He is a likeness then not only of the nature of the Creator, but the divine way of intelligibly and freely existing and operating. Such a creature, as was pointed out in regard to his talent of knowing, was necessary if the creation was to be the intended complete image of the Creator.[70] Because he has the potential to do this, and because by doing it, he exercises spontaneous creative power toward his own completion of being and the increase of beings in the universe, he is dynamically always increasing both his own and the universe's likeness to its Maker and his.[71] This independent and governing mode of existence and operation is clearly superior to every other creature's operative existence so much so that it is this command over actions which is the source of that uniqueness in the human person which makes him so different from all others who have no such choice, and which shows him in observable operation to be supremely unique in perfection and worth, because he is thereby a supreme likeness in creation of the free and intelligible nature by which the Creator acts. The supreme manner of subsisting with control over his own operational existence reflects in him a far greater similarity to perfection itself, which is as intimately in the universe as man is, and yet so infinitely transcends it in free and autonomous operation, an activity different in kind from the material operations of the rest of

69. Cf. Leo XIII, *op. cit.*, p. 171.   70. *C.G.*, II, c. 46.
71. Cf. Harvey, *The Metaphysical Relation Between Person and Liberty*, p. 68 ff.

things.[72] Man also reflects this in that he too is independent of reality, "in the world" indeed, but freely not "of the world" in that he is not chained to any one inclination or action or object as is the rest of creation, though he controls and freely uses elements common to him and all other natures.

It is his rationality that gives man this superiority of choice and dominance over himself, over his actions, and over the goods he may make use of, and it is in the operation of this free activity that man not only is constituted in a greater operative perfection, but achieves his own further perfecting, his further actuality; and then also, with the retroaction of values, he himself gains even greater perfection because the perfective use of his powers has perfected the universe more, by his free creation of further actualities in it. He not only is perfective of himself and the universe, but actually the master of the means of perfection themselves, a position of likeness to the omnipotent and free Creator's governance of Himself and all else, which is immeasurably above the irrational creatures who are not free movers, but only moved. This *is* man's nature. This supremacy *belongs* to him. And the final reason for all this superiority in existence and operation

---

72. Too many modern writers, struck by this, and by the necessity of emphasizing man's independent freedom, have submerged the *ratio* of it, which *is* man's reason. Outside of that false emphasis, there are many modern scholastic expressions of the importance of this superior operational talent, which reflect the same viewpoint St. Thomas himself asserted in his writings. Read the whole context in Lenz, *op. cit.*, pp. 139–166, but especially p. 147: "Der Unterschied zwischen Person und Sache besteht nicht so sehr in der rationalitas oder Geistigkeit selbst, sondern in ihrer Rückwirkung und Auswirkung für die Subsistenz. Als Formelelement der Person möchte ich nun nicht mehr die Subsistenz schlechthin bezeichnen, sondern die höhere geisteigerte Individualität und Subsistenz der geistigen Natur, die sich besonders in ihrer Freiheit bekundet. Weil sie ein vollkommeneres 'per se esse' hat, hat sie auch ein vollkommeneres 'per se agere' . . . die positive Vollkommenheit, wodurch eine communicatio ausgeschlossen wird, ist bei der Person grösser, sie hat *eine grössere Unabhängigkeit,* vollkommenere Einheit, höhere, innere Konzentration und Ganzheit, *grössere Selbstmacht.* Sie ist in eigenblichen Sinne, Prinzip und Herr ihrer Tätigkeit, deshalb hat sie Eigenwert und Eigenrecht. Und zwar ist es schon hier ganz klar, dass die Person diese ihre Würde und Vollkommenheit nicht von aussen hat, nicht etwa als Teil der Gemeinschaft oder auch als pars principalis des Universums, sondern aus sich, als *ursprungliche Gabe.*" (Italics ours.)

is the reason why it was originally communicated to him: the divinely constituted goal, the completion-goal for man, a *special* existence-end and operation-end belonging only to the human person and possible only for such a spirit, the first and final reason for, and the proof of, his immensely perfected supremacy over all other creatures, the final person-goal of free persons.

UNIQUENESS OF DESTINY. The man who manufactures something makes it fit the purpose he first has in mind. So the Creator. As what we observe and analyze in the natures of creatures gives us the idea of their proper purpose, so the knowledge of their purpose, more than anything else, bestows an understanding of their natures. It has been the unanimous conclusion of history and science (except for a modern and brief shortsightedness) that "nature does nothing in vain," that functions not only have end-results, but the same functions the same results, and that this end purpose is the "cause of causes," the causal-aim which instigates the activity of a causal-source. It is the last and final explanation of the nature and functions and perfective actualizations of creatures.[73] In this question, it has been apparent that the whole universe with its almost limitless variety of natures and functions and immediate ends, is integrated by having the same source originally and the same goal finally, from which each one originates and back to which each moves finally, each in its measure and manner.[74] It is clear from what has been said

73. *De Ver.*, q. 10, a. 6; I–II, q. 1, a. 2; I *Sent.*, d. 3, q. 2, a. 2.
74. *C.G.*, III, c. 22. Gilson summarizes the Thomistic position with his usual clarity: *Thomisme,* p. 588: "L'ordre entier des créatures dérive d'une seule cause et tend vers une seule fin. Nous pouvons donc attendre que le principe régulateur des actions morales soit identique à celui des lois physiques; la cause profonde qui fait que la pierre tombe, que la flamme s'élève, que les cieux tournent et que les hommes veulent, est la même; chacun de ces êtres n'agit que pour atteindre, par ses opérations, la perfection qui lui est propre, et réaliser par la même sa fin, qui est de représenter Dieu: 'unumquodque tendens in suam perfectionem, tendit in divinam similitudinem.' Toutefois, chaque être se définissant par une essence propre, on doit ajouter qu'il aura sa manière propre de réaliser leur fin dernière dans la mesure ou elles participent à sa ressemblance, il faut bien que les créatures intelligentes atteignent leur fin d'une manière qui leur soit particulière . . . par leur opération propre de créatures intelligent et en la connaissant."

already, that the completing of each being in operative existence and functions is a *growth in likeness* to existence and
perfect goodness itself, the source and end and model of
all, the cause whose reflection must be in varying degrees in
all its effects: *agens agit sibi simile.*[75] This impressive view
then which Thomism gives of the universe in its final explanation, is that each has an immediate end in the completion of its own potentials, and each lesser capacity also finds
in that being which immediately exceeds it in capacities its
own immediate goal of perfection, so that in the ascending
hierarchy, each creature finds its goal in its immediate superior, and the combination of all of them finds its goal of
completion and perfection in the perfection of itself, and
also, through man, its part in the integrated perfection of
the whole universe. Man alone, the creature masterpiece,
finds his goal directly *ad extra,* in his God. Human powers are
beyond the rest, so the human essence and existent person
are beyond others, and he finds his purpose is far beyond the
rest, a goal different in direction and in directness, the supreme in kind. All the parts of the universe are for the perfection of the whole, but man alone goes further and finds
his extrinsic end in the enjoyment of his God, because as each
less noble creature is for the nobler, man alone finds none
nobler within his created range, but God Himself. All other
creatures are for God finally, and He is their end indirectly,
but man has God for his direct end and represents Him with
visible creation's sole intelligent image.[76]

It is an inescapable conclusion that the creature whose superiority we have been outlining, than whom we can find

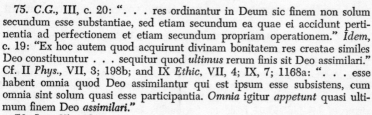

75. *C.G.,* III, c. 20: ". . . res ordinantur in Deum sic finem non solum
secundum esse substantiae, sed etiam secundum ea quae ei accidunt perti-
nentia ad perfectionem et etiam secundum propriam operationem." *Idem,*
c. 19: "Ex hoc autem quod acquirunt divinam bonitatem res creatae similes
Deo constituuntur . . . sequitur quod *ultimus* rerum finis sit Deo assimilari."
Cf. II *Phys.,* VII, 3; 198b; and IX *Ethic,* VII, 4; IX, 7; 1168a: ". . . esse
habent omnia quod Deo assimilantur qui est ipsum esse subsistens, cum
omnia sint solum quasi esse participantia. *Omnia* igitur *appetunt* quasi ultimum finem Deo *assimilari."*

76. I, q. 65, a. 2, c.

none higher upon earth, has no other creature above himself then, to be his goal. He alone of all of them must be his own immediate goal, not just in the functional end of each of his powers, but himself the first end-purpose of his total person. The end of all functions is their perfection of function in actuality, and the end of all functions actualized in a man is that man-person. This functional end in man himself, because of his spirituality and consequent lack of limitations, presents itself as a quasi-infinity, a potential indetermination. This point cannot be over-emphasized in setting out the superior value of man, who is in the true sense *unique* in this respect, the only creature whose operations and goal center upon his individual *self*, and which must do so because of his conscious and intelligent nature and powers which inherently make him a self-end.[77] Because man knows and can therefore choose, and can control his own functions and means to ends, and control his choice of proximate goals, he is "limited" under God and by his own nature, in a far from rigid way, and directs himself to himself as his end. He alone, as an individual then, as one human person, *is* an end, and rising above his own species, assumes an importance possessed by no other creatures, which are only for their species. He alone moves himself and directs his individual actions to his individual goal with his own unique command over his own powers. He alone in creation operates toward and for his chosen goal as a *true agent*, a controlling and deciding power in himself, while all other creatures are rigidly moved by their natures, as instruments for their species, for ends over which they neither exercise nor possess any control or right to control. Their species exist and operate in themselves, only for the human species, and those species and the human

77. *C.G.*, III, c. 28; also Smith, "Human Social Life," *op. cit.*, p. 291. Cf. Emmanuel Kant, *Kritick der praktischen Vernunft* (from Reimar Verlag, 1908), vol. 13, p. 87, for a very keen insight into this human situation: "Everything in creation, except one thing, is subject to the power of man, and can be used by man as a means to an end, but man himself, man the rational creature, is an end in himself. He is the subject of moral law and is sacred by virtue of his individual freedom. Personality exhibits palpably before our bodily eyes the sublimity of our nature."

species in final analysis, for the individual human person.[78] Only a human person can consciously command many of the powers in his nature; all other creatures are commanded by theirs. And because of this, in the realm of purpose and goal, only in the human species, which is one of free individuals with a power of rational choice, is the immortal and incorruptible spiritual individual above his species, a permanent and commanding individual agent who manages his own energies and drives, for himself, for his chosen proximate reasons and goals, and for his own individual and personal good and satisfaction. Obviously, this is such superiority in a human person, that he is in a class apart, the sole creature who is in any way more important as an individual than his own class. The point begins to be, not just that the human species is by far the most gifted and superior in creation, but that *this or that* man is of more value than all the individuals of any other species, or all the other species together. His own human species is important because of these human individuals who compose it, because they alone as individuals are spiritual and permanent. Other individuals of other species are expendable. Not man; he alone is free, spiritual, permanent and priceless. In this light, he can be seen as so far superior to anything else that comparison becomes difficult: it is like comparing the monkey wrench to the hand that can turn it at will. And when one appreciates the uniqueness of man in this respect, it is clearly seen how much greater, how much more extensive and intensive a likeness he is to the Creator than any other creature. He alone participates in the true agency of God, and is related to others as God is, as agent to instrument, as commander to the commanded, as person to thing.

Since man alone is a true agent, and the other creatures instruments, they *must* in their irrational and unfree existence, find their goal in him alone who acts on account of himself, and freely so acts. Others can only follow their natures as instruments do and perfect an instrumentality which

78. I–II, q. 1, a. 2; *C.G.*, IV, c. 55; and especially *C.G.*, III, c. 113.

is naturally directed towards helping the human person to reach his goal by using them. He is not only then the peak of creation as something above other creatures, but is the focus of their being and existence, that to which they all point as *their* immediate goal.[79] While on the one hand he is part of the universe, on the other he is the center and peak and integration of the universe, something surpassing the whole, and so different and free that he constitutes something for which the universe is, and for which it is activated, as an instrument for which he is the purpose in use and control. This position he achieves because he alone partakes of divine intelligence, by which the Maker of creatures is their Maker and related to them as Ruler to ruled. A human person knows himself and them, and consequently can direct himself and them, so that other creatures, in being directed by their own implanted natures and by man, must operate for man. Only intellectual natures can exist *propter se,* and the fact that man alone in visible creation is such, and that other creatures are instruments for him, is a fact evident from universal actions and the fitness of such a relational procedure, which man has always followed and which irrational and inanimate creatures are obviously fitted to. Each creature shows by its habitual natural acts that it was so born to act that way, as Aquinas has put it in a carved phrase: *"sicut agitur unumquodque in cursu naturae, ita natum est agi."*[80]

79. II *Sent.,* d. 1, q. 2, a. 3: "Ipse enim duplicem ordinem in universo instituit; principalem et secundarium. Principalis est secundum quod res ordinantur in ipsum; et secundarius est secundum quod *una juvat aliam* in perveniendo ad similitudinem divinis . . . ex parte operis ipsae creaturae tendunt in divinam bonitatem sicut in illud cui per se assimilari intendunt. Sed quia optimo assimilatur aliquid per hoc quod simile fit meliori se, ideo *omnis creatura corporalis tendit in assimilationem creaturae intellectualis* quantum potest, quae altiori modo divinam bonitatem consequitur, et propter hoc etiam forma humana, scilicet anima rationalis, dicitur esse finis ultimus intentus a natura inferiori. . . ."

80. *C.G.,* III, c. 112. Cf. Lenz, *op. cit.,* p. 154: "Durch die Vollkommenheit ihrer Natur überragt sie die anderen Geschöpfe, weil sie allein Herr ihrer Akte ist und sich frei zur Tätigkeit bestimmt. Ebenso zeichnet sie sich aus durch die Erhobenheit und Würde ihres Zieles, weil sie in ihrer Tätigkeit nicht durch das Universums, sondern unmittelbar durch Erkenntnis und Liebe, Gott, das Ziel des Universums erreicht, während die anderen Geschöpfe nur

All creatures will find their final end in their Creator to whom their nature's law directs them in existence and in all operations which depend upon His *concursus.* But the point of prestige here is, first of all, that man alone can be his own end too, and that he is their end also, and that all others attain their final end through him, that they complete their immediate purpose in him, and that through him they not only attain their final end then, but participate in his final end as they are contained in his composite and find therein an end higher than their own nature's. They reach God indirectly, *via* man for whom they are. Man is immensely superior to them because their lesser potentials and lack of self-direction make him not only superior in his possession of what they lack, but make him the goal of what they have in their existence and operations. Their functions find completion insofar as they function for man, and man alone will have the unique distinction and dignity of aiming at God directly and containing within him the power to possess that God.

It is already obvious from our previous analysis of human nature, that the Infinite alone can be the goal of man's existence and powers. Whatever he has in common with lower creatures in this order of ends above all, nothing exists to compare with him except God Himself, in whom alone man finds his completion.[81]

Only man is capable of aiming at God directly, and only he is able to possess the infinitely spiritual. Other creatures can attain only the particular, because their natures participate in divine goodness only in existence or in living, or knowing present particulars by their senses or imagination. Only the human rational nature knows the essence of good and can directly move toward and attain the universal.[82] And since the only *actual* existent universal as such is God,

---

über den Menschen an diesem Ziele teilnehmen. So ist es klar, dass der Mensch nicht bloss als Teil, sonderns als Personganzheit im Universum steht. Als rationale Kreatur hat er nicht bloss einen Mittelwert durch und für das Universum, sondern Eigenwert, während die anderen Geschöpfe nur Mittel für den Menschen sind."

81. *C.G.,* IV, c. 54.
82. II–II, q. 2, a. 3, c. Cf. Maritain, *Scholasticism and Politics,* p. 64.

and the only actual spiritual potential capable of embracing such is man, man alone among creatures is fitted and prearranged by nature to move toward and find God directly, and attain Him wholly. The human person alone, by knowing and loving, can reach the infinite-knowing Himself, and so has, in a special manner not given to any other creatures, God Himself as his goal.[83] He is under God's plan and governing in a higher and special manner. This is evident from the only kind of goal and the only manner of attaining it (in knowledge and love) which fits his nature and his alone. None of those who lack intelligence could have this goal or be competent to embrace it. They indeed share somehow in the perfect and communicative existent, and reflect Him as their source and end. But man manifests that he is made for the universal *directly*, and shows, as they do not, that he is capable of *possessing* Him. Others attain their end insofar as they are, or live or even know by sense. Man alone attains it by knowing and loving. They can attain God only in and through man, and none of them is built to possess the universal at all, nor the spiritual. In goal, in immediacy of direction to it, in capacity of attainment and manner of possession, a human person is so superior to the rest of creatures that he is uniquely alone in nature and manner of existence and in purpose. He alone is spiritual and knowing and permanent, a perfection of participation in being and a resultant likeness to perfection which is so supreme that he is much more different from than like lower creatures. As he uses them and completes them and elevates them, and as they belong to him and find their end in him, he is to them as their proximate good.

COMMAND OF CREATION. Because of his rationality which includes both his intelligence and his rational will, man is not isolated in his superiority. It is the summation and climax of all man's superiority to other creatures to point out that he is not only existing and operating in a unique and supreme position by himself, that he not only has a destiny toward which all lower natures are pointed also in and through him,

83. I, q. 65, a. 2. c.; *C.G.*, III, c. 147; Gilson, *Thomisme*, p. 245 ff.

but that the very rational nature and supreme goal which places him so far above other creatures, constitutes him in a particular active and godlike command-relation to inferior creatures. All creatures are under the governing intelligence of the Creator. However, a human person is under it not only in a way different from and superior to others, but under it in such an intelligent manner that he is constituted in relation to others much as God is, in a governing relationship. The divine nature which creates, conserves, foresees, and governs, is named Providence. As man participates in divinity and shows a likeness to it, he evidences therein his real and natural sharing in that providential activity of command.

The concept of Providence involves two things quite distinct, although one necessarily follows from the other in the case of divinity, and it would seem also in the case of humanity, which shares in divinity in the measure of man's sharing. Providence, strictly speaking, is the Creator's knowledge of the natures He has created, the relations between the whole order existing among them, the planned ends for all of them, and the graduated superiorities of their ends. Consequent upon this knowledge is the following out of that planned and known order, the execution of His providential plan, which is His rule over creatures as He intelligently directs them to their known and proper ends according to His intention. His pre-existent knowledge is an eternal thing; the execution in governing is a temporal measure, except for immortal man.[84] In this order of ends and execution, we have seen that man was made superior in nature and operation because he was *planned to be* superior in purpose and aim and destiny. He is not only superior matter in his complexity and extent of operation, in that he includes, coordinates, and elevates elements common to other creatures and even includes in active use or vestigial "carry-over" the very organs of lower creatures, but he is immeasurably above matter because he shares the spiritual whose immateriality is by nature inde-

84. I, q. 22, a. 1, c., and a. 2, ad 3; I–II, in re the final end of man. Cf. Garrigou-Lagrange: *Providence*, p. 158.

pendent of the limitation of matter, the very contradiction of it. So the human person is consequently not limited in operation of understanding or choice of immediate ends, not limited to the comprehension of his own nature nor by blind laws of a nature. Besides, since this creature alone is a person who is living in a uniquely excellent manner of existence, he is the only creature supreme as an individual, and far different in a superior way, to all the individuated units in creation which remain individually subordinated to their species. In this species, the individual is the supreme value, and permanently so. The principle which the Aristotelian and Thomistic philosophy applies to such an order is that such superiority, such perfection, particularly in the case of perfection in individual humans, is thus constituted by the order of ends and the effective powers of nature in a regulating position over inferiors which are less perfect.[85] Because of this more perfect position and especially because he is an individual whose value leaps beyond his species, *qua* species, man can never be only a *means ad genus,* as others are. The positions are contrary: others are to be looked upon only as instruments, while spiritual man can never be such, but must be a true agent. This means that by very nature his independence is such as to make him not only superior, but so peculiarly superior as to place him in *command decision over all the others* who by nature remain only blind means or instruments. Such is the Thomistic position and since this applies to *all* persons by nature, and prohibits their being used as irrational and ruled creatures, it is a position whose implications for value-standards in the relations between humans, and the relation of humans and irrational creatures, are far-reaching and of great social significance.

The theory is best seen again, from the aspect of the participated-divinity which man is and the resultant image he

85. I, q. 96, a. 2, and *Comm. Caietani* ibi notatum: "unicuique convenit praeesse vel subesse, secundum conformitatem ad gradum suum." This is a principle constantly accepted throughout Aristotle and St. Thomas: the imperfect is not only inferior to the perfect, but *for* it; perfections flow down from perfects to imperfects. The scientific moderns emphasize more the "emergence" of the more perfect from the imperfect.

is, not only in nature and end, but consequently in existence and living operation. Since he is rational, he is so because he shares in the divine intelligence. But it is the divine intelligence which has created, and which plans and foresees ends and the ordering to ends. Therefore, by his sharing in rationality, man is sharing in that activity of intelligence called Providence. The point is not just that he is a subject of providence, which he obviously is, but that his ability to understand natures and ends makes him participative of divine providential intelligence, as no other creature is. He grasps, as divine intelligence originally knows, his own goal and the goals of others. He can foresee the ordering of natures to those ends, and the means chosen, and the plan of all.[86]

It is clear that all creatures are subject to divine providence and so in some way subject to divine and eternal law, regulated by it and measured so in actions, as is shown in their very inherent drives to their natural and proper actions. But one creature alone *provides* consciously and freely for himself and others, and recognizes in his nature that participation in eternal law which is for him then the created *natural law* of his rational nature. This means a very different and *active* participation in the foreseeing intelligence of God which constitutes human person in a likeness superior, and even contrary to, the inferior participation and likeness of other creatures. Moreover, he is under providence as a free agent, as one who is by that rationally free nature, in control of his own actions, capable of a choice of means to ends, and therefore partaking of the free and causal control of the intelligent and free principle agent who creates. The Thomistic argument based on these facts is that such intellectual and voluntary relation to God, which makes him participative of God's foreseeing intelligence *and directive will*, immediately puts man in a relation to creatures which do not so participate, as of agent to instrument, a godlike relation which is uniquely imitative of both the understanding and of the directing Providence. He and lower creatures have by no means the same kind of providential relation to the Creator,

86. I–II, q. 91, a. 2, c.

but rather they are to man more as man is to God, and man to them more as God is to them, in a shared measure, of course, but really sharing in the foresight and even the causal and free directing of Providence, the right and capacity of rule. The observable fact that lower creatures are more moved by men, or blindly by their own natures, shows they have principally the characteristic of instruments, while the rational nature of man which evidences its recognition of its own nature's needs and the human person's evidence of his personal dominion over his own actions, show that they have the characteristic of agency which acts by itself, for itself, freely. From this it is clear that what shows itself to be an instrument must be an instrument *for something,* and the very fitting of their natures to man's need shows them to be instruments for man who manifests himself in turn as a free governing agent. He manifests himself as *competent* to use them, they only as competent *to be used.* Human persons, then, exhibit in their operational existence a relation to divine Providence which is not only that of the governed, but of the participative governing.[87] To our modern minds and psychological outlook, it seems too abrupt, if not something of a gratuitous assumption to draw a conclusion of human dominance over the rest of creation immediately from man's participated rationality, so that one insists that it is his very rational nature to dominate, and others' to submit.[88] But the implications of his rationality give more strength to the doctrine. It is from the observation of what naturally and universally takes place that induction seeks the *rationale* for

87. The cumulative force of this thesis in Thomism can be got only from the full study of its treatment in Aquinas. The argument is explicitly based upon the very nature of man as intellectual, and implicitly upon the experiential evidence man has always had of how natures in action fit this relationship naturally: *"sicut agitur in cursu naturae, ita natum est agi."* It is both an application of the principle *operatio sequitur esse* and an inverse application of it into arguing the natures and relations of created "esse" from their characteristic operations. I, q. 21, a. 1, ad 3; *C.G.,* III, cc. 64, 77, 78, 81, 112, and particularly c. 113.

88. II–II, q. 66, a. 1, c.; *C.G.,* III, c. 81: "Quia tamen aliquid homo de lumine *intellectuali participat, ei* secundum providentiae divinae ordinem *subduntur* animalia bruta, quae intellectu nullo modo participant." Cf. II–II, q. 168, a. 11.

man's instinctive use of and dominance over the rest of creation. All the experience men have shows such instinctive actions of rational men with irrational creatures, and confirms
this reasoning. We know rational man can grasp goals and
the means to reach them. From his own nature, he can understand his own goal. By that same nature he can understand
much of the created natures around him and can thus grasp
also what their goals are and how their goals are arranged as
subordinate to his and therefore intended for him in his attaining his own higher goal. In this way, he grasps the total
and final purpose of all, and many of the planned means
toward reaching it, which are secondary ends themselves.
Only man and God can do this. God's so knowing is called
Providence. Moreover, life-experience, and the life-experi-
ences of history, show that man *needs* the use and help of
other lower creatures in the attainment of his own goal, a
goal he not only foresees but now sees he must strive for, and
a goal which his very nature and natural powers demand be
striven for. Therefore he looks upon other creatures as *made
for him* by their very natures and purposes, and so naturally
uses them as he proves himself able to, and by instinctly as-
sumed right of nature and purpose. God is his human completion-goal directly, and he alone of creatures, as the only
one master of his own actions, is a proximate end in himself,
a fact he rationally recognizes in himself. But by their very
make-up and their lack of intelligence, man can see that other
irrational and determined creatures must find God through
him as their proximate goal, and this order of ends thus puts
him in a command relation to the rest of creation, insofar as
he not only has the ability to use them for his purpose, but is
bound to help achieve the final end of all creatures which he
can recognize for all and they cannot at all. They obviously
are unable to use themselves freely, nor can their own powers
move by nature to any goal beyond the perfection of their
species toward which they rigidly move by the blind dictates
of their nature, whose ends depend upon an ordered motion
planted in them by an intelligence outside of them which
makes of them only instruments. But since man shares that

intelligence, he is, in the measure he shares it, partly their end and can be their consequent master. "From the very fact that he understands divine providence . . . he *can* govern himself and others."[89] He alone shares something which makes of him an agent who uses and directs, and they without sharing such must be intended only as instruments for the use of those who share.[90] This plan, because he participates in the intelligence which made it, man sees by his intelligent nature and instinctively puts in operation, never questioning the validity of his position of mastery over irrational creation and his rightful free use of them. The Thomistic theory of the *raison d'être* of such a position is not just an *a priori* assumption with no relation to facts, but rather the scientific attempt to explain what is naïvely obvious in practise, a power daily proved and a right of use taken for granted by all men and never resisted by lower creatures with any effective and universal success which would invalidate the thesis. The individualized unbalance of the relation and the historical difficulty of its execution is a historical problem connected with the theology of original sin and not germane to philosophy.

In actual experience, as if putting the relation to experimental proof, man finds that non-rational and instrumental creatures fit the part of instruments for him and his needs. They do not naturally and entirely resist his use of them and the dominion here spoken of is precisely only this: the natural need of, and native competence and right to *rational use*. It is not only that this higher rational level *can* use a lower, but that the assimilation of the lower by the higher so fits the higher, and the lack of the control and use of that lower so impedes the higher, that empirical evidence shows one must be made for the other, as necessary for its very conservation

89. *C.G.*, III, c. 113.
90. I–II q. 91, a. 2, c.; cf. Gilson, *op. cit.*, p. 245: "L'homme, qui vient prendre rang immédiatement après les anges au point de vue de la perfection, n'apparait cependant qu'au terme de la création dont il est la veritable fin. C'est *pour lui* que sont crées les astres incorruptibile, que Dieu divise les eaux par le firmament, découvre la terre noyée sous les eaux et la peuple d'animaux ou de plantes."

in existence, and therefore subject to its control and use. There *are* needs, and observably, lower creatures *fit* them when used, a fitness shown throughout creation, even in the use by the blind instinct of non-human animals, of creatures less than they. Even the simple elements show themselves naturally fitted for compounds, as do inorganic compounds for the organic and living, as plants exhibit themselves neces- sary and useful for animals. So all of them, and animals par- ticularly, show themselves patterned in their elements and powers to fit the needs and be the instruments of accomplish- ment of man's existence and powers, the means for actualiza- tion of his perfection-goal.[91] All these creatures are them- selves for man's use. Some are for food, some for clothing, for transportation, for innumerable aids to the realization of his capacities, particularly to the actualization, finally, of his power of knowing, that power which makes him so like the understanding and foreseeing and directing Creator.[92] Inso- far as these other elements are directly fitted for his animal needs and directly or indirectly are instruments for the com- pletion of his intellectual potentials, by which he reaches his intellectual and universal end, he is superior to them in a governing way and he therefore *directs* them to that use by right of his rationality which sees the proper use, and in this way directs, along with God, the whole universe to its end. Man is the master value of the irrational universe, as the value of man is God. This is the full notion of his mid-posi- tion, his *"nodus et vinculum"* status, the *"horizon et con- finium"* relation he has to others.

This power over and this right to the proper use of crea- tures external to him Thomistic philosophy saw corroborated and "modeled," as it were, in man's own composite. They took this dynamic microcosm he individually coordinates and masters within himself as the coordinate and particular evi- dence of his rational right to use and control external mate- rial elements and forms which are only twin to what he in- cludes in himself. Over his own composite, no one can doubt

91. *C.G.*, III, c. 22.
92. *De Pot.*, q. 5, a. 9.

his factual and customary control and the legitimacy of his natural self-rule, his use of his reason as the principle of his authority and power and the use of his rational free will as its implement, whether he exercises a "politic dominion" or a "despotic rule," such as he has over the vegetative functions of his corporal elements.[93] As the material elements in him are under his control, he is the created unit-model in himself of the relation of Providence to all creation. In this dynamic of existence and operation, and not only in a static nature and a superior-inferior ranking relation, do lower elements and lower creatures whose natures are for man's use, therefore, attain their end in and through man who is their end and his own also, and whose Creator is his end directly and theirs only indirectly through him.[94] Since this power and right man evidences constantly by his own power of choice and his consequent life-long dominance over his own actions of soul and body, he manifests a natural quality or ability to be a true agent, a free, creative causative power in his own right, and not a rigidly moved instrument. He is not led, he leads himself. Therefore, the Thomistic thesis says, by his natural power and because of the natural appetency of his nature, and therefore by natural need and right to exercise his powers towards his completion and actualize the potentials imbedded in his essence, he leads lower creation, in him, to a higher level as he not only incorporates it into himself but understands and uses it, completing its own material and proper functions, for his own higher and proper end. And just as his

93. Cf. *Comm. Caietani* in I, q. 96, a. 2.
94. Aristotle, *Politica*, Bk. I, c. 5, 1254, p. 1132 (McKeon Ed.): ". . . it is clear that the rule of soul over body, and mind and rational element over the passionate, is natural and expedient . . . and the same holds good of animals in relation to men." (It is well known that Aristotle carried this principle into the realm of men too. Cf. *C.G.*, III, cc. 112, 121. Cf. Lenz, *op. cit.*, p. 148: "Der Mensch steht über den Tieren und herrscht natürlicherweise über sie und die gesamte Schöpfung, die nicht wie er nach dem Bilde Gottes ist. Alles ist des Menschen wegen und zu seinem Nützen gemacht.")
We think the argument, cumulatively taken, has force and is corroborated by facts, but it is noticeable how the Thomistic commentators and interpreters have only repeated the thesis without argumentation, although the original Aristotelian principle that the less perfect is always *for* the more perfect, etc., is not so immediately evident.

own spirit unifies and controls and uses toward their immediate proper ends all the material elements included in his ruled composite, so he faces all external and similar material units from the same advantage height of a command relation. Just as he is, observably in himself, a creature who freely governs the matter which he alone in creation understands, so he is meant to govern matter outside himself.[95] Whether this is an argument which follows *ex necessitate* or only a corroborative evidence from a parallel instance, it does stand as a valid corroboration, at least, of what is constantly observable in men's relation to the rest of creation, both in their natural assumption of a right and their universal practice of the use of that right by the constant and successful competence they exhibit. The parallel has been accepted by the majority of men in all ages, at least in practice, as it is accepted by scientists and legalists still.[96]

The important implication in this whole doctrine is rarely pointed out, and its omission leaves the sequence somewhat hanging in the air. The "leap" from a participation in intelligent understanding to the execution of the understood order is not in the nature of things a necessary progress. However, it seems to be in this case of participation something of a legitimate connection, not only because man shares that essential intelligence which is *at the same time* a directing will, but because there is separate evidence in man that he shares also that goodness which is the creative and directive and ruling will of God. Thomas does not repeatedly link the two

95. I, q. 96, a. 2, c.: ". . . in homine quodammodo sunt omnia; et *ideo* secundum modum quo dominatur his quae in seipso sunt, secundum hunc modum *competit ei* dominari aliis." Cf. *De Ver.*, q. 18, a. 7. (The interesting word here is of course *"ideo."*)

96. Delos, "Rights of Person, State and Race" in *Race: Nation: Person*, p. 48: "The same mastery is exercised *a fortiori* over the surrounding world. This too, man grasps by knowledge . . . intelligence comes to know the laws of this surrounding world, and hence takes command over it; for to know the laws of the universe is to be able to direct its operations and utilize these . . . to make them subservient to the advantage of man."

It is not easy to see how Delos reached an *a fortiori* position; "rights" may be tested by and even corroborated by "abilities" but they are not identical, and the one does not necessarily flow immediately from the other, or else one can justify the dictum that "might is right."

powers in actual words, but all the meanings and implication of his whole development of the philosophy of man allow of a legitimate and close relation, although there is not in the conclusion *ex intelligentia sola* as such, or even in the conclusion drawn from man's personal dominion over his personal acts, any necessary consequence that he has equal right over creatures inferior to him but external to him. Nor have others been too careful in elaborating the doctrine. Only one commentator mentions the dual premise from which one can much more legitimately draw and much more clearly see the conclusion.[97] The point is that since in man directive power and right to use is neither essential in being nor identical with intelligence in his essence as it is in the divine essence, one cannot immediately jump from shared intelligence to rightful and competent rule of other creatures. In man however, we find two essential powers shared, which are one in God's nature. Because man shows intelligence, he must share the intelligence which is Providence and understand the natures and ends of creatures. But besides this, though part of his rationality, man shows a distinct sharing in divine goodness in his will to universal good and in that free play of choice of means which is, in human free will, the image of the freedom of spontaneity of God. In this, then, and in a needful

97. *C.G.*, III, c. 111, *Comm. Ferrariensis:* "Advertendum . . . Thomas *assumpsisse* hanc propositionem: unumquodque inquantum participat similitudinem divinae bonitatis, intantum *participat* similitudinem *divinae voluntatis.*" That is, man shares not only the intelligence which knows but a will which rules.

De Ver., q. 5, a. 8, c. This seems perhaps Thomas' best expression of the doctrine: ". . . maxime propinquae sunt Deo creaturae rationales, quae ad Dei similitudinem sunt, vivunt, et intelligunt; unde eis non solum a divina bonitate confertur ut super alia influant, sed etiam ut eundem modum influendi retinent quo influit Deus; scilicet per *voluntatem*, et non per necessitatem naturae; unde omnes inferiores creaturas gubernat et per creaturas spirituales et per creaturas corporales digniores, sed per creaturas corporales hoc modo providet quod eas, non facit providentes sed agentes tantum; per spirituales autem hoc modo providet quod eas providentes facit. Sed in creaturis etiam rationalibus ordo invenitur. Ultimum enim gradum in eis rationales animae tenent, et earum lumen est obumbratum respectu luminis quod est in angelis . . . et inde est quod earum providentia coarctatur ad pauca; scilicet ad res humanas et ad ea quas in usum vitae hominis, venire possunt . . ."

collaboration with his understanding, man shares the directive will of God, and so is participative not only of providence strictly speaking, which foresees, but of the divinity which executes the understood order, the ruling will of God. Further observation and analysis corroborates this: man not only does so operate, but his insight into himself and into others shows him that their ends are in him, that they are to be for him as instruments, and that his power over them is legitimate, because he alone is under Providence and divine governance as also participant in both, that he is the supreme and unique *individual* who shares a God-like rule of creation.

He alone has this planned position in the universe. By participating intelligence he sees the arrangement of creation and by participating will he cooperates rightfully in the carrying out of the direction and control of that order intelligently instituted. He alone is that image of God who shares in both divine foresight and divine directive right and power, by his understanding and free will. Since his intelligence itself can intelligibly contain all things by its understanding of their nature and purpose, man is also given as part of his rationality a rational will to control, which gives him a natural right and ability to use for himself creatures useful to him and his end. As he is governed in a special, free manner by the highest perfection and actuality and intelligent cause and will, so what he shares has conferred upon him the dignity of his own intelligent and free causality and agency. He whose rationality is a relatively unlimited, undetermined and free power, governs all irrational creatures who are more limited than he, all those whose natures are material and determined *ad unum,* and whose ends are both temporal and inferior, and yet useful to his higher operation and end. The naturalness of this chain of command in being, whereby the higher and more complete includes and uses and directs to its own ends and so perfects the less perfect, reaches its created climax in the human person who is the focal point of their attraction in being and the center of attractive force for their dynamism in operation, who is, under God, the directing and knowing personal ruler of their blind and impersonal instrumentality. The creative Providence governs through him, and for him, as a kind of participating and secondary providence. He is the appointed and properly created agent for the execution of the divine plan which he alone is given ability to recognize, and he shares also in the divine ruling will which directs and controls and uses the units and their proper movements in the universe-plan. He so shares God as to be himself, under God, a kind of god for matter. Since alone in creation *he and God understand,* and *only he and God govern by nature,* man is then not only superior to others, but is by his very nature, dominant and ruling of them, as they are by their nature fitted to be ruled and used. Consequently, anything done contrary to such a planned and observable arrangement is contrary to such natures and is thus useless in the case of irrational creatures, and is useless and frustrating to the natures of human persons. What is *in* nature cannot be obstructed with any abiding success. So with the human person, it is unnatural and in the long run useless to attempt to be destructive of what is their natural and inalienably rightful position of authority over the rest of creation, as if they were of the ruled nature of animals. Any such attempt is an attempt to destroy the unique and natural image of a Creator who cannot Himself be subject, an obstruction of their individual and personal likeness to, and their intended imitation of in operation, and increasing assimilation into, that being and that providential nature who is *Ipsum Intelligere et Velle.*[98]

98. We do not bring into discussion the distortion and disintegration of this dynamic of governed and governing creation which was caused in historical man by the disintegrating force of original sin. That only increases the difficulty of accomplishment and does not invalidate the natural states of right and power.

The force of the treatment St. Thomas gives this question seems to us to be satisfying when posited as a cogency flowing from the cumulative effects of many aspects of observable facts and the reasoned insight into human nature, rather than by convincing from any one aspect. That man's rationality immediately and directly demands a right of governance is not too apparent and cogent an argument, simply because of the distinction between understanding, and right to use, and power to use, and because we have many instances in life where the power to control does not demand the accompaniment of a legitimate right to control and use, or where the understanding of a

* SUMMARY. Man's relation to the rest of creation is such that he is in a position of extreme superiority over all other creatures, not only because he shows himself to have a complexity of nature and operational powers which is greater than their possession and use of the same kind of powers, but because he possesses a power of rationality which is completely foreign to all other visible creatures. By this power he not only understands the others whom he surpasses, but possesses the competence and right to use them for himself. All these superiorities are created in his nature, and the final reason for them is seen in man's uniquely permanent and divine destiny, in contrast to the temporary and irrational existence of all others. His innate potentials show him to exist on a level far above others, and this very eminence is enhanced when it is seen that the natures of all others, and his inclusion of them within himself, so related him to them that he commands them for himself, integrates them into the unified and greater perfection of both himself and the whole universe and in being such a "proximate god" for them, is the intermediary through which all the rest of creation "becomes aware" of its God and images Him in a conscious, intelligent and formal worship. Because of his rationality, man is creation's god, and as such, of a dignity or value incomparably beyond any other's. It remains, then, only to investigate his relation to the Creator Himself, to see the exact level and location of his dignity, lest confusion over his godlike status should make him confuse himself with God Himself, and so lose his own proper worth.

---

purpose does not immediately imply right of control for that purpose. It would seem *only in a divine nature* that these attributes are immediately united and identified in one, and only by careful reasoning does one see that the human participation in both intelligence and will place man in a ruling eminence imitative of divine governance.

CHAPTER FOUR

Man and Creator: His Perfection

FACT OF THE IMAGE. The dignity of a human person is only partially seen from his great superiority over the rest of creatures. It is fully understood only when he is seen in his own special relation to his Creator. This chapter will point out that the rationality by which he so far surpasses other creatures also makes this creature, and him alone, the natural image of the Creator's nature. To be such is not to be different in degree only, but in kind. They are, and they live, because they temporarily share in being and existence, and in this they are obscurely "like" God. But man lives in the way God lives, intelligently, and from the image that man is, one can tell not only *that* God is, but somehow grasp a little of *how* He is. This treatment of man as uniquely "the image of God" owes its first real development to St. Augustine, who developed the theme from Holy Scriptures, and from a Christian adaptation of the Platonic theory of Ideas. But St. Augustine's handling of the theme is scriptural and theological and complex and trinitarian, and often arbitrary. While St. Thomas admittedly took his development from Augustine, he put it on clearer philosophical grounds, and preserved only so much of the unforced development of the theory that he is the true and best philosophical source of this classical and persistent doctrine. Although it is not without much profit to read Augustine *in toto* in two sources particularly it is difficult to use him as a source too often, because it is almost impossible to disentangle the philosophical premises and arguments from the theological and scriptural. And after Aquinas, the literature lets this theme fade out, or takes it for granted, either because to some the doctrine is obvious and needs no argument, or to others, because they increasingly belonged to a world more homocentric and egocentric than theocentric, and such a world, while it would become distortedly conscious of the independent superiority of man to creatures, would grow distortedly unconscious of the fact that man was not a god, but only the completely dependent and faint image of one.[1]

The image man is, is different from the irrational likeness seen in others. Only an image reflects in some definite way the powers or attributes of nature, something of the *interior* of a thing. On man's "more noble" side then, he is more than the likeness which all other creatures are, as he is the only rational creature. This no other has in common with him, even in lesser degree, but man has in common with the angels.[2] Because he is an "image" he remains, of course, a "likeness," since image is a species of likeness in general. In one sense, insofar as every creature represents an idea in God, everyone is an image of that idea, though not an image as is man, of the very intelligent nature and intelligent operating of God, the nature-act in whom that idea is. Everything is like the picture in the mind of the artist, and only man is related to God *somewhat* as a son to a father, being the image not only of an idea of the Creator's, but of His intelligent nature. It is true that all creatures are a likeness insofar as they are, and live, as each one substance is one in itself, and has a certain order to it, but by the image of divine intelligent nature in his human intellectual nature, though in a human way, man alone, properly speaking, is an "image" of God.[3] He alone directly participates in the Divine Nature in his undivine measure and manner; he alone is *like in in-*

---

1. For Augustine-sources, confer *De Genesi Ad Litteram*, in its treatment of the text "ad imaginem Dei."; but chiefly *De Trinitate*, Bks. IX–XIV. For some collection of Augustine's treatment and commentary on, cf. Gilson: *Introduction à l'Etude de s. Augustin;* and Vernon Bourke's *Augustine's Quest of Wisdom.*

2. I *Sent.*, d. 3, q. 3, a. 1.

3. The terminology here is dangerously close to what is usually reserved for the analogy in theology and the supernatural image, but we feel it can legiti-

telligent nature. Other creatures can be traced back to a producing intellect, but man alone *reproduces* that intellectual nature in some way, reflecting as it were, the "species" and the essence.[4] In him you cannot see divinity, but you can see *what it is like.*

Not that the body is excluded from a likeness of God such as other material creatures show. Since it is unified with man's actions and relations are attributed to the person who energy, it has even a greater likeness, but it cannot be the image of God in His nature, since it is material. However, it is so connected with man that it is in a wide sense, and secondary way, included in man's divine imaging, insofar as man's actions and relations are attributed to the person, who is both soul and body. There is a kind of image in man's personal generation, though it is physical too, where man comes from man as "God is from God," and inasmuch as man is the principle of men as God is of the whole universe. Moreover, there is a certain image in the way the soul is total in the total parts of the body as God is in creation, and in the relation of superiority and governance which man has to the rest, as God has to him and the rest, and insofar as man is

---

mately be used here. An approach to the solution of the mystery of man's "natural image" as distinct from his supernatural, will be found treated later.

Aug., *Serm.* 43, c. 2 (PL 38; 255): *De Gen. ad Lit.*, c. 12 (PL 34, 347–8); Damascenus, *De Fide Orthodoxa*, lib. II, c. 12 (PG 94, 920); Greg. Nyssa, *De Hom. Opif.*, c. 16 (PG 44, 184). These Fathers of the Church did not philosophically develop the doctrine here, but they are well aware of it from Genesis and often use it.

II *Sent.*, d. 16, a. 2, ad 2, and a. 4; *C.G.*, IV, c. 26; *S.T.*, I, q. 93, a. 2, and a. 6. Note: The development of the distinction between "vestigium" and "imago" and the full implications of the imago are not yet too clear in the *Sentences*, and sometimes seem to contradict the later clarity of the *S.T.*

4. I, q. 93, a. 2, ad 4: ". . . quaelibet creatura est imago rationis exemplaris, quam habet in mente divina. Sic autem non loquimur nunc de imagine, sed secundum quod attenditur secundum similitudinem naturae. . . ."

I, q. 93, a. 6, c.; "Potest ergo hujusmodi differentia attendi inter creaturas rationales et alias creaturas, et quantum ad hoc quod in creaturis rationalibus, repraesentatur similitudo divinae naturae. . . . Nam quantum ad similitudinem divinae pertinet, creaturae rationales videntur quodammodo ad repraesentationem speciei pertingere . . . (in aliis) apparet in eis quoddam vestigium intellectus producentis. . . ."

Cf. II *Sent.*, d. 16, q. 2, a. 2, and *De Ver.*, q. 10, a. 1, ad 5: "in assignatione imaginis, mens locum divinae essentia tenet."

their end proximately as God is totally and finally. But these reflections partake of image only *secundum quid* and only because they presuppose the basic and real image of mind.[5]

The divine image properly resides in man's intellectual soul, which is essential to man as the above mentioned relations are not primarily, since they flow from his essence and operations. Since man alone is an image because of his intelligence alone, the image of God exists in his spiritual and rational principle, not in his body, which is like God in the way all other material creatures are like God, who is not material, but spiritual, and yet has the likeness of them in His spiritual intelligence. Man's corporal side, although it is immensely elevated by association with his spiritual side, is not of itself rational and so not an image properly speaking.[6] It is mind alone that makes man different from beasts, and in mind only is he properly an image.

Clearly there is an immense difference between this creature and others when one directs attention to the different ways in which they represent their Creator. All creatures are made like the likeness of them in the intellect of God. Of man too, there is in the divine intelligence a likeness, but that likeness is in some small measure and faint degree a likeness of God himself, because the likeness which man is, is not only already a likeness in the divine mind, but is also a likeness of the nature too, as nature, that original kind of being and existence of which man is directly, however obscurely and faintly, the existent double in creation. He is not

---

5. I *Sent.*, d. 3, q. 2, a. 3, ad 1.; II *Sent.*, d. 16, a. 3, solut.; I, q. 93, a. 3, c.; a. 4, ad 1; *In Epist. I ad Cor.*, lect. 2.

6. I, q. 93, a. 1, ad 2; and a. 6, c.

With respect to corporal indications of image, Augustine uses a corroborative argument which Aquinas also makes brief use of and which is not without some significance, although it strikes us today perhaps as something of whimsy. Cf. *De Gen. ad Lit.*, c. 12 (PL 34, 347–348): ". . . quid habet homo excellentius . . . nisi quod ipse ad imaginem Dei creatus est? Nec tamen hoc secundum corpus, sed secundum intellectum mentis. . . . Congruit et corpus ejus animae rationali, non secundum lineamenta figuraque membrorum, sed potius secundum id quod in coelum erectum est, ad intuenda quae in corpore ipsius mundi superna sunt: sicut anima rationalis in ea debet erigi, quae in spiritualibus natura maxime excellunt. . . ." Cf. I, q. 93, a. 6, ad 3.

merely a likeness of a likeness in God's intelligence, but an image of God Himself, who is *Ipsum Intelligere;* so he is, by participation, His created intellectual double. From other creatures, one could conclude that only an intelligent God could make them, as from an object refracting light we conclude a source of light. But from man one can conclude something of what God is like, what intelligence *is,* as from a picture of another, or the echo of a voice, or a face in a mirror, or better, like a small mass made radioactive and then seen in its own glow. Since this image is caused by a participation in nature, we speak in analogical terms evidently, and not of an image *ad aequalitatem.* Man is not God, only His faint and imperfect image.[7] It is not that man

7. *De Trin.,* lib. 12, c. 11 (PL 42, 1006). St. Augustine saw the position very clearly, that the image is not sufficient reason in itself for human honor. "Honor enim hominis verus est imago et similitudo Dei, quae non custoditur nisi ad Ipsum *a quo imprimitur.*" Cf. *C.G.,* IV, c. 26: ". . . intelligere et velle sunt ipsum esse divinum . . . et propter hoc, sic consideratur divina similitudo in homine sicut Herculis in lapide; quantum ad repraesentationem formae, non quantum ad convenientiam naturae. Unde et in mente hominis dicitur esse imago Dei." (Note: As far as we can judge, "convenientiam" in that context is not just a "likeness" but means an identical and equal repetition.) Even in *C.G.,* Aquinas has not yet reached the certainty he seems to have reached, or at least the clarity of I, q. 93, where it becomes increasingly clear that, although there is no question at all of equality, there is an imaging of divine Nature. *In Epist. I ad Cor.,* lect. 2; I, q. 93, a. 2, and *Comm. Caietani.*

Perhaps it is not without some value to quote a far different writer, such as Berdyaev, who sees with admirable clarity and humility the distance between the image and the original, and yet, in that very context, gives evidence of a current careless use of terms and the somewhat emotional rhetoric which obscures the philosophic truth in a question so important and yet so dangerous because of its well-nigh incredible intimacy of image-relation to God. "Personality is the creator and bearer of supernatural values and this is the only source of its wholeness, unity, and eternal significance. But this must not be taken to mean that personality has no intrinsic value. It is itself an absolute and exalted value, but it can only exist in virtue of superpersonal values. In other words, the existence of personality presupposes the existence of God; its value presupposes the supreme value—God. If there is no God as the source of superpersonal values, personality as a value does not exist either; there is merely the individual entity subordinate to the natural life of the genus. . . . Personality is the moral principle and our relation to all other values is determined by reference to it. Personality is a higher value than the state, the nation, mankind, or nature, and indeed it does not form part of that series." *Destiny of Man,* p. 72.

This is an example of a rather common custom of signifying man's inde-

is a perfected and completed image, but is created "into the
image," that is, in *some* image, and with perfectible powers
to improve that image.[8] And yet however perfected he becomes man is always a very imperfect and incomplete image
of the original, since it is the infinite God he is the image
of, and there can be no question of an *ad aequalitatem*
image. Man's tremendous superiority over irrational creation never implies independence of his Creator, nor anything
but an immense distance between them. The human person
indeed finds his dignity embracing a kind of super-human
value, just because of the superhuman person he is the image
of. He does share somehow, though minutely, in divine intelligent nature, but it is the very essence of his dignity that
he is only dependently participative of and faintly reflective
of it. Any misrepresentation of the image for the original immediately destroys the dignity of the image in that it denies
the very essence of imagery. We have value only because
God is what He is, and He gives it to us. ". . . We are persons
because we are the work of a Person; we participate in *His*
personality even as, being good, we participate in *His* perfection; being causes, in *His* creative power; being prudent, in
His providence; and in a word, as beings in *His* being. To be
a person is to participate in one of the highest excellences of

pendent type of existence in freedom by calling man an "absolute." It seems
to us that this usage exactly misses the whole point unless one is to proceed
ad absurdum and call him a "relative absolute." It is this kind of terminology
which has led to attitudes and practices which presuppose a homocentric
creation exclusively and absolutely, a position which confuses the dependent
image with the absolute original. And it is this manner of speaking which
has led us to discard many modern writings as not particularly helpful to this
thesis. Since the concept of man's dignity hinges upon the use of an analogy,
it is not too clarifying, and is dangerous, to multiply the metaphors in attempting to explain the *rationale* of his dignity.

8. While individual differences have been treated in some small measure
in Part I, and will be traced more in the perfecting living of man in society
in the third chapter of this part, it should be remembered here again that
man is not a static creation, but can further complete himself, and also that
there are differences in perfections among human beings and therefore differences in the clarity of image and its root perfectibility. Cf. I *Sent.*, d. 3, q.
3, a. 1: ". . . alia autem, quia plus et minus participant de Dei bonitate,
magis accedunt ad rationem imaginis."

divine being."[9] It is no necessary part of an image to be *equal* to the original of which something is the image. This is immediately clear in a mirror-image. Equality is a *perfect* image, or an identity in nature. And man is not any perfect image of the infinite God, but immeasurably far from Him, since his human essence limits him (naturally speaking) to only a finite imitation.[10]

In man the image is of God's nature, but *in* another kind of nature, like a president's picture on a dollar bill. And yet, the "image" examples Thomas uses are not very apt, because the image in man is not static; it is an operative thing, it is an actual sharing in another's real nature, something the statue and canvas do not do. His examples fit irrational causal likeness much more than the human-divine relation. It is perhaps not correct to say man is an image as a son is of a father, and yet there is somehow something more apt in that example, if one can preclude any equality in this particular relation. It is as if a living son were to share one small part of the father's nature in a real, active manner. It is as if he were to be like his father because he thinks, but totally unlike in that he thinks in a totally different way. The difficulty is caused by the uniqueness of this relation which is between infinity and finiteness, essential intelligence and created contingent intelligence, so that the necessity of remembering the analogy of being in logic and in terms, and the fact of participation in reality, makes an example from human relations most inadequate. But the image is more real, and is some-

9. Gilson, *Spirit of Medieval Philosophy*, pp. 204–5. Also, Gilson, *Thomisme*, p. 421: "la personne n'est pas autonome, sauf en ceci qu'elle de Dieu. . . ." It seems belaboring the obvious to stress this point, except that human persons, particularly in recent history, have so persistently repeated the contradiction of Adam in trying to make the image the original. Then man's dignity is totally destroyed in that he neither remains the image nor becomes the original. The value and perfection of an image is the value and perfection of an image only.

10. I, q. 93, a. 1, c. Cf. Edw. Pace: "World Copy," *Catholic University Bulletin* (1899), p. 210. ". . . God, knowing His own being, knows it both as absolutely His and as an original which may be imitated, a copy eternally set. . . . Imitability, an attribute of the divine essence, declares itself in divine ideas . . . The same absolute excellence that makes His being imitable is also the bar to an adequate imitation. The copy is perfect and its setting; in the copying comes imperfection, and with it the more and the less."

thing more than an impression upon paper or marble or canvas. Augustine has seen this, and expressed it pithily and beautifully: ". . . you are the stamped coin of God. And you are better than such, since you are the minted image of your God which is alive and intelligent, so that you even know whose image you bear and in whose likeness you have been made, while a coin knows not that it carries an image on it."[11] There *is* some sharing of the same nature, and so something more of image even than in a mirror, *something* of the shared resemblance a son has for a father, though it is clear that only God Himself can truly be the equal and perfect image of Himself. In this aspect, I think the statement of Gilson interpreting St. Thomas is more valid than St. Thomas' own words. Gilson claims that since rationality is essential in man, it is man's essence to be God's image, while Aquinas says in one place that man "is not essentially an image." The difference is only apparent if Aquinas means to contrast man's dependency and contingency with God's essentiality. Man need not be, and therefore need not be an image. But if man is to be, *qua* man, he must then be rational and must be an image of divine intelligence, even though he can be like God only in proportion to his limited essence.[12]

LOCATION OF THE IMAGE. The divine *image is* in the very intellectual nature of the soul, in its inmost constitution. The nature was made for its intended goal: man's intellect was made to the image of God in order that he become the like-

11. Augustine, *Serm.* IX, c. 8; PL 38, 82.

12. I, q. 35, a. 2, ad 3; I, q. 93, a. 1, c.: "non tamen est similitudo secundum aequalitatem, quia in infinitum excedit exemplar." Also, q. 93, a. 1, ad 3: "rei ad rem coaequandam pertinet ad rationem perfectae imaginis."

I, q. 93, a. 6, ad 1: ". . . non quia ipse *essentialiter* sit imago, sed quia in eo est Dei imago impressa secundum mentem, sicut denarius dicitur imago Caesaris inquantum habet Caesaris imaginem." Cf. Gilson, *Spirit of Medieval Philosophy*, pp. 286–288. Cf. footnote 14 *infra*.

Although the works and statements were perhaps better not used as philosophic sources, since they are involved more with supernatural life, contemporary medieval ascetics and mystics make more constant use of man's participation and imagery than St. Thomas does, or at least more strongly. Cf. St. Bernard, *In Cant. Cant.*, 82, 8; *De Diligendo Deo*, c. VII; William of St. Thierry, *De Natura et Dignitate Amoris*, and his *Epist. ad Fratres de Monte Dei*, II, 16; Cf. *C.G.*, III, cc. 24 and 25.

ness of God in his love. And this resemblance, this natural and dynamic imitation, is the final test of the excellence and value of the human person: his resemblance to absolute value, the measure of his likeness to God Himself, the estimation of his original share and his growing participation in the being and existence and nature of God, a capacity belonging to the human person alone among creatures, *der einzige Ort der Gottwerdung*.[13] It is man's intellect which constitutes man precisely in his unique degree of perfection, and the exact reason why he is so ranked. The fact that he alone participates in the nature which is *Ipsum Intelligere* gives us at the same time the true position of man: the very *raison d'être* of his superiority is the very principle of his dependence. This cannot be forgotten, else one gives not only a distorted picture of man, but wipes out the very essence of his value in trying to make an image an original. That is a half-portrait of man, who is not totally, but partially intelligent. It is a lag from the mistakes of later Renaissance humanism which did not see that the supremacy of man was not *a se* a human supremacy, but a kind of divinized humanism, which must immediately imply dependence, a superiority which derives its excellence and value from the original to which it is inferior. If man's value is not, in final analysis, a derivative and participative thing, he loses all value, because obviously he is nothing absolute and permanent in and from himself. The portrait is dear only because of the original it reflects.

The point in question in estimating man, is to recognize that this image is neither accidental nor intermittent to him, but *of his very nature*. The image of God is coessential with man himself; he cannot be man without being rational, and he cannot be rational without being so by participating in intelligent divine nature. His essential specific difference in

13. A statement of Max Scheler's, taken in a sense he probably did not mean and yet in a way truer than he intended perhaps. Scheler's well-known work, *Die Stellung des Menschens im Kosmos*, has not been referred to because it is beyond our purpose to give a critical evaluation of the post-Kantian and semi-pantheistic final position of the unfortunate Scheler. Cf. Augustine, *De Trin.*, lib. IX, c. 12; PL 42, 972.

species is an image of the divine essence. That which is
proper to his intellectual nature is precisely the image of
what is essential in divine nature.[14] This is the means by
which he alone is united to divine nature and directly imitative of it. Intelligence is *common* to God and man, and
natural to both, though man's is a meager participation in
that divine nature, and shares it only in his human manner
and measure. Moreover, strictly speaking, since God is complete and constant actuality, man's intellect is an actual imitation of the divine only insofar as it is active, and when it is.
But since the wellsprings of man's intellectual activity are the
natural dispositions toward this, and the powers to act men-
tally, the natural possession and presence of the potentials is
a virtual imitation. And finally, because of the manner of
divine intellectual activity, which is immediately intuitive,
the human image is much more in the final and full intellectual grasp than in that process of discursive reasoning by
which man reaches comprehension.[15] God is permanent, continuous, immediate, and infinite intelligence. By some small
participation in this nature, man has permanent, intermittent, mediate, and finite intelligence which is a true image of
God, actually so when man is actively understanding, and
virtually so always, in the sense that his nature has an abiding possession of the powers to understand and the natural
disposition to use them. Our further investigation of the hu-

14. I, q. 93, a. 9, ad 2: ". . . *essentia animae pertinet* ad imaginem, prout
repraesentat divinam essentiam secundum ea quae sunt propria intellectualis
naturae." Cf. Augustine, *De Vera Relig.*, c. 44 (PL 34, 159); *De Diver.
Quaest.*, q. 51, no. 4 (PL 40, 33–4); *De Trin.*, Bk. XIV, c. 4 (PL 142, 1040).
Augustine stresses the fact that because of the intellectual imitation, man is
in direct contact with Truth: "haeret enim veritati nulla interposita creatura
. . . non enim aliter incommutabilem veritatem posset mente concipere. . . ."
Cf. Gilson, *Thomisme*, p. 480.

15. I, q. 93, a. 7, c., and ad objecta: ". . . primo et principaliter attenditur imago . . . in mente secundum actus . . ." Cf. *De Ver.*, q. 10, a. 3, c.
I *Sent.*, d. 3, q. 4, a. 1, ad 4: "secundum optimum sui assignatur imago in
anima, ideo potius assignatur secundum intelligentiam, quam secundum
rationem; ratio enim nihil aliud est nisi natura intellectualis obumbrata, unde
inquirendo cognoscit . . . quod intellectui statim et plena luce confertur."
(Note: Our interpretation of this text is perhaps arbitrary, since it is not too
clear what, in this instance and at that stage of thought, Aquinas meant by
"intelligentia" in contrast to "ratio.")

man person's imitation of God, is to point out then how his intellectual operations do imitate the divine intelligent operation, both in the understanding itself and in the rational desires which must follow his knowing.

IMITATION IN OPERATION. The important side of *the human person's relation to impersonal creatures* lies not so much in the superior possession of elements common to both kinds of creatures, but in his rational relation to them, by which he is related to them and "contains" them intelligibly as God does. It is by the shared "light" of divine intelligence that man understands all the rest of creation. As in divine intelligence are contained the *"rationes aeternae"* of all things, so in human intelligence are contained the intelligible images of things known. We see all things, as it were "in God," in the light of His shared intelligence, so that we are dignified by that image of Him in that we are related to them in a way He is.[16] And this imitation of God is an image bringing man closer to Him than to other creatures because all things known are contained in a human person as God contains them, in a spiritual and simple manner, as the thing known must be held in a knower.[17] This is the last piece in the perfection of creation, that there be a person-creature who contains or can contain the rest, as God Himself holds in His mind and essense all He has made. Man has been seen as a miniature cosmos, and even a miniature god, and it is no puzzle that such a creature sometimes mistakes himself in practice for his Creator. When man imitates God in his creativity by physical powers, and more so by thought, he becomes even a higher image, because then, like the Creator, he leaves in what he makes the tracing of that model-likeness in his mind according to which idea he made the produced, and according to which original idea and intelligible species he must make things. That process is a perfect human reproduction and duplication of the Creator's own creative process and His intelligent relation to creation. Man too makes things and does things like his own nature, an imita-

16. I, q. 12, a. 11, ad 3; I, q. 84, a. 5, c.
17. *C.G.*, II, c. 46; Cf. Gilson, *Thomisme*, p. 332.

tion of the Creator who made man also in imitation of His nature, and man does this by a rational process by which he therefore operates in imitation of the intelligent nature of God.[18] As God is, so is man in his limited way; as God operates by intelligence, so does His human intelligent image.

In all man's creativity, even with material powers inasmuch as they operate by the force of the life-energy radiating from his spiritual and rational soul, there is that imitation of the Creator which is in all instances a reflection of the communicating divine goodness that man shares. In this, man has a level of imitation of God which is peculiar to him and peculiarly God-like.)He not only shares God statically, as it were, in a still-life picture of divine goodness, and not only shares Him in that dynamic way that other creative powers do, in that they share the activity of communicating goodness and are creative causes themselves, but man is also a fuller and sharper image of the communicating divine goodness in that he influences other beings in the same intelligent manner that God does, by foresight and rational will. As seen before, human persons reflect the foreseeing intelligence and will of God not only in that they can understand and desire the understood good, but that they so share in Providence as to share the understanding of other creatures and their ends, and in their personal unification of understanding and willing, they share therefore the direction of creatures to their ends as a secondary and partial Providence. Man alone is an active and free cause as God is, and the sole image of the intelligent causality of God, the rationally free creativity of divinity. Particularly in that superiority already pointed out, wherein he cooperates in the creation of other human personal images, and, in a certain way, *furthers* even the creation of spirit in them insofar as he is capable of and responsible for their rational development, he more and more clearly evidences that he is the agent-image of God upon earth, as if God's "day of rest," once the human image was made, was not only a natural but almost necessary sequence, considering what man was made into. He

18. *C.G.*, II, c. 45.

can understand all natures and the over-all plan, understand his own part in it and the goals of all; he is capable of attaining the completion of the plan in himself and for the universe in others through him, so he is such an image as to seem the visible countenance of the creating and governing intelligence, and, for lower creatures, their image of their destiny-goal which is the same Creator. (We do not consider here historical man who has much weakened this ability at imitation and the resultant clarity of image.)

Of all visible creation, only the human person *knows himself*. This person-creature has already been pointed out from many aspects to be the supreme likeness of God, the uniquely God-like *chef d'oeuvre* of creation. Now we see more and more the real root of his imitation of God, as we look at man more and more closely and find more and more in his immanent rational activity the participated intelligence of God which so resembles the internal and essentially intelligent activity of the Creator, without considering any activity *ad extra*. Like God, man knows himself. Alone among creatures on earth, but in common with God, he is *self-aware*; he can turn in upon himself and understand himself and so he can consciously love himself. This is the very operative essence of divinity itself, and the imitation man is of God is clearly not only static but dynamic, and not only of formal causality, and not only of divine nature, but a natural imitation of the essentially operative nature of God as active.[19] Obviously, the mind of the human person is not the mind of God, nor does it know in the same immediate way. But in its human way it does do precisely what God does by intelligent operation, and therefore it is not only far, far superior to any creature other than rational, but is the only creature which truly images God. Like God, he imitates the activity of God, and not only exhibits himself, therefore, as the image of divine intelligent

19. *De Pot.*, q. 9, a. 9: (speaking of a likeness higher than vestigial or causal) ". . . Alio modo, secundum *eandem rationem operationis;* et sic repraesentatur in creatura rationali tantum, quae potest *se intelligere* et amare, *sicut et Deus,* et sic verbum et amorem sui producere, et haec dicitur similitudo naturalis imaginis; ea enim imaginem aliorum gerunt quae similem speciem praeferunt."

nature, but like God, can recognize the image in himself.[20] He not only is of great value, but knows his own worth in seeing value within himself. Man alone is not only the supreme perfection and value of the rest of creation, but is of a value beyond comparison with other creatures in that he can discover within himself the image of absolute value, and that by the same process and by the same internal standard, man can be himself a valuer, not only of the rest of material and immaterial creation, but of himself. Man is the value of and also the valuer of all else, as the God whose image he is, is the value and the valuer of man himself. And because he can recognize and evaluate, man can see in himself his direct end in that infinite value he is the image and participant of.

It is because of this that man loves himself, that man sees himself as his own proper goal, that he sees his own relative perfection in imitation of absolute perfection, as the desired end of his operations, and that he sees, because he *is* such an image and so imitates God Himself, that all else which is temporary must be for him and he not only for God, but that such an image as his and such an imitation must not be only temporary, but must continue to be, because that is the kind of spiritual image he is. This he sees deeply because his rational soul, wherein lies the image, forces him to see it and recognize himself for what he is, the visible image of the intelligent and eternal divine nature. Only man has an end in himself and beyond the universe, and so, within the circle of the universe, because he knows himself for the image he is, only man can and must love and desire himself as God does, as the object of his intellect and will. The instinctive natural appetency for preservation in existence seen in all existents, which is some imitation of the perpetuity of God, is not like the knowledge of it and consequent *rational* desire and certainty of it, which the man-image has.[21] Man loves himself freely; and, even beyond the dignity of his free choice, he

---

20. Augustine, *De Trin.*, Bk. XIV, c. 8 (PL 42, 1040): "Ecce ergo mens meminit sui, intelligit se, diligit se; hoc si cernimus, cernimus . . . non quidem Deum, sed jam imaginem Dei." Cf. Mullen: *Essence and Operation,* p. 112.

21. *De Pot.*, q. 5, a. 9, ad 7; *C.G.*, III, c. 112.

shares here perhaps more than in anything, something of the natural spontaneous liberty of love which God has for Himself. The nearer one is like the infinitely spiritual Creator, the less is one determined by anything outside oneself and the more capable of determining oneself. This, man is, and in this ability he cannot be compared to creatures at all, only to God. When he determines himself about himself, he is exhibiting a liberty of will which seems something beyond liberty of choice of a means to an end: he is already loving the proximate end and exercising the spontaneous choice of *good*. Only God and a human person can know themselves; only those two can love themselves. It is because of this that man *must*, by exigency of nature, love himself, as God does. It is specifically in this rational desire and satisfaction that, by that acting nature, he is the image of intelligent love itself and must imitate what he is.[22] Whatever participates in goodness, must be, in that measure of its participation, an object of desire. And whatever shares in intelligence must love the goodness he recognizes and shares in. But obviously, a human person cannot be more than what he only participates in, and so cannot love the participated more than the unparticipated, insofar as he knows it. The object of rationality in knowing and loving is God. In himself, man must and does know and love the image.[23]

THE MYSTERY OF IMITATION OF DIVINITY. This is the mystery of man's natural knowledge and love of an infinite God. The object of the human person's intelligence and will is intelligence and goodness itself. Before treating this image and imitation of divinity in object, brief mention must be given, at the risk of repetition, of the *naturalness* of the finite human's relation to the infinite divine, because the apparent antinomies in the relation have made it the subject of cur-

22. The sequence of ideas is perhaps somewhat eliptical. For a full sequence, and the treatment of the metaphysics which forces the necessity of this conclusion, *vide supra*, Chap. II, in re Goodness and Natural Appetency.

23. It is quite possible, especially for man as he historically is, not to love the image, *qua* image, and to mistake himself for the original. However, *actually*, it is the image, the reflected and participated being in himself, which he loves.

rent discussion. The relation has become the subject more perhaps of confusion than of discussion, and much of it is needless. It would appear sometimes as if the point at issue were whether or not God *is* the object of man's will and intellect. That *cannot* be the point at issue, because He *must* be the object. There is no problem of object, only an attempt to understand the operation by which the object is reached. The question can only be *how* it is possible. And in discussing the question, it is necessary to keep very clear the distinction between human capacities, human mode of operation, and the functional object of the human operation. There can be no dispute upon the obvious: the object is evidently non-human and infinite; the subject is as obviously human and finite; the method of operation of the subject must be human and finite, because the natural principle of operation determines the manner of any nature's action. And as long as the question of the *how* of this relation is discussed philosophically, any object or method of motion toward it which is known from other sources than reason, and asserts truths above reason, cannot be confused with the issue. Where theology teaches the reality of a divine object to be attained in a divine manner, it teaches of divine powers bestowed to do so. The philosophical question can only be how it is that a finite person can naturally attain an infinite object of reason and will, how it can even recognize and move toward it.

Too many of the discussions upon the topic promise to outline a Thomistic theory and to support it by quotations from Aquinas, without considering enough the context in which the words were used, and wondering whether the philosopher was speaking of man in his "natural" state or as he historically is, in a supernatural state or exclusively intended for it. It seems to us that the recent insistence of some upon the transcendental relations of being, should always have been the starting point in any discussion of the relation of the infinite to the finite. The question is really not new; it is the ancient problem of the transcendent and the immanent, and the analogy of being has been the only satisfactory answer to the how of that relation which has escaped the errors of extremes. Even when one discusses upon that premise, the same premise must be remembered in the very use of the terms "finite" and "infinite" so that the term "infinite" is clearly used either in a relative or absolute sense. There can be no clarity when the principle of matter and form is taken beyond its scope and then has to be discarded because the field of discussion is not concerned, except accidentally, with the material. But the principle of act and potency, as expressed in essence and existence, must be used still to cover the whole field of transcendental being and there one can see some explanation which gives some satisfaction to the human mind. When the term "infinite" is used in relation to human persons, whether of powers or of functional object, it can mean no more than that personal spiritual powers are not limited to any one nature as we see material powers to be limited, and further, that they are not limited to a defined number of natures. But it can never mean "infinite" in the absolute sense which embraces all simultaneously, *tota simul et perfecta.* The "infinite" of creatures cannot be identified with the infinite of the Creator. The "infinite" of creatures is a descriptive adjective borrowed from our negative concept of a non-finite God, and merely expresses our imitation of Him in some respects, without ever implying equality. "Infinite" among personal powers surely means not limited by matter or external substances, but does not connote the absence of limitation by internal nature. Even in his spiritual powers, any creature is necessarily limited by his own created and finite essence, even when he possesses a spiritual power whose scope of activity allows of indefinite extension.

Some of the modern proponents seem to have taken the most sensible path in emphasizing this: that the capacities of the human mind are unexhausted except by the illimited, although the finite mind is such in essence that it cannot at once be all it seems able to be progressively; it is not capable of attaining its own "capacities"![24] It does seem to have "infinite" capacities, indefinitely expanding. However, our thesis

24. Cf. O'Mahoney, *The Desire of God,* passim; Dugan, John S., *The Desire of God in Modern Scholastic Philosophy,* outlines three prominent theories and a Thomistic criticism, with its own offering of a "solution."

of the human imitation and image of God, when understood in the light of participation in being, can be no little help in this question. There is no doubt whatsoever that St. Thomas taught that the primary and final object of rational operations is the infinite God, the all-intelligent and the all-good, whether the person so striving recognizes his object as such, or not. Man's natural desire of intellect, and his rational desiring of will for God, is a rational functioning of that natural attraction for the universal in which he shares being and existence. His rational appetency is possible because he participates in divine intelligence too, and this does not infringe upon the supernatural in its technical and theological sense. He is "naturally" participant of divinity without being divinity, and "humanly" imitative of divinity without becoming divinely what is imitated.[25] There is no advantage in becoming involved in quibbles about certain meanings in some Thomistic texts when the whole doctrine is rather clear from the over-all scanning of his writings. For instance, there has been much question of such phrases as the contrasting words used in I, 93, a. 4, and C.G., III, cc. 111–112 about the "aptitude" and the "habit" and the "act" of loving God. When other texts are considered, it is almost obvious that the Cajetan commentary is correct in saying that the terms were not used exclusively but to point out the progression and *predominant* manner of possessing God in different stages in the historical life of man.[26] What is true of the pure spirits is true of man

25. I–II, q. 91, a. 2, c.: ". . . lumen rationis naturalis . . . nihil aliud est quam impressio divini luminis in nobis . . ."

C.G., III, c. 25: "Desiderat igitur homo naturaliter cognoscere primam causam quasi ultimum finem. Principalis omnium causa Deus est. Est igitur finis hominis cognoscere Deum." (Cf. I *Metaphy.*, 1)

Augustine, *De Trin.*, Bk. XIV, c. 4 (PL 42, 1040) and *S.T.*, I, q. 93, ad 3: ". . . hoc ipsum naturale est, quod mens ad intelligendum Deum ratione uti potest . . ."

C.G., III, c. 20: "bonitatem autem creaturae non assequuntur *eo modo sicut in Deo* est, *licet* divinam bonitatem unaquaeque res imitetur secundum *suum modum.*"

26. I, q. 93, a. 4, c., and *Comm. Caietani*; C.G., III, c. 111, and *Comm. Ferrariensi*, where the interpretation is rather forceful, yet seems quite consistent with the words of the text: ". . . creaturae vero rationales sua operatione attingunt Deum, tum ipsam Dei essentiam secundum seipsam intelligunt et contemplantur, ipsumque Deum in seipso amant."

in respect to his spiritual side. He can have an "unlimited" object and unlimited capacities insofar as he is non-material, and yet remain limited in actualization and in very capacities by his own finite essence. He has being and existence in common with God, but is fenced in by limitations in his participation consequent upon his specific essence. His rationality is in this respect like the angels', whose "act of existing is limited and restricted to the capacity of the receiving nature—they are *unlimited from below and limited from above,* that is, limited as to the act of existing received from above, unlimited because their forms are not limited to the capacity of some matter receiving them."[27] Without stepping into theology, one can say that the human essence excludes man from God's manner of operation, but not from a "passive potency," an aptitude he participates in, to receive actualization into that manner, if the active power to so participate is given. How this can fit human nature is not too difficult to apprehend from the analogy of imitation and image and participation in divine being and existence. Gilson's treatment of this relation in his *Spirit of Medieval Philosophy,*[28] under this aspect of participation and image, seems consonant with Thomas' statements, and is a superb exposition of the whole solution. Human love is never anything but a finite participation in God's own love of Himself consequent upon the same shared process of human knowing so that the end of human love is also its cause. Man's creation was an act of love and an act creative of shared love-capacity in that creature. God causes the loving of Himself in other beings as the image and imitation in other beings of the love He continuously is generating in Himself to Himself. He puts in created essences an appetency for His perfection, analogous to the eternal act by which He loves Himself, and by which then men can love Him. This is, in participated image, the accomplishment of that complete circle Thomas and Aristotle were so fond of: *"quaedam enim circulatio apparet in amore, se-*

27. *Ente et Essentia,* c. 5; Tr. *On Being and Essence,* A. A. Maurer, CSB, Toronto: Medieval Institute, 1949.
28. Cf. Chapters XIII and XIV especially.

cundum quod est de bono in Bonum." Our quest of God
is God's shared love in us, our finite participation in, and
therefore, our image of God's own love of Himself. Strictly
then, we *do not acquire* love of God: it is in us, His participating images, and we perfect ourselves as we develop it in
awareness, as we educate ourselves to it. The particular
and finite approach to the universal in this case is not of dis-
crete wholes and parts and separate species only, but is an
analogue, a participation, a phase of one creative good.
Man is not divine, but *by nature* there *is* in him some *measure of divinity* in nature and species of operation, though not
in mode. So there is something common between him and
God, some connaturality by which he naturally knows and
loves Him who completely transcends man, because He is
also immanent in him.

Image from Object of Intellect

IMAGE IN KNOWING. The ultimate "Why?" of man as an
image of God, which is at once the *rationale* and perfection
of the image in operation, lies in the destiny of a human person, lies in his final destiny as achieved and possessed, and
in that goal as something being progressively striven for and
reached in increasing measure while on earth. There is an
infinite difference in the method of knowing and loving
between God and man. But there is in common that very
knowing and loving, and there is *full identity in the object* of
the knowledge and love of both man and God. It is God Himself. However little we can comprehend of it, the full story of
divine being and life is told when we say that God knows
and loves Himself infinitely. And the full story of man is told
when we say that he *is*, only in order to know and love the
same God.[29] Whether persons recognize the functional-aims
of their intellect and will or not, it is philosophically clear that
they are directed, naturally and inescapably, to truth and

29. Cf. Smith, *Some American Freedoms*, p. 152. There is no need to quote
numerous authorities for support for a doctrine so common among so many
philosophers and so central in all the works and life of Aquinas and Augustine and their whole line of predecessors and successors.

goodness, the absolutes, and that in the *direct* striving for this, which we name God, we find the root reason for man's being an image of God, the *raison d'être* of his life and actions, and of his perfection in operation and his essential imitation.[30] The image of God in man's personal nature is a natural aptitude to know and love God, with consequent operative capacities to do this, including a rational recognition of the created functional aim of these abilities. The image grows in further and further immanent acts of intellect and will by which self-perfection remains most human, and yet in that same human imitation, becomes most divine when the object of those acts which perfect himself is identical with the object of divine intelligence and will, God Himself. The original is super-human, the image is human; the identical perfect and final and primary object is divine, but our mode of operation is human. It is to be emphasized that the coincidence of object and the inevitability of the operations of rational nature toward that object mean there is but one path to the perfection of nature, which is the perfection of the divine image in man, and so but one aim and activity for the integration and happiness of that nature: the persistent motion toward that object and no other. Since this is so, and motion toward it makes the human person closer to it and more and more like it, it is to be emphasized that the image, though there in the beginning, must continually change into a resemblance less and less potential and more and more actual. The image is not a still-life image; the picture *moves,* expands, clarifies. And this it does best and most directly in that activity which is motion directly toward the original,

30. Cf. I, q. 103, a. 1; I–II, qq. 2 and 3; I–II, q. 55, a. 1; *Opusc.,* III, 149, *et alibi.* Cf. Lenz, *op. cit.,* p. 151, for a fine synopsis of the whole treatment: "Je weiter die menschliche Person auf dem Wege zu ihrem letzten Ziele in der Erkenntnis und Liebe Gottes fortschreitet, umso mehr steigert sie in sich die Ebenbildlichkeit Gottes, mit der ihre Vollkommenheit und Würde zusammenfallen."

Also Geiger, *op. cit.,* p. 226: "Le retour de toutes choses à Dieu, leur source première . . . consiste essentiellement en ce que, suivant sa nature propre, chaque créature se réalisant elle-meme, réalise la similitude de la Perfection Première, les créatures intelligentes seules ayant le privilège de faire retour à Dieu *directement,* en le connaissant et en l'aimant."

the rational operations which move straight toward the object of which they are the image, in direct imitation of the natural operations by which their object Himself moves to Himself, in the actions of intelligence and will directly knowing and loving God.

However aberrant may seem the paths at times, the necessary functional aim of the rational person, the goal of his rational living (and rational natures must operate rationally or destroy themselves), is and must be God. And the most direct and perfect imitation of God, the straightest path to the object, is knowing God Himself. This is the unique human goal for which man had to be given unique powers. Since the goal is divine, he was given, in image of God, "divinized" powers.[31] Other creatures indicate the causal power of their Creator, but their likeness to Him is faint in that they pursue only derivative objects with powers not directly indicative of the natural powers of God. The human person has a power like God, operates intellectually as He, to the *same* object of such powers, as He does. *This*, directly and clearly, is the *very image* of Him, and although the likeness must be an analogous one in any relation between the infinite and the finite, it is really an image and a quite clear one, particularly when focused directly upon its object which is also the original of which it is the image.[32] To be knowing God is most God-like.

---

31. Augustine, *De Trin.*, Bk. XIV, c. 4 (PL 42, 1040); S.T., I, q. 93, a. 7, ad 4; II–II, q. 10, a. 12, ad 4; q. 81, a. 7, c.; C.G., III, cc. 25 and 37.

32. *De Ver.*, q. 10, a. 6, c. The statements here, although explicitly explaining the image by the use of the word "Trinitatis" are as applicable with "Dei," and an excellent summary of the Thomistic position. "Invenitur autem in anima nostra aliqua similitudo (Divinitatis) increatae, secundum quamlibet sui cognitionem, non solum mentis, sed *etiam sensus* . . . sed in illa tantum cognitione mentis imago Dei reperitur, secundum quam in mente nostra *expressior* Dei similitudo invenitur. Ut ergo cognitionem mentis secundum objecta distinguamus, triplex cognitio in mente nostra invenitur. Cognitio, scilicet, qua mens cognoscit Deum, et qua cognoscit se ipsam et qua cognoscit temporalia. In illa cognitione qua mens temporalia cognoscit, non invenitur expressa similitudo (divinitatis) increatae, neque secundum conformationem quia res materiales sunt magis Deo dissimiles quam ipsa mens; unde per hoc quod mens earum scientia informatur, non efficitur Deo magis conformis; similiter neque secundum analogiam, eo quod res temporalia, quae

However, insofar as the operation of a person's intelligence is an *imago Dei*, the imitation is such no matter what is the immediate and particular object of the operation. It is only that the image is perfect when there is both imitation in operation and identity in object. Yet there is in experience, and in uninjured creative intention, although fainter and indirect, a true identity of object even when the rational powers of a human person are exercised upon creatures, material or spiritual, insofar as in them, man finds not only participative being and goodness, but the tracings or images of God too. We know Him first, *through them.*[33] In other irrational creatures we "trace" God, and in other persons we see Him better and recognizing Him most in our own image, we there indirectly best see *Him.*

This rational activity, by which we know and love our-

sui notitiam parit in anima, vel intelligentiam natura ejus; et sic non potest per hoc increatae (divinitatis) consubstantialitas repraesentati. Sed in cognitione qua mens nostra cognoscit se ipsam, est repraesentatio (divinitatis) increatae, per analogiam, inquantum hoc modo mens cognoscens se ipsam verbum sui gignit, et ex utroque procedit amor . . . Sed in cognitione ipsa qua mens ipsum Deum cognoscit, mens ipsa Deo conformatur, sicut omne cognoscens, inquantum hujusmodo, assimilatur cognito. Major autem est similitudo quae est per conformationem, ut visus ad colorem, quam quae est per analogiam, ut visus ad intellectum qui similiter ad sua objecta comparatur. Unde expressior similitudo (divinitatis) est in mente secundum quod cognoscit Deum, quam secundum quod cognoscit se ipsam; et ideo proprie imago (divinitatis) in mente est secundum quod cognoscit Deum primo et principaliter; sed quadammodo secundario et sic quod cognoscit se ipsam et praecipue prout se ipsam considerat *ut est imago* Dei; ut sic ejus consideratio non sistat in se, sed *procedat usque ad Deum.* In consideratione vero rerum temporalium non invenitur imago, sed similitudo quaedam, quae magis potest ad vestigium pertinere. . . ." (Italics and parentheses ours. The distinction is not of operation here but of object.)

33. I *Sent.*, d. 3, q. 2, a. 1.

Augustine, *De Trin.*, XIV, c. 8 (PL 42, 1040): "mens meminit sui, intelligit se, et diligit se; hoc si cernimus, cernimus . . . non quidem Deum, sed jam imaginem Dei."

I, q. 93, a. 8, c.: "Attenditur igitur divina imago in homine secundum verbum conceptum de Dei notitia, et amorem exinde derivatum. Et sic imago attenditur in anima secundum quod fertur vel nata est ferri in Deum. Fertur autem in aliquid mens dupliciter: uno modo, directe et immediate; alio modo, indirecte et mediate, sicut cum aliquis videndo imaginem hominis in speculo, dicitur ferri in ipsum hominem . . . (through seeing His image in oneself:) non fertur mens in se ipsam absolute, sed prout per hoc ulterius potest ferri in Deum . . ."

selves, is an activity imitative of the divine activity by which
God infinitely and essentially is related to Himself and identified with Himself. We find out *that* He is from creatures;
we find out *that* He is, and something more of *what* He is and
how He is, from ourselves. This discovery and its consequent
reactive attraction of will, is an imitation of the activity of
the Godhead, although indirectly identified with respect to
object, since the operative imitation is focused not upon the
original, but upon the image. This indirect imitation of God
can be perfected itself, as we become more and more aware
that it is His image we know and love within ourselves, and
as we "educate" our imaged mind and will to operate more
and most consistently in creation and in ourselves upon objects which are more and more noble and godlike, more and
more close to that good, and that true, and that beautiful,
which in any creature is the likeness of Him, and can be explicitly recognized as such by intelligent creatures. Although irrational creatures do not specifically imitate God
in their operations, and do not pursue Him directly, or even
indirectly in His image in persons, yet persons themselves,
through such creatures can indirectly imitate in operation
and pursue in object the original of the likeness. This not
only increases the image in man by clarifying his intellectual
object, and perfecting his operative powers, but in doing
so, is so perfective by practice that it makes him more readily
capable of *directly* imitating God and focusing upon Him
directly as his direct and express image, achieving therein a
coincidence of operation *and* object.

Evidently, he cannot know all of God nor love Him infinitely. Only God Himself can accomplish that. Man must approach Him first through sensible things and always in a finite measure. But he can then step off from the material and
even the imaged spiritual and focus his rational faculties *directly* upon God.[34] He must start with the particular, mate-

34. Augustine, *De Trin.*, Lib. XII, c. 7; PL 42, 1004–48: ". . . secundum
rationalem mentem ubi potest esse agnitio Dei, hominem factum ad imaginem
ejus qui creavit eum . . ." and cf. c. 12.: ". . . in mente eo est imago
Dei, quo meminit, intelligit, et diligit Deum, quod est Sapientia."
Cf. I, q. 12, a. 12, c., and ad 2.

rial, and very faint likeness, but he has divinized powers which can lead him beyond these to their original source. His rational personality is perfected in his constant search for truth through truths, his constant striving for good, as he rises from contingent beings to the absolute being, from countless piecemeal truths to the absolute truth, from the multiplicity of partial and limited goods to the supreme God who is the plenitude of being. By his godlike power of intelligence, he enriches his own being and increases his own imitation and image by becoming vicariously, as it were, all beings. As he learns the natures of lesser beings, he not only sees more of the creative whole, but imitates more and more that Creator with a like operation as he intussuscepts their forms. And in tending to the partial and limited goods found in all good things, his intelligence and will are gradually prepared for the destined perfection of embracing the truth and good directly in Him who is the original of all these images. The closer a human person approaches to an intellectual focus upon the supreme intelligible, instead of this or that intelligible, the more perfecting and perfected is he in his operations and the more directly bent upon imitating the original of his image.[35]

For this, finally and primarily, was man made; in this he precisely and most perfectly is the imitation and image of God and progressively achieves increasing assimilation to Him and into Him. In so acting he is most *man*, most a *person*, and precisely so because in doing this is he most godlike. "To contemplate and to tend to Him is the supreme law of the life of man who, created to His divine image and likeness, is powerfully impelled to the enjoyment of his Creator. It is not indeed by any force or energy of the body, but by the understanding and the affection of the will that man is inclined towards God."[36] It is in this that man reaches his

35. *C.G.*, III, c. 25; *De Pot.*, q. 9, a. 9.
36. Leo XIII, "The Chief Duties of Christian Citizens" (*Sapientiae Christianae*), text in *Social Wellsprings*, vol. I, p. 143. Cf. III, q. 4, a. 1, c., and ad 2: "humana natura . . . nata est contingere *aliqualiter* ipsum Verbum per suam operationem, cognoscendo et amando ipsum . . . est *capax Dei* . . . propria operatione cognitionis et amoris . . ."

peak of operation and his progressive earthly destiny, in the operation of his unique, godlike rational powers, *directly* upon the object which is the direct object for him alone, his knowing and consequent loving of God Himself. In this operation and in attaining this object, he completely transcends the rest of creation and imitates God by the very fact again of that transcendence. He alone ends in his beginning.[37] Only man possesses God.

In this, a human person reaches his destined and due dignity as he achieves the real divine assimilation in that conformity with the original and primary goal of his nature and functions, his finite but connatural union with his infinite Maker. The point is that all this is *real* and in *man's nature,* and he cannot operate with contrary goals without frustration. Power of function must perform its function![38] Only the human person can reach out by intellectual understanding and rational love, his own special and divine-like way of perfection, to the very substance of God, in the measure he knows anything of the divine substance in his mind, and so holds within him the likeness of it.[39] To know the perfect is perfection in knowing. Moreover, he can increase the image, and therefore his natural satisfaction and integration, insofar as he increasingly directs his rational powers upon their primary functional aim, increasingly upon the direct knowing and loving God. In this he not only is achieving their completion and perfection, but is paralleling the divine operations themselves and giving evidence in imitative operation of whose image he is.[40]

In sum, the more the human person's knowing is not only directed upon God Himself, but is more constantly active, the more does he imitate and become the perfected image of the *ipsum intelligere* who is continuous and infinite activ-

---

37. *C.G.,* II, c. 87.

38. *C.G.,* III, c. 25. It is unfair to the writer of it to quote any one part only of such a well-knit and comprehensive survey of man as seen here. But note: "non sufficit igitur ad felicitatem humanam . . . qualiscumque intelligibilis cognitio, *nisi divina cognitio adsit,* quae terminat *naturale* desiderium."

39. *C.G.,* III, c. 25.

40. I, q. 93, a. 4. and *Comm. Caietani* de hoc.

ity: *similia similibus cognoscuntur*. This is the one human activity which is common to a creature and Creator. Though not carried out in the same manner by God and man, the human person does have the ability, by the very perfecting of his imitating powers, to perfect the manner of knowing God and of becoming more and more the image of Him as he becomes more and more rationally self-sufficient, and more and more independent of created likenesses in his direct knowing of their Creator.[41] It is the very topmost peak of man's image that by his act of knowing God, he comes sometimes even to perceive some little of God's manner of intelligent operation in knowing a very little of God's own immediate knowing of self, a very great resemblance of God in man, a very divine activity and truth in a human person.[42]

IMAGE IN LOVING. It is particularly in the rational consequences of knowing God that the essential dignity-value and perfection of the human person can be most clearly seen. What is known, insofar as it is and is good, must be reacted to as metal to a magnet. It is in man's will then, that man's close approximation to God will be best seen. His will is not only the image and imitation of God, but through that participation, can achieve a union with the unparticipated which is so much more than what we mean by image, that image cannot truly and completely express the full dignity and "divinization" of man. By his understanding, focused directly upon its supreme intelligible, he can achieve not only a similarity of operation with God, but an identity of object. By his will, following that same object, he can achieve fuller and fuller *union with* an ever-distinct object, without the connotation of separateness so predominant in the concept of "image." The movement of the will shows more clearly to us the return of the participated back to some manner of fusion with the original unparticipated, however distinct the personal substances remain. This is the actual sharing of the same good, the result of the attractive radiation from goodness and its creature communication, seen in the direct re-

41. *C.G.*, III, c. 37; cf. Maritain, *Degrees of Knowledge*, p. 290.
42. Augustine, *De Trin.*, Bk. IX, c. 11 (PL 42, 970); *C.G.*, III, c. 25.

turn of partial goodness in humans back to the source and object of their wills, the *union toward identity* with Him who is total good. The more directly human wills move toward Him and the more they transform their potential union with Him into actual participation, the closer and more intimate the joining of the two, the more they become *one* good and one spirit, the more God-like does man become and the more he shares the absolute value itself and so the more priceless and divine is his value. This is again, the imitation of that original movement which prompted his creation, man's attractive and retroactive motion to that original creative love, and so this is the most perfect imitation and assimilation to supreme value-good. Assimilation here is to be taken in its full modern sense, which is not only a growing likeness to, but some manner of being *taken into*. The analogy which explains participation in the goodness of being, above all genera and species, allows this as a rational and satisfactory explanation of man's reflection of and actual sharing in God Himself! This is *of his nature*, and is inescapable, and is then not only the standard of measurement of his value but the measure of his integration and satisfaction, because his will must thrust toward such union with an ineluctable *logique du coeur*, as Pascal called it, because it must actualize itself, must complete or perfect itself, and in so doing, at the same time attain the perfection of which its own is a sharing and toward which it was destined and for which destiny it was given its powers. In his beginnings, a human person is made in a path which is grooved to God, set in motion by the same love-will he is to end within.[43] It is because of this that human nature must be dissatisfied with particular goods either in quality or quantity, whether a particular human person realizes at the moment what dissatisfies his nature or not. He may and cannot help love for them, because they too share good. But he alone was made for universal good, and made to attain it directly and with increasing ability in life, as his intelligence is to grasp Him

43. I, q. 112, a. 1, ad 4; I–II, q. 98, a. 5, ad 2; *C.G.*, III, c. 116; *De Malo*, q. 6, a. 23.

directly, above the indirect indications of creatures. ". . . men, created by God to His image and likeness and destined for Him Who is infinite perfection . . . realize the inadequacy of earthly goods to produce happiness. . . ." Hence they feel more keenly in themselves the impulse toward a perfection that is higher, an impulse implanted in their rational nature by the Creator Himself.[44] If the likeness of truth and goodness can attract man, it is only because they are miniature and faint representations of the original and total he is made for. If they exert attraction for him and he cannot help his impulse to them, then the direct motion to goodness consequent upon the direct understanding of intelligence, must, in comparison, totally inflame him and draw the whole man completely to it.[45]

It cannot be over-emphasized that this attraction to his God is in a human person's nature, and *cannot be escaped* without disintegration of such a nature, without that nature acting non-rationally and becoming less and less *human.* Either such a person becomes more and more divine by participation and imitation, or becomes less and less human: the achievement of the completion of human nature *is* that actualized sharing the divine which is the perfection of his potentials to God.

Human love is never anything but a finite participation of God's own love of Himself, so that, by this participation, the cause of human ability to love is also its completion and destined end. God causes in that He generates love in Himself, and causes it in other beings as an image of that loving self, and causes it creatively in others so they must be imitative in their love-operation of that love-activity in Himself which *is* Himself. They have in their natures a native and ineradicable drive toward that completion of potentials which

44. Pius XI: "Christian Education of Youth," text in *Social Wellsprings,* vol. II, p. 90.
45. Aquinas, *Commentarium in Psalmos,* Ps. 41, v. 5: ("delectasti me Domine, in factura tua."): "Si igitur creaturarum bonitas, pulchritudo, et suavitas sic animas hominum allicit, *ipsius Dei fontana bonitas,* rivulis bonitatum in singulis creaturis repertis diligenter comparata, animas hominum inflammatas *totaliter ad se trahet.*"

is within the limits of their essence the attainment of His perfection, a natural impulse analogous to the eternal act by which He loves Himself, the same act they share in and by which then they in turn can love Him. Again, this is that *"circulatio"* Aquinas was so fond of. There is no distinction amounting to separation between true love of oneself and the love of God: created love, being participative of divine love, has the same object and moves to the same union. (Aberrations of this natural process are not considered here, because they belong to the distorted image and imitative ability of historical man and do not affect the essence of a human person, only the speed and difficulty and measure of attainment.) Even to love any created good is to love its resemblance of divine good, and since it is this resemblance which makes the good to be good, the real heart of the object loved is sovereign goodness. It is impossible to love the image without loving the original, consciously or no. And then, for human persons whose intelligence makes them explicitly aware of what and who is the original, it is impossible for their natural wills not to prefer the original to the image, even in themselves. To love oneself, who is the participated image and analogue of God, is to love God, and the action of such love is the operative imitation of God who is a continuously active love. True love of creatures, and especially of self, His only created image, is an increase of that image and a further imitation of God's love of self, because it is simultaneously the love of Him.[46] If this progresses *naturally*, according to rational nature, and consistently, the imitative process takes that voluntary nature, as it did its understanding, upwards in completion and perfecting, to the direct love of Him, which is immediately imitative of His activity, and imitative of Him in its destined permanence. This is the perfection of the human person who is himself the perfection of creation, the sole image of and only direct imitator of God, a human person who is *naturally divinized* by participation in divinity and increases the imitation as his participation is naturally transformed from a potential into an actualized

46. Cf. Gilson, *Spirit of Medieval Philosophy*, pp. 269–303.

and active condition, until his relatively infinite thirst of soul for knowing and loving is satisfied in his possession and his awareness of possession, as far as his finiteness allows, of the absolutely infinite perfection for which he is clearly destined by the very powers of his nature. He approaches more and more to a finite reduplication of and participation in divine life as God lives it in Himself in heaven. Obviously, there alone stands the final value and dignity of man: the more he shares in God and the more he is thus naturally like God, the more his active living is a humanly reflected re-presentation of the divine living. The more noble is he in nature and operation the more priceless is he, and the more beyond comparison with any other creatures. The more he "becomes what he is" by nature, the more he must be treated himself for what he is and the more he must treat other images for what they are: the reduplicating images of God. Dignity is goodness, which is perfection, which is completion in existential being, which is God. By that must man be measured and by that destiny he must measure himself and his actions, and from that nature and destiny take his own awareness of his essential and permanent value and prestige. From the nature of the God whose shared existence and powers he has, he can take his assurance of possessing the same God. Because the intellectual seeing of God is to bring human nature to the very peak of its expression and wholly to actualize this "humanity" which is otherwise realized but brokenly, we are sure that by gathering them up and bringing them to a pointed perfection, happiness will warrant all the acts, all the desires, all the joys which, agreeing with the noblest and most "human" needs of our nature, are beforehand like the state of the soul whose boundless hopes will at last be fulfilled.[47]

THE SUPERNATURAL IMAGE. Nowhere in this thesis are we in the domain of grace and revelation. When we speak of participation in divine nature, and its image in human persons, we are using the common analogy of being, and asserting the fact of that participation only within the limits of hu-

47. IV *Sent.*, d. 18, q. 2, a. 3; cf. Gilson, *Moral Values and Moral Life*, p. 48.

man nature's sharing what is common between infinite and
finite intelligent being. Within the limits of human nature
and the human mode of operation according to that nature,
man participates in the intelligence which is the divine nature, but which *is* and which operates in Him, in a totally
eminent and divine way.

Grace is another realm from our present field of inquiry.
By this absolutely divine gift, the human person has infused
into him, and so shares, what is completely beyond his nature, and what is properly and exclusively divine alone. By
grace he shares in that divine nature in a divine manner,
though remotely, though still in a finite measure: *in eodem
genere et eodem modo, sed non in eodem gradu.* Where natural participation is sharing what is *common* to God and human creatures, grace shares what is *proper* only to God,
sharing in intelligent divinity *as it is divine,* sharing the Godhead *as He is in Himself,* not just as He can be known and
loved by us, but as the "interior" nature of God knows and
loves as He is triune in persons. By grace, man is given a
quality of soul which enables him to be disposed to know
God intuitively as God knows Himself, and to love Him directly as He loves Himself, being given an essential disposition to the same formal object and uncreated operations,
which God has Himself in Himself. The natural participation in divine intelligent nature enables us to know, and to
know Him *as we are,* while grace enables us to know Him
as He is, and as He knows.

A divine nature, as such, and a divine mode of knowing
as divine, is foreign to the field and capacities of philosophy.
Our natural participation speaks of the common and human
analogical participation in what is also divine, but by our
human and natural, and created way of knowing and loving,
never of a human's participation in the divine nature in His
own divine manner of possession and operation. This warn-
ing is given not only to protect the interpretation of the terms
here used, but to give also a glimpse of how poor and trun-
cated is the picture, grand as it is thus far. By nature, in us

one can see what God is like; by grace, one can see God.[48]

SUMMARY. The comparison of man with his Creator has shown that his position of dignity includes much more than his superiority to other creatures. The very *rationale* of his dignity, from which his superiority flows as a consequence, consists in a relation to his Creator which constitutes him as *imago Dei,* as the image of God in nature and the imitative parallel in operation. Man is the image of God in his mind, and then in his will, and in the operation of these faculties in knowing and loving. He images God in all their operations, but eminently so when he pursues with them the same object as God, which is God Himself. He is not only intelligent, as God, and able freely to love, as God does, but by those very powers, can direct his rational energies upon God directly and expend his divine-like powers upon precisely the same infinite object upon which intelligence and love itself directs His infinite energy. This re-presentation, as it were, of the nature and activity of God upon earth constitutes man in a worth and dignity which from its very nature is evidently comparable and measurable only by the standard and rule which is the infinite God Himself, and man's dignity is something of an incarnation of the Creator in creation, in man's measure, but with a divine model.

48. Cf. I–II, qq. 109–114; *In Joann.,* c. 1, lect. 4 and lect. 8 ad fin; c. 17, lect. 6; Garrigou-Lagrange, *De Gratia,* pp. 90–121. (This is a comm. on I–II, 109–114.)

CHAPTER FIVE

Man and Men: His Perfecting

THE SOCIAL PERSON. The full picture of what man is must include *how he is*. The portrait must reveal not only his essential nature and its image dignity, but his existential nature and the actual growing world of his value-potentials. The investigation of such a human person and his value has shown that an essential of his worth and dignity lies exactly in the fact that he is dynamic, that he not only possesses the dignity of a creature superior in perfections, but that he grows, that his energy potentials push toward the completion of that inherent perfectibility which is both his present worth and his promise. This climb of man to completion can be shown only with the picture of the climate in which he operates and the ground over which he moves. The human person's power-values are actualized only in the person-milieu in which he acts, the stimulant environment which is labeled "society." It is precisely part of human dignity that, like God, he is not isolated by nature from other persons. Human destined dignity is achieved (or annihilated) only in and through societal action. In reciprocal actions, a human person "accumulates" perfections through others, and communicates to them the sharing in his own, or the stimulus to develop their own. Completion of the intended human dignity is attained or lost by each one's personal handling of his relations with other persons in communal living. Men "make" or "break" themselves *and others* by their mode of human or non-human living among others, or even by their attempts *not* to live among others. The community of persons is the necessary growing ground for each individual person, because only through and in that environment can each separate person "grow" by development of his spiritual potentials, his personal values. Unlike lower creatures, the creature of intelligence does not belong directly only to the efficient order which inserted him into the cosmos and the ontological order in which he is. It is natural, and natural to his position of dignity in creation, that he belong also, and he alone directly and consciously so, to the teleological order of intelligent, purposive groupings of persons, the conscious grouping of rational human persons together for a common aim: *human* perfection, *full* person-worth.

The very nature of each individual person is to live in community with other persons. So the individual person and the community of persons are fitted to each other. From the beginning and by nature man has been made for society, which is then a natural environment and instrument for him, so that what was wanting to his nature and yet beyond the power of individual attainment with only his own resources, he might attain by association with other persons.[1] Many of the essential powers and consequent acts of a person must suppose other persons for the movement of energy into act. To love, to speak, to own things, can be understood only when other persons exist and are related to each other. The "I" must demand a "you," and a "we" is as necessary for human existence as any "I" and as natural for the functioning of any individual person as are his own powers to him. In fact, it is the "we" that adds the full proper dignity to each "I." The actual living of a human person can take place *humanly*, only with other persons and with and under the person of God, where the union of the images with their original is accomplished largely by the instrumentality of the union of image with image. The very powers of the human individual person demand for the accomplishment of their functional aims and the achievement of the whole person's intentional and final end, a scale of communities and a

1. Leo XIII, "Human Liberty," in *Social Wellsprings*, vol. 1, p. 128; Luigi Sturzo, *The Inner Laws of Society*, p. 12. Cf. *C.G.*, III, c. 117. Aquinas speaks in some twenty passages of man's being *naturaliter sociale*.

range of social function which parallel those individual powers and offer the milieu in which alone they can operate to
complete actualization and reach full human worth in the
actualized completion of quasi-infinite person-potentials.
Aquinas has expressed that necessity in a pithy statement
and perhaps with no little cloistered humor when he says that
social life is necessary for the progressive practice of perfection, and that "solitude belongs to the already perfect."[2]
Man's energized nature exists, it is true, for the actualized
perfection of his individual and independent person. But the
subsistent independence of that nature is no absolute thing
and does not connote independence from any other help
toward the perfected actualization of its powers. His individual essence achieves existential completion only through
his coexistence with other such person-natures. The end is
self completion; the means in the strictly causal sense are
the *self* powers of his own nature, but the necessary instrumental climate is found in the interactions of personal, co-
existent living in common with *many* other *selves.* Man lives
actively in a family, a civil community, a human race, a religious organization, a vocational group, and in these intro-
active, operative, personal worlds, he actualizes his potentials and increases his imitation, in action, of the God whose
image he is by nature, so that the accretion of perfections
on to that person builds and molds him into a closer likeness
of God, lifting him to the intended excellence of his full godlike image and complete human worth and dignity. He not
only has needs which he cannot supply in isolation, but powers whose expression (and they demand expression by force
of nature) need fellow-men, both for accumulation and communication. The community life is grounded in his nature
and in the insistent drive of his nature for further actualization. It is true that before any active life and social interac-
tion, there are potential and actual perfections independently intrinsic to that nature, and that the operative powers

2. II–II, q. 188, a. 8. Cf. I, q. 105, a. 6; III, q. 8, a. 1, ad 2; *C.G.*, III,
c. 98; Rommen, *The State in Catholic Thought,* p. 189 ff.; Mouroux, *The
Meaning of Man,* p. 124.

effect realized perfections not essential for the definition of man as man. But social relations and activity are necessary for the realization of a *full* man and the attainment of his matured value in life. His intended perfection and therefore his nature's satisfaction in his fully realized human worth depend upon and demand a hierarchical satisfaction attained by the effective operation of powers whose inner natural drive to operation he cannot withstand, yet whose insistent energies cannot satisfactorily function without the stimulus or help of other persons and their drives and powers. All this is the development of his personality, the operational expansion of his person, which can be accomplished only through that interactive community of persons called society. He needs not just a world of matter or even of living things. His true sphere of creative evolution is in a world of persons. There he can mature to full growth and dignity as a person, as a developed rationality and God-image, by the help of fellow-images. He is free to complete himself among others; without others, he is extrinsically determined not to. "We are in some sort our own fathers, because we bring ourselves to birth as we will." [3]

It is only this wider unity of a supra-individual world which allows an individual human person to achieve his full meaning and dignity, to completely actualize his own personal potential worth. Since the rest of that human society is constituted by individual persons, each person is bound to it by his very nature. He is unique, but he is a unique participation in a common human species and a true expression of that common value in all his human actions. He is one with other human persons by many "expressional ties" of similarly operative natures and powers, and by the "positional ties" which bind many persons to his person in familial and social interdependence. Since he must be a part integrated into the social whole and must stand in a certain human relation not just spatio-temporal but ontological and teleological and

3. Greg. Nyssa, *Vita Moysis*, PG 44, 327. Cf. Sheed, *Communism and Man*, p. 104; Cox, *Thomistic Analysis of the Social Order*, p. 46 ff.; Smith, "Human Social Life," *op. cit.*, p. 306.

intelligible to the whole body of thinking members who ✕
make up humanity, he cannot divorce his operative living
and perfecting and expansion of personality from them. And ⌋
since this whole body is made up of those active persons who
live and move in those interdependent and dynamic relations
to each other and in their operative perfecting into the fullness of human dignity through the functional relations flowing from their organizational interlocking in society, each
particular member is integrated into the group and expands
his perfecting operations through the "functional ties" of society.

There is great potential perfectibility in man and essential
inherent value and dignity, because his being and nature and
powers and above all his intelligence constitute him in the
image of the Creator Himself, absolute perfection and value.
But the image is both finite and alive. It can and must grow
and perfect itself by the expanding and continued operation
of its own potential toward its own recognized goals. This
dynamic character of the human person, the actual perfecting
of the image, and the consequent completion of his full
worth and dignity, can be seen only where it can be accomplished: in the acting communities of persons who must complete themselves with and through each other. Man's perfected value by nature as the intelligent image of his God is
the prime value-aim for group societal life, as human life in
human societies is the necessary and surrounding instrumental milieu for the realization of each individual's perfectible
potentials. It is essential to the dignity of a human person
that he is social, that he alone like the original he images
consciously and intentionally operates as one person among
other persons unified by their common nature. He has powers
to be perfected into a complete image; he has by that same
nature and those same powers, the ability to bind himself
into intelligent communities with intelligible aims fitted to
perfect his individual person-image. There is no full and
true picture of a man and his worth, as there is no chance of
progress toward full grown human dignity for any man, except as a man among many men.

THE PERFECTIBLE FACTORS

The dynamic development of the human person takes place in and through the reciprocal activity of communal living, and while the actualization of many potentials may take place simultaneously, it is patently impossible to treat such development analytically, just as it actually takes place. There must be a separate discussion of the functional values which are perfecting, the positional relations which are conducive to or perfective of the person, and the potentials perfectible, and all of these factors linked in their developmental activity with their model perfection. However, the very theme of this chapter makes it evident that in reality none of these factors acts in isolation or even in succession. Only their analysis is sectionalized.

THE BODY. It has been made clear that it is not man's body which is the *id quo* specifically making him a person. Yet it is the *whole man* who is the person, and his body is part of his composite being. As such, its development in a human being is a personal development, since its life-principle in him is the rational soul which does make him a *person*. Furthermore, its development in constitution and in operative ability must be credited to him, the person, and therefore has some place in the perfectible and perfecting development of the human person. The corporal powers must be used first for the very sustaining of his life in order that his rational soul can operate, as it must, through his body, and that in societal activity, it can express itself through that body. For this then, it can develop more and more as the agile and perfectly accommodated instrument, and is of no small importance in the total view of the dignity of man. It is in his use of things of the earth that it must develop and in its proper assimilation of them that it can hope to impede the health-obstacles to the functioning of his soul. His process of nutrition preserves him in health and strength, and its growth parallels and is a necessary aid to the growth of personal soul. Moreover, it is through the body that is expressed that perfection of divinely imitative man that is generation, man's creative imitation, and this perfecting operation, by which man perfects himself in realizing the preservation of his race, is a social affair. There is no intention here, and it would be a distortion of reality, to minimize the role and importance of a person's body in the process of perfection in society. Because of what he is in make-up, man could not possibly develop without the assistance and through the medium of bodily facility and co-operation.[4] But it is not man's body which is peculiarly responsible for his distinctive personal dignity nor for the perfecting process toward completion of his personal potentials. That is the province of his rational powers and any philosophical outlook or cultural custom which has exclusively focused its view or practice upon man's corporal achievement has so obviously distorted the true reality of the human person that such errors against reality merit no careful consideration or refutation in a philosophical analysis, even though they need constant check in social practice because of man's propensity to accept as the most important and satisfying, and even as the whole, that corporal part of him which impresses him most directly, immediately, and vehemently. Moreover, this study is not primarily a critique of errors about man, but a positive approach to the truth of his dignity, from which attained eminence it is hoped the errors may then present themselves to a refutation which needs much less demonstration. Because they are more the cause of his dignity and more what makes him *personal and human,* it is his spiritual energies which deserve more attention, those rational values and powers which indicate the increasing perfection of man in society *as a person,* and which insure his personal perfection and happiness in an abiding way, since they are superior and more desirable.[5] It is not so much the centering upon the body, but the exclusion of these spiritual powers which are the truly distinctive *human* powers, which dooms to social failure and personal frustration all the philosophic errors and social materialistic dictatorships which so attempt to handle *humans* without realization

4. III, q. 65, a. 1, c.; II–II, q. 129, a. 6, ad 1; *In Ethics,* lect. 1.
5. I–II, qq. 31 and 87.

apparently of the human hierarchy of values within persons.[6] It is man's mind and will which make out of a mob, a society, and of man, a person.

THE MIND

In the very heart of a human being lies a radical and ineradicable tendency to expansion . . . a personal attraction from God. Man is called to *enrich himself* in body and in spirit by every kind of cultural activity, and by gradually establishing his dominion over the world; to *possess himself* by way of an infinitely more intimate activity of mind and will, leading to a full self-awareness and self-mastery, and to *give himself* in an unforced generosity . . . in communion and love.[7]

There we find a masterful expression of the perfecting of man in social living, and in that personal progress which must be the effect of the actualization of his rational powers, of his intelligence, and then of the realized activity of will following his mind's knowing. It is his mind which is the distinctly human cause and guide of the *expansion* of his person, his feeding upon the intelligible food offered him by other persons, his internal spiritual and personal awareness of all this, and his reciprocal communication of it, a rational and personal activity which in turn is the further actualizing of his own powers.[8] Man alone, being an end in himself, exercises his human powers for himself, and has his own perfection as a destined end, after the destiny which is his Creator's honor, and the perfection of the divine ordered plan of the whole universe.[9] And this perfecting of himself for himself is accomplished through the actualization, the operation of intelligent potentials. It is an internal, spiritual and rational proc-

6. Smith, *op. cit.*, p. 293.
7. Our summation of: Smith, "Human Social Life," *op. cit.*, pp. 305–309.
8. It might well be noted that whatever is said of the actively developing person, through his rational faculties, implies a dignity true in each measure for any and all human beings. Whether or not their rational faculties temporarily operate or are temporarily impeded in their operation, even from birth, is a condition which is accidental and immaterial to the thesis and never excludes any such human person from the common dignity belonging to all who naturally possess the components of human essence.
9. I, q. 65, a. 2 (and *Comm. Caietani, ibidem*).

ess for which social environment offers the milieu and instruments. And it is a constant and lifelong process of building up and rectifying and molding his rational personality, which will attain a full stature only in a future life. It is the development of his soul-life which is peculiarly human and is the secret and measure of his personal dignity as a human. It is in this process that the ontological person finds further dignity in the increase of the psychological and ethical personality, an added operative, and second perfection founded on and caused by his first ontal perfection.[10]

The notable point here is that the actualization of those powers which specifically make this creature human, is brought about in activity which is reciprocally social. *This* individual needs other persons for the development of his powers which specifically make this creature human is taneously helps the development of others' as their perfections are communicated to others. It is society which is the necessary instrumental atmosphere and yet it is the individual person who orientates all the social forms by his rational recognition of an intelligent use of their instrumentality and the direction of their usefulness toward a rational end which is common to all but essentially and distinctively *personal.* Each person, by the natural potentials of nature and their inherent drive to perfection, is set in motion by the Creator toward the achievement simultaneously of his own rational perfection and the completion of others, each a minister of providence for himself and for others.[11] There lies in this drive to rational perfection the necessity not only of active rational operation, but of a proper activity feeding upon proper rational food, toward a proper person-goal. If the mind and will are allowed to exercise a mutual influence to lead the person to stupidity and false goals, neither can attain its native and creator-intended fulness or dignity, and

10. S.T., I, q. 73, a. 1, c. Cf. Gilson, *Spirit of Med. Philos.*, p. 202 ff.; Cox, *op. cit.*, p. 36.

11. Leo XIII, "Rerum Novarum," in *op. cit.*, vol. 1, pp. 180–181; Duffy, T. F., *Papal Teaching of Principle of Subsidiary Function*, Washington: Catholic University of America Press, 1949, p. 7; Sturzo, *Inner Laws of Society*, p. 55.

misuses both itself and society.[12] *My* development depends upon society, but also the value-level of society depends upon the contribution to it of my rational perfecting of myself. Since the perfection of others so depends upon *this* person's use and right use of his rational faculties, since not only his own dignity but theirs depends upon this, each has in his hands, in some degree, the measure of the personal perfection and value of other persons, and is participative in social life of the rational causality of the Creator. I am by nature set "for the rise and fall of many in Israel." I am bound to the development of my mind for their perfected dignity as well as my own because it is an integral part of my destined and dignified perfection that the Creator wills me, and gives me the power to be, a partial cause of the dynamic and developing nobility of other persons through my own energy and intelligence and love.[13] By nature, *I am* "my brother's keeper" (and my own) by and because of my intelligence, and the realized dignity of many persons depends in some measure upon *my* rational digestion of socio-cultural food.

It is only within an ordered society, which is what should be meant by a "civilized" society, that such rational development can take place, because only such a community gives opportunity for personal rational powers to actualize themselves in a way connatural to them, and only such an environment offers the material which is intelligibly digestible for the perfection of each one's personal powers. This fuller development of the powers which precisely make this creature human and personal, and their proper full development upon objects fitted to rationality, is what is known in its end-result as culture, that integrated and symmetrical actualization of all the faculties proper to a human person as rational.[14] Such

12. Cf. II–II, q. 47 (*De prudentia*); Leo XIII, "Immortale Dei," in *op. cit.*, vol. 1, p. 80.

13. Aquinas, *Comm. supra Evang. Joannis*, cap. 1, lect. 4. Cf. Wagstaffe, Sr. M. Joseph, *Philosophy of Culture*, Catholic University of America Press, 1949, p. 23.

14. Cf. Wagstaffe, *op. cit.*, pp. 31–33; p. 60; and Johnson, George, *Curriculum of the Catholic Elementary School*, Catholic University of America Press, 1919, p. 51.

proper development must increase the worth and dignity of
the individual person, because it is an operative expansion
of personality upon discerned, appreciated, and accepted,
true and graded values. It is the filling up of personal and
operative being with the created and predominantly immaterial intelligible fragments of uncreated being, and truth,
and goodness. So it is then that the degree of "culture" possessed by each person is at once the measure of the degree
of his development of his person-powers and of his perfection, and consequently of his worth or dignity.[15] It is by the
proper operation of his rational powers that a person escapes
more and more from immersion in matter which is of less
value than spirit, and by that proper activity possible within
civilized communal living that he elevates the community
itself from a "mob" to ordered society. The thrust of intelligent actualization is the spiritual dynamic which provides
the energy necessary for both that personal and social effort
which can achieve both culture in the socially-united persons, and ordered civilization in the organized group. This
achievement must come from *within* persons, and therefore
this development of the human mind is the greatest agent of
social progress and the surest measure of both individual and
social worth because it is indicative of the superior process of
the integrated actualization of spirit which is more imitative
of its Creator and the true, destined goal of human-image
perfection and universal progress.[16]

Full personal dignity is measured by the perfection of the
person. But it is his intelligence which radically makes him a
person and is moreover the chief perfectible factor in the
completion of his personality. Insistence upon this seems
either a truism or, if couched in more rhetorical terms, some
"mysticism" of impractical appeal, unless one looks at the
effects of the historical forgetfulness of it, the consequent
social "inhumanities of man," the devaluation of the indi-

15. Cf. Delos, J. T., *La Société Internationale et les Principes du Droit
Public*, pp. 75–78.
16. Dawson, *Progress and Religion*, pp. xiii, 82, 263, *et alibi*. Cf. Mohan,
Thomistic Philosophy of Civilization and Culture, Catholic University of
America Press, 1948 *passim*.

vidual, and the resultant personal and social bewilderment
and unhappiness. The lack of the proper development in the
most conducive surroundings toward the connatural goal of
intelligent perfection, the repugnance toward it in an anti-
intellectual "culture," had caused the denial of metaphysical
reality altogether in many instances, and so the denial of the
primacy of the spiritual. This has been, according to as reliable an authority on culture and civilization as we have,
Professor Dawson, the "fundamental Western error."[17] The
refusal to follow the natural bent of an image-intelligence
was unable to smother man's natural thrust to realize his
potential worth in some way, and led man to imagine he was
creative intelligence itself, from which his arrogant mistakes
led his children to cast off intelligence itself as an impossible and impractical and inhibiting value in life. Man was
magnified to an unreal size until the bubble burst and he
shrank to less than his true and due size, as he has gone from
an exaggerated individualism to a "much more shameful and
painful anonymity in impersonal collectivism." Thinking was
never free to create its own principles and make its own
gods in its own image, but only to be governed by reality.
We cannot annihilate what *is,* or change the hierarchy of objective values; we can only discover, accept, and exist according to them. The inevitable result was that the spiritual
potentials and values were thrown overboard and that meant
throwing over exactly what makes creatures persons—and
valuable. The result has been the destruction of the *human*
in man, and his specific *raison d'être.* After the exaggerated
rationalistic individualism stemming from the Renaissance,
and the inescapable later degradation inherent in its falsity,
man had to lose his position of unique superiority and sink
back into material nature, into being a subordinate part of an
impersonal mechanism. "Sensory truth . . . ushered in the
Age of Incertitude . . . and such incertitude cannot be toler-
ated indefinitely. It is inimical to man's happiness, his creativeness, even his survival." And today's Marxism may be
seen as the "culminating point of the modern tendency to ex-

17. Dawson, "Christianity and the New Age," in *Essays in Order,* p. 224.

plain that which is specifically human in terms of something else." "Contemporary fatalism . . . has proclaimed to the entire world that man must be regarded as simply the passive channel through which flows a stream of cosmic process wholly determined by natural law, which *leaves no room for personal action.*" The only remedy must be found in man himself, in the renewal of an understanding of that human image of divine intelligence and the earnest attempt to realize the full and proper potentials of that intelligence. Man cannot live as *human* without belief in and susception into himself of objective values, least of all, of those values of the higher, spirit-life which specifically make him human. That faith which was the inspiration of the whole modern development, the faith in the power of intelligence, was destroyed by being carried to an extreme beyond the image-measure. But its corrective now is not the loss of due respect for intelligence and due development of it. This is the distinguishing and chief perfectible factor in man as man, the outstanding and unique and natural possession of human persons alone in creation. Only a striving which focuses energy chiefly upon the actualization of *its* potentials in its own right, and as governing other potentials, can preserve the environment around men which is conducive to their perfection and personal satisfaction, and the social functions which are the perfecting instruments of him, and so achieve that intelligent and intelligible human goal which endows the human person with the worth proper to his image and imitative powers, the progressive re-presentation of the original intelligence which is at once his perfection and natural happiness.[18]

18. Eminent authorities in the fields of sociological history and thought have been quoted very briefly for viewpoints of the modern error, though the error and its tragedy seem blatantly clear to us. Authorities were used lest the view seem singular or without scholarly or respected support. The unanimity of conclusions and the force of conviction in such authors allows even the term "appalling." Cf. Dawson, Wust, Maritain, *Essays in Order,* including the "General Introduction" by Dawson. Also Sorokin, *Crisis of Our Age,* and Weaver's *Ideas Have Consequences.* There are almost innumerable aspects of this anti-intellectual situation, and almost as many reliable and respected authorities upon it, but this study is not a criticism of the errors against human nature and dignity; it is a positive assertion of it.

THE WILL. The will must act within and upon environment; its activity is enhanced by other wills within a social group. By nature, the will tends to follow the lead of the intellect. It is a perfectible of personality as is intelligence and should complete itself parallel to and led by the governance of intelligence. However, the will is free, and in its freedom is the dominant factor in the perfecting of personality, the motor-energy of actualization. Without proper use of his liberty, radicated by nature in reason, he has no truly purposeful activity and is betrayed to conquest by impersonal and lower forces. So the manner in which this dignity of liberty is exercised and developed is of the greatest moment for man, since upon its use depend the greatest good or evil.[19] The point that needs understanding today in the development of free persons is that personal freedom is a power and right of choice of means to ends, and of choice of immediate ends, not of choice over human order and assigned ends of human nature. We are legitimately masters of means as long as they are to our end and only in this direction do we find proper dignity.[20] The perfection of the human person by the perfecting of his personality powers is a set and assigned thing. His perfecting must consist in progressive imitation of Him in whose image his nature is made and toward whom his potentials move to action. It is the unreasonable attempt to exercise freedom of choice over the ends themselves which impedes the completion of human personality and shows itself to be unnatural by the tension and sadness and dissatisfaction it evidently effects. Man is free and independent because he is the suspended image of his intelligent Creator; he cannot be suspended to himself in his created nature and powers and the attempt to accomplish such ruins personality. ". . . This denial of creatureliness, this affirmation of the relative as an absolute, this denial of an image which is indelible is the cause of pain and error and self-frustration . . ."[21] True

19. Cf. Leo XIII, "Libertas Humana," in *op. cit.*, vol. 1, p. 115; Harvey, *Person and Liberty*, Catholic University of America Press, 1942, p. 76 *et alibi*.
20. I, q. 63, a. 8, ad 3; q. 82, a. 1, ad 3; *De Ver.*, q. 24, a. 6, c.; III *Ethics*, c. 2; II–II, q. 64, a. 2, ad 3.
21. Sheen, *Philosophy of Religion*, p. 243; Leo XIII, "Rerum Novarum," in *op. cit.*, vol. 1, p. 181.

dignity and satisfaction must lie in habits of will which, in the created image, parallel in action the will of the increated and creative original. The real human value, then, and real personal excellence lie in *good* habits in a perfection of will, which coincides with objective values and the model good it imitates. It is this innate freedom which gives man the capacity for assuming responsibility before a group and sets him apart from the rest of creation, and it is the recognition of his ability to think for himself and choose means, his freedom to judge honestly, that is the tribute from other human persons to the image-dignity of human intelligent and free personality, and its underlying, abiding person. It is because of the necessity of realizing to its full this power that communal groups must be, and because of it that they are dynamic groups which develop an individual person's free worth and, in doing so, increase their own group value.

It has been seen that, by nature, man imitates God in his tendency and power to communicate the goodness of his being and to create under God, new being. Because of this, the moving energy of his communicative will demands a society through which he can communicate his own goodnesses to other persons in imitation of his Creator, and to fulfill the demands of his own inherent goodness which is essentially distributive; and secondly, the dynamic potentials within the individual person for free development need society because his will needs the social group for the materials of goodness he can choose and upon which he can then freely operate in achieving further goodness himself by incorporating them or their effects into himself. This reciprocal movement of will in the group is something without which the individual cannot achieve perfection and his due human dignity. It is part of a personal nature to have an inner ontological urge to communicate the goodness of knowledge and of love. Only society can provide him with the conditions of existence and development he needs to satisfy this driving energy to communicate perfection, the stuff of his decisions, his choices, his desires, his loves. He cannot accomplish this in isolation nor can he, even in society, disassociate his self development from the development of other persons whose personal perfecting he is closely tied to because of that superabundant good in the being of his own will, which must by the very nature of goodness communicate itself to others.[22] The operative progress of this free energy to love must find its primary field of activity in other persons and such are found only in society which offers that stimulus of a person-milieu.

But the truly full perfection and dignity of that communicative will is conceived only when the will-energy is driving in proper channels towards its nature's proper goal and not misusing its freedom to the destruction of its own dignity. It is the individual's choice of other person-images, recognized as images, as the objects of communicative-love which is most imitative of human nature's model, most satisfying to individual human persons above any and all material objects, and so most perfective of his supreme dignity under God as the imitating image of love itself. That is why the Thomistic position has always been that the inner drive impelling man and society to a higher state of realized perfection cannot be the spiritless dialectic of Marx or Hegel, nor the irrational emergent evolution of Morgan and Alexander, nor any such unaware and blind *nisus* only, but the conscious and uniquely personal and imitative impulse: *assimilari Deo*. The will is a perfectible in man and this is its proper object of desire: love itself and the images of that love, and the increasing assimilation to love in practice. So this, by force of nature itself, which man cannot escape without personal and painful frustration, must be the object of persons living among persons, not just the will's exclusive concentration upon the accumulation of desired material possessions.[23]

Since the importance of personal rational will for society and of society for the perfecting of individual wills is a relation not difficult to see, and since the functional perfecting

22. Maritain, *Person and the Common Good*, particularly p. 38; also his *Scholasticism and Politics*, particularly p. 68; Smith, Enid, *The Goodness of Being*, p. 86. Cf. Chap. II *supra*, re "Goodness."

23. McDonald, *Social Value of Property*, p. 147 ff.; Harvey, *Person and Liberty*; and Ferguson, *Philosophy of Equality* give those fuller treatments of modern fallacies upon this question of false objects of will and false emphasis in desiring. It is not our present purpose to list or criticize them.

of it will be more clearly understood in the treatment of man's positional and functional relations in society, there is little need to belabor the point here. It may seem best to synthesize the point with expressions of it met in two authorities whose eminent sense and prestige in philosophy and in *Staatsphilosophie* is unquestioned and weighty.

".. . All human community is, in the first place, a *unitas ordinis* between persons; it is not only the limitations, the narrowness of individuality, that calls for life in a community, but even more, the will, the urge of persons to let others participate and to participate in others' personal value, by this is produced an exaltation of life in a community. We may now add that the act of *love* is the most constitutive one for community life . . . it seems it is more the acts of love that open to one person the inner values of another person in his singularity . . . if you do not take this into account, the material element will become too important; the biological, racial, economic, and geographical elements will have exaggerated import . . . (they) are determinative factors of community-building, but not supreme; they are transcended by personality, by which they are made relative, and they thus become servants to the person."[24]

". .. There can be no word said on morals that does not directly concern the history of personality. It is the person, as practical reason, whose activity weaves the web of human life; it is the person which, destitute in its essence, ceaselessly enriches itself with new knowledge, with new moral habits, that is to say, virtues, with practical habits, that is acts, and thus gradually building itself up, issues at last in those human materpieces whom we call sage, hero, artist, saint. And these masterpieces endure, imperishable as the person they constitute, deeply sculptured in the very substance of an immortal soul destined one day to regain its body in immortality."[25]

These are the *human* factors perfectible in man. His actual perfecting of his personality in society must be seen through the operation of these potentials in the social relations formed by his positions in relation to others, relations

24. Rommen, *op. cit.*, pp. 46–47.
25. Gilson, *Spirit of Medieval Philosophy*, pp. 205–206.

created by his very social and personal functions. The human person *expands* into society and his own individual personality finds its expansive and progressive perfection there.

PERFECTIVE RELATIONS. Since society is an organized grouping of persons, it is a milieu which offers to the individual person perfective relations to its composing units, which become the personal climate in which he develops his personality and actualizes his potentials for greater perfection and personal value, in which he is able to make his imitative abilities operable and complete his image-nature. The very origin and primary scope of social life is the conservation, development, and progressive perfection of the human and social person.[26] The social "body" is not exclusively for the whole, as the physical body, but is in the end arranged as an instrumental environment for the advancement of all and of every single member, *utpote personae sunt*. And the different related inner organized units of society are natural arrangements through which the different potentials of man for perfection can be realized and integrated into the perfection of the whole person by that varied but unified social participation. Through all of these he can attain that conscious effectiveness and significance which is required for his full development. He moves toward realization of his destined dignity and the completion of his image-nature, only in the ascending spiral of milieus seen in his operative living in a family, a vocational group, a community, a state, a human race.[27] The first of these human groups, the most intimate to him and most important to his development, is the first group within which his personal existence begins: the family.

THE FAMILY. The observable functioning of the familial unit and the deep-seated drive of human persons seen in that functioning is evidence that nature intends the family and the home to serve above all other units for the development of individual members of society until they reach the physical, mental, moral, and social stature of mature men who

26. Pius XII, "Mystici Corporis" in *Catholic Mind* (Jan. 1943). Cf. Pesch, H., *Lehrbuch der Nationalökonomie* (Pustet, 1905, Freiburg im Br.), p. 381.
27. Cf. Cox, *op. cit.*, p. 150.

can upon their own initiative then realize the further development of their person-image. The family gives indication
of a *microcosm* in social life, parallel to the over-all order and
integration of the whole universe. Its first evidence of the
human and personal imitation of a free Creator lies in the
unification and integration of this unit into an image of divine arranged order in the world, a work left to the free con-
struction of human persons, who discover and arrange their
hierarchy of values here according to a divine plan for them,
and similar to the planned hierarchy in the whole universe. So
it is the natural and necessary relation of persons in a family
group which first puts each person in a position to develop his
personality, his initiative in knowing and loving, and therein
gives him the personal surroundings which are the human
means for the perfecting of his own personal humanness.

The family is the first grouping natural to and necessary
for efficient personal living. In the first place, it is the environment which supplies the necessities of physical life, a
sine qua non of rational, personal development. Aquinas
rather limits to the wider social life, to offer means for what
he calls the "perfect sufficiency" of living, where the civil
group helps him not only to fulfill physical life, but moral
life, or the intelligent living of the rational spirit. Such a
statement seems to result more from a predilection for neat-
ness of division than for reality. The family itself offers means
to rational development earlier and more influential and
even perhaps more varied, than the civil group.[28] And the
same kind of statement, made by Rommen, while it too applies very aptly to civil life, should first be true, and even
more true, of family life, else we run the danger of narrow-
ing family life and its developmental influence to that very
level of biology which misses the whole social point and importance of family living. As long as there *is* this familial social group, it is a grouping of *persons* primarily instrumental
in developing the spiritual personality and full human values.

28. *In I Ethic.*, lect. 1. Cf. Rommen, *op. cit.*, pp. 44–45; cf. A. L. Ost-
heimer, *The Family, A Study in Social Philosophy*, Catholic University of
America Press, 1939.

It must presuppose personality. ". . . Forms of social being
. . . are necessary not on account of mere biological urges
which men have in common with irrational animals, but in
order to perfect our personal life . . . If biological urges
were their exclusive basis, it would lead necessarily to depersonalization, and destroy human dignity. Only if social
being is a form of living together of persons, can the end of
the community be effected without the sacrifice of personal
values. Only then is possible this *coincidence* of the common
good and private good of the individual person, the double
character of all social being, that it is above the individual, is
a common objective, and still is justified only by serving persons. Only so can we understand the idea of subjective rights.
. . . They arise from the service character of all forms of social being, for all forms of social being exist for the sake of
persons."[29] The *unitas ordinis* and the "positional ties" of social
groups, and most of all of the family, are service-organiza-
tions, operative and perfective environments for the perfecting of individual persons. And the family most immediately
affects the attractions which instigate the development of
those potentials which are specifically personal and human,
the operative development of intelligence and the growth
of communicative goodness in love received and learned and
given. Again, it is the growth in the perfections of actualized
knowing and realized loving which belong exclusively to
person-images and are imitative of the divine Person, and
for the perfecting of these powers the family most of all puts
the individual in positional relations in which he can achieve
such perfecting, wherein he begins to "take the world into
himself" in knowing, and to project himself into the world in
loving, an ability only rational creatures show, and in which
lies their unique godlike worth.

The deep drives in the human personal nature demand
their satisfaction in a complete functioning, and the family,
properly speaking, as a group begun by two but attaining its
own definition and completion only with more than two,
with the inclusion of dependent and undeveloped units in

29. Rommen, *loc. cit.*

children, allows for the completion of those potentials. That is why the individual person is not complete, his due dignity not achieved, and therefore his demanding person not satisfied, unless the process of generation consequent upon love, finds its own consequents in children. It is true that personal love itself expands the small individual self and makes it coincide with others, departing from self only to complete self in others. But human love, and particularly conjugal love, which is a distinct species of it, since it is a total person-relation thing, and not just an animal instinct, not only finds its satisfaction in the expansion of self into another person loved, but must find its satisfaction in that completion which creates. For this, the relations of the family were instituted and intended.

Love is not only *centripetal* in the increase of self, but *centrifugal* in its essential giving; it is not only this in the completion of two human persons and in the complementing of two species of persons, the masculine and feminine, but in perfecting itself must realize its completion in the creation of another and similar person-creature. This is particularly true because love of such a sort cannot find completion of its imitation of creation, for which complete image of creative activity it is made and intended, unless it finds that complete creative activity which includes the conservation and care and guiding development of a similar and self-caused creature. The family provides for the participation in such divine creative activity only when it continues to "create" the perfecting personality of the child in the familial education of that undeveloped intelligence, and in its habituating of that unpracticed will into progressively actualized loving. This is the abiding condition the family offers for the continued and destined perfection of human personalities into their due perfections, and in the very doing of it the guiding members of the family not only indirectly imitate the original Creator, but directly do so insofar as they are exercising their image faculties upon other images of Him, and in that can even consciously imitate the activity of God in knowing and loving Himself.[30] To love the created image good is to love also the

30. Cf. I, q. 44; *De Caritate*, c. 12, ad 16; *C.G.*, III, c. 24.

creating good, the absolute, the model, and so to further reach the perfection of one's own image of Him. This continuance in creating the very masterpieces of creation, by the cooperative functioning of two persons and God in creating persons, is a unit function which for completion, and for personal satisfaction in one's own drives and potentials, *must* include much more than the momentary function of physical generation, and even more than the full realization of the inclusion of the whole person in that conjugal love; it demands, of its very nature, the accomplishment of the intended end of that generation, in order that the powers of transmitting a development of intelligence and love, of exercising one's powers of instruction and love upon one's own creation, be allowed to operate in an abiding manner and growing perfection, in imitation of one's own Creator. This extension of one's own person in the child is a natural perfection of a human nature and power, and demanded for the concomitant perfections attained in relation to that personal creation. The full dignity of the human person, the completion of his potentials, cannot be achieved without the created object of conjugal love and the resultant ties and relations which foster the further development in the parent of parental dignity, which is his closest imitation of creative Divinity and fullest image-perfection. Of this truth, and its deep-seated magnetism in human persons, there is daily evidence in the daily preference shown by parents for children above all impersonal gains. There is even further evidence in the dissatisfied tension of those who deny their nature and dignity by not so preferring.

Moreover, the family presupposes and offers the various relational ties providing opportunities for development of personal intelligence and love, between the created members of that family, as between brothers and sisters, opportunities of perfecting dignity and worth not exactly repeated in any other relations. There is, in the completed family, that mutual and reciprocal activity of intelligent and loving living which most constantly and intimately develops human beings, from their most plastic stage, toward their individual and personal completion. The relations between mother and father, between parent and child, between brother and sister, are natural ties which more than in any other social group offer the instruments of imitation of God and the almost infinite expanding and sharpening of His image. In this group most of all is the intelligence of one influential upon another, and the union of love most closely achieved and most imitative of the divine. There is, in any human personal image of God, an incompleteness which can be filled in no way but by the generation and the *continued rearing* of other person-images. This *is* human nature and the dissatisfaction effected by its obstruction is evident enough today to prove its normal necessity. And for the child-image, there is an obstacle to the development of his image and his imitative powers in the absence of true family environment, which cannot be supplied otherwise, whatever other potentials he may have developed in other ways. The point is so obvious and so well proved by experience and so easily seen to be natural, and the strangely divine imitation of parents in generating and in rearing is seen so clearly in the physical imaging of parents by children and in the personality and character imitation of them, that it should be without need of words or proof if history had not shown that a blindness to this is more than possible. The human person-image is not full grown, nor can it be, without the creating of the family and the abiding development of rational powers in that family, and the conscious impeding of such an accomplishment is doomed to failure and personal dissatisfaction, since the nature itself cannot be lastingly obverted by any violence against its drives. The full and due dignity of a person is here most achieved or most destroyed, and in very great measure a human person tends to be what his family made him, a divine image greatly sharpened or largely blurred, a person of human worth more, or less, realized.

THE STATE. The second positional tie available for man's development in personal perfection and dignity is his relation to the civil community, a kind of larger family including many more persons and activities than the family group and therefore more and varied opportunities for the perfecting of personal potentials. This group, too, is natural to man as a "social animal," though lacking the physical relationship of the family. It is necessary to realize that it is man's rationality which places him in this order, and makes of a state something in that spiritual and personal order, not a physical thing. Since this is so, it is easily seen, as before pointed out, how contrary to the natural order and end of civil societies and to God-instilled dignity, indeed for the very nature of the rational image-person, is the so-called "secular state," which has no regard for man's necessary ontological and teleological relation to God and therefore is not the true and proper state with a right functioning and end. It is in this sense that it is impossible for a true democracy to be an efficient state "for the people," and at the same time be a "secularized state," because the very backbone of a democracy is the assertion of the individual and inalienable dignity of human persons and the heart of the individual's dignity is his being constituted in nature as an image of God. Moreover, no false functioning of an amorphous "equality" constitutes the proper nature of a state or allows for that kind of civil and social activity which offers a proper and ordered instrumental atmosphere fitted to the nature of man, and conducive to his true personal development. There must be a hierarchy of organization in the civil state as in man's own nature, as in the family group, as in the universe itself, a carrying out of the natural created subsidiarity of creatures which is their graduated value and the opposite of that total and false leveling-off of collectivism which makes integrated unity impossible among persons who evidence patent and widely varying abilities and talents and values.[31]

These above-mentioned truths have been stated to exclude from our notion of a civil grouping, and its consequent relations to persons and their progress, any false notion of a state, which would inhibit their dynamic perfecting and be destruc-

31. For further words upon the present papal proposal of recognition of the principle of subsidiarity, confer the M.A. thesis already alluded to: Duffy, *op. cit.*, p. 26 ff.

tive of natural human dignity. The state must be accommodated to the natures of human persons because their presence
and natures are necessary to and constitutive of a civil state.
Such a community is not beside or above the individual persons, but in them all together, a moral unit grasping them and
organizing them and integrating them into a social whole
which indeed can be logically distinguished as a particular
and accidental mode of coexistence, but never as any physical reality existing separately and independently from its
individual and personal members. It is the rational, the *intentional* object of individual persons which constitutes the
distinguishing essential of such a true socio-personal grouping, the common end or good of the group constituting its
formal and final cause. Whatever that end is, it is *given* in
human, personal nature, and is in the very order intended in
the universe, here consciously seen and willed, and made the
conscious and obligated goal of human persons through their
knowing sight. However objective the end may be, its attainment comes only from the subjective, the seen and willed
actions of individual persons, the common pursued object of
individual wills which is the principle of social unity and the
object of social cooperation among persons. It is part of the
value of a person that *he* creates society for *his* needs.

It is necessary for the understanding of the proper relation
in worth of the state and the individual person, that this true
idea of such a social group be grasped and remembered. It is
a *personal* grouping, constitutive of persons and *for* persons,
and both perfective of their native dignity and evidence of
it. The civil community itself has only a secondary value,
ontologically; though real in being, it is not any substantial
and independent existent being as is the human individual.
As stated in the first chapter, the use of "person" for any
group of individuals making up a "moral person" is a fiction
of law and must not be confused with the actual individual in
being or in value or dignity. Only individual persons are substantial beings, and all social forms belong only to accidental
beings which depend for their existence upon an existence-in-
another. What value and prestige they have accrues to them

only because they are *from* individual persons and *for* them and never possibly above them. True, this social grouping adds its dependent being to the individual and increases his value: the more he is integrated in society and the more actively influenced by it in a proper rational manner and the more influential he is in it, the more being and perfection and dignity does that individual person acquire. But the society which is created by persons to help persons cannot possibly out-value them. In the order of values, social groups are centered upon and dependent upon individual persons, and never the contrary.

It is to personal rationality that the state owes its existence as such. This civil-social form exists in the person-sphere and adds an end of rationality to the concept of any grouping such as an animal herd. But it is the rationality stemming from individual persons and from God originally, which makes that social state as different from animal groupings as man is from an animal. If that is not there, and individual persons are impeded from the exercise of their rational freedom when a civil group acts as if it were a separate and higher physical entity which could deny the development of individual powers and values, then there exists a denial of the concept and reality of human society, and the group is a herd. The very nature of social existence and the definition of a state and its kind of being must be got from personal individual being, from rational, free, active, individual substances from whose greater value and dignity the state itself has dignity. And therefore the state cannot exclusively or even primarily aim at a material goal or in doing so it perverts its natural constitution, betrays its members who are not material nor have a material perfection, and necessarily fosters disintegration among its rational person-units and destroys the personal dignity for which it was created as the instrument of development and protection and perfecting. Grundlach uses "intentional being" to emphasize the formal element of all communities. That places the founding of all forms of social existence in the teleological order. "A community is destined for and intends the realization of a specific good which demands the solidarist co-operation of a multitude of persons and consequently is a common good." This idea of the state is particularly important when treating of the worth of the individual person, because the superior value of the person and his position of dignity is at once manifest in the fact of that very relation where it is so mistaken today. This emphasis on ends and values is the deepest and most important foundation of any community because in the realization of these ends and values the human person individually perfects his very nature and reaches his due dignity. The community "receives its consecration by its service to the perfection of persons."

In the order of being, individual persons, because they alone as such are rational and substantial, are first. In the order of ends, the community is immediately before the individual, but only because the end of the community is necessary for the perfection of many individuals and so superior in the same species of goodness.[32] That is, the earthly common good is superior to the earthly individual good, a kind of quantitative superiority, but without jumping into the eternal good of the individual which in one individual alone is superior to the merely earthly good of many.[33] Persons are immediately directed by their own nature and end, to their individual and eternal goal, to the community as a whole, but only that this temporal and social end may be a means! Only that the attaining of the common end or good may be the means of their individually attaining their individual perfection. It is from this then, and as always, from individual persons, that the common good gets its value, because it is linked to the perfection of its person members, not only in a coincidence of ends, but also by a kind of reciprocal action, in that the attaining of the common goal which is more valuable than any one individual's, is at the same time the means for

32. II–II, q. 141, a. 8; Aristotle, *Ethica*, I, 2.
33. Cf. Pius XI, "Education of Christian Youth," in *op. cit.*, vol. 2, p. 91; Pius XII, *The State in the Modern World* (Summi Pontificatus), N.C.W.C., 1939.

each individual's attaining that individual perfection which coincides with his final destiny, but is supra—mundane, super-temporal, and imitative of divinity. [34]

It is not our purpose to give a critical analysis of the erroneous and destructive philosophies and practices which have constructed unnatural states and upset the due relation of state to individual person, and so attempted to destroy the proper superiority and dignity of the individual human person. This has been more than adequately done already. In all these cases, whether it has been exaggerated individualism or its inevitably consequent opposite, collectivism, the root error has been a misconception of the due position of the human person in his supreme value and his relation to civil groupings and civil authority and civil goals, [35] a blindness to the dignity of the human person, or a refusal to accept it, is the central error and human tragedy of our day. That is why this is an attempt to outline the correct and natural relations of the individual person to the social group, wherein his dignity receives not only its true original value in his nature, but finds in the group the milieu conducive to his natural and necessary perfection. Something is contrary to social nature if and when it forces the individual person who comprises the unit of the social group to smother his natural dignity. This is resident in him in his divine image-nature and by that very imitative nature, gives him a destiny higher than the material or temporal goal of the group. *It cannot be surrendered or stamped out.* The attempt to do so indicates not any lack of worth in the individual; but it only proves the

34. The question of the exact nature of a civil community, and therefore of its correct natural relation to an individual person is, however important, a complicated and subtle question. The too-brief exposition we have given owes its attempted explanation chiefly to the cited work of Rommen, particularly the chapter on "Social Being," pp. 33–56, and through him to G. Grundlach's article "Solidarismus, Einzelmensch, Gemeinschaft" in *Gregorianum*, vol. 17, 1936.

35. For an analysis of the destructive relation of liberalism and communism to the human person, cf. Ferguson, *Philosophy of Equality*, pp. 195–216; Wolfe, *Problem of Solidarism*, pp. 1–60; Sheen, *Philosophy of Religion*; Sheed, *Communism and Man;* and the further sources noted in those works.

useless error and inevitable failure of the state which tries
to contradict nature itself.[36]

The important point in the relation of the individual to
the state is that the relation is dual and reciprocal. The individual person needs the social environment as a necessary
condition for the development of his implanted potentials to
greater and godlike worth, and the social environment needs
the individual for its preservation and development.[37] It is
for this reason that there is the dual relation of the individual
to the state, where the supra-temporal end of the individual
makes of the common social end in turn à means to individual perfection. Man is ordained to two ends, an ultimate and a
proximate. The first claims the full totality of his being, the
second does not. In relation to the immediate and temporal
social end of the whole group, he is an inferior part, but in
relation to the eternal individual destiny, he is a substance
autonomous of the social group and above it in value. The
ultimate end embraces the proximate and civil group-end
which, in that respect, makes of the social group-goal itself
a means toward the attainment of that ultimate goal which
is only for the individual person and sets him above the
state. So man can play in society a dual role, functioning both
as a part ordered to a whole, and as an autonomous substance
to whom society is subservient as a means for personal perfection.[38] It is the relation which is dual and the functioning
which is double. It is not a split between individual and person. That is impossible because *the person is the whole composite*, and by definition is not an individual plus something
else, but a species of individual. *Individualität und Personali-
tät sind nicht ezwei Stücke, sondern der Doppelbetracht des*

---

36. Cf. Smith, "Human Social Life" in *op. cit.*, p. 303.

37. *De Regimine*, lib. I, c. 1.

38. Ferguson, *op. cit.*, p. 120 *et alibi*, puts this very well, following Welty
in his viewpoint (*Gemeinschaft und Einzelmensch*). St. Thomas simply and
clearly shows the coincidence, in final analysis, of the two goals which need
each other and become identified in the good of the individual: ". . . qui
quaerit bonum commune . . . ex consequenti etiam quaerit bonum suum
. . . quia bonum proprium non potest esse sine bono communi . . . quia
homo oportet quod consideret quid sit sibi bonum ex hoc quod est prudens
circa bonum multitudinis." Cf. II–II, q. 46, a. 10, ad 2.

Menschen. Beide haben ihre Funktion im Sozialen und für das Soziale.[39] The same unified person acts in perfecting himself, though drawn by two goals, the social one being contained in the ultimate and exclusively personal one. Only insofar as he is constrained to remember other persons also, and cooperate to the advancement of the group, is he subordinate to the civil setup. But at the same time, the end of the civil setup is *for him* and he cooperates toward it only for *his* good, in the eternal viewpoint. Without going further into explanations of this relation, it has been necessary to outline the position because of modern misconceptions of the importance of the individual and the predominant misconception in civil rule that he is only an individual until totally subordinate to the state. For all that matters permanently, he is of such a nature and such powers and such consequent worth and suprasocial dignity that he is immeasurably above the state which is to him only a temporary instrument for completion of his person-value.

The person is prior in time and perfection to society, and while in the Thomistic position he is admittedly subordinate to the state as a *totum,* because the unit he is cannot be subordinate any other way, he is not subordinate *totaliter.*[40] He is not subordinate according to all that he is and all that he has. Such a total subordination is only to the God-original he imitates and totally depends upon.[41] By its innermost and truest being, the individual person belongs to another and more perfect society, the universality of being, that whole which is the infinite, God Himself.[42] Society just does not exhaust the potentials of the whole person. Man is ordered first to God, and then to society only as a means to God, so that while social groups are the instruments of his perfection, the root and also the content and measure of his native value are independent of society and above and beyond it. His intrinsic value or dignity does not flow from society, but to it.

39. Welty, *op. cit.,* p. 138.
40. II–II, q. 65, a. 1.
41. I–II, q. 21, a. 4, ad 3. Cf. Welty, *op. cit.,* p. 282.
42. Dawson, *op. cit.,* pp. 239–240.

He is, with respect to society and his final supra-temporal end, a kingdom of his individual own, a God-image with a personal destiny toward and personal powers for attaining the infinite in personal accomplishment and therefore to partake of and resemble the infinite in value and dignity. So there is, for his developmental perfecting, a "bi-polar relation between the individual and society: a mutuality in the order of ends characterized as the relation between potency and act."[43] This being and life and personal goal are eternal, sacred, and *natural* to him, so that nothing of what he is or what he is to be can, without internal tension and loss of due and satisfying human dignity, be impeded by himself or totally or permanently controlled by a temporal civic group.

Society is *for* man, a natural milieu conducive to his completion of personal self, the perfecting of an immortal and dynamic person-image of God. And since man's native worth is such, participative of and measured by the divine, the state can only be characterized by a "service-relationship" and never properly or satisfactorily claim the characteristics of absolute command which can make of individual persons things to be exploited by a group which the individual in reality excels. Only man, the individual person, and not society in any form, is permanent in existence, endowed with reason and free will. Only he is the image of God.[44] His natural gifts have a value surpassing the immediate interests of the moment, as the natural and inescapable drive of those gifts can be not satisfied in a person by any exaggerated or primary concern with or grasping of the material and temporal, nor rest long under any form of government which frustrates that nature by impeding the satisfaction of his natural spiritual desires, no matter how much of the material is supplied him. Man is not made to increase the value and dignity of society, but society to give him the chance to perfect his individual and personal worth by the opportunities it gives him in personal group relations to perfect his spiritual powers and

43. Ferguson, *op. cit.*, p. 123. Cf. Welty, *op. cit.*, p. 280.
44. Pius XI, "Atheistic Communism," in *op. cit.*, vol. 2, p. 352.

satisfy his spiritual nature, either directly or indirectly by removing material obstacles or providing material aids toward the free development of spiritual powers. It is in this way that man is aided by the group and by government regulating the group, to complete his individual and personal worth, to expand the original seed-value of his nature into the fullness of dignity.

The perfectible factors already mentioned are naturally the ones which are given the wider opportunities for individual development by the civil community, not perhaps influences so strong as the family's, but more varied and numerous than ones offered by familial surroundings. While, like the family, the state is interested in the material betterment of men, since it is a human group, it is distinctly the *human* or personal aims which this grouping of persons has for its goal of advancement, by offering an environment conducive to the progressive completion of those potentials which, once actualized and in the measure actualized, measure the perfection of the individual person and the dignity of his image-nature. This has been stated very recently in a most encouraging manner by the spokesman for a large and powerful civil community: "We work for a better life for all, so that all men may put to good use the great gifts with which they have been endowed by their Creator. We seek to establish those material conditions of life in which, without exception, men may live in dignity, perform useful work, serve their communities, and worship God as they see fit. . . . These may seem simple goals, but they are not little ones. They are worth a great deal more than all the empires and conquests of history. We should ask for continued strength and guidance from that Almighty Power who has placed before us such great opportunities for the good of mankind in the years to come."[45] The environment for growth in bodily perfection must be provided, and active help given, since not only is the body part of the unit-person, but a person's body is often more dependent than animals' and has not the fully independent equipment of animals; though it progresses further,

45. Harry S. Truman, "State of the Union Message," Jan. 9, 1950.

it is particularly more dependent on creatures of its own species.

But beyond this type of needed help, which is, as it were, a needed individual environment for development of rational powers, the need of other persons, so evident for advancement in rational life, is naturally supplied by the civil community. Persons thinking and willing, particularly loving, are directed to other persons, and depend upon other persons' stimulus and guidance for their progress in manners of operation properly efficient; "perfect self-conscious is reciprocal to 'we-mindedness.' "[46] Since perfecting of mind and heart is impossible in isolation, and cannot be realized fully within the family, it can find its needed opportunities only within the larger groupings wherein it can reach self-sufficiency and that full connatural operation of powers which is due to its inherent potentials and demanded by their attracted pull toward the completion of their divinely settled destiny. Only that is true human value. This proper development demands the integrated orderliness of the properly "civilized" community, which means an intelligent and human coincidence with the planned and natural order of person-creation fixed by the Creator, a dynamic order whose primal values, aims, and activities are first directed to an expansion of *spirit* in man, not just the accumulation of material *things*, which cannot possibly constitute the destiny or satisfaction of a creature who is not just matter and whose dignity and deepest drives spring from his immaterial spirit. It is only within such a community, following a godlike order of proper values and evaluations, that the individual human person may so develop his distinctively human rational powers as to realize that kind of perfection which his nature demands, whether at the moment he recognizes it or not, a dynamic and spirit-completion which is, and must be by created nature, imitative of the activity of divine intelligence and love. That is why the civil community itself, composed of dynamically pro-

46. Rommen, *op. cit.*, pp. 221–223. Cf. Leo XIII, "Diuturnum Illud," *Allocutiones* III, 109.

gressing individual spirit-persons, must itself be a group spiritually dynamic, working always first for the perfection of the native functional goals of intelligence and will, and keeping material goals in view only as the instruments of that rational perfection and satisfaction of spirit. Only with this aim and in this direction, and governed by this evaluation of human goods, does the group and therefore its constituent individuals move toward the ideal actualization of true human and personal dignity, which is rational, which is an achievement not of material quantities possessed, but *must be by nature* an attainment of immaterial values, an assimilation into persons of greater spirit-wisdom and rational love.

Social union and perfection, while stimulating individual perfections, depends upon individual, personal, volitional acts. It is society which offers the individual the necessary opportunities for attainment of due dignity; and yet it is the individual who makes possible that opportunity and governs it, who groups with others to create that dynamic social surrounding necessary for dynamic individual spirits. Only in society can man "experience full incarnation." And yet it must be remembered that the very fact that he is a *member* denotes his uniqueness and differentiation from others. He is not to be submerged in the group, but through it to expand his spiritual powers whose continued proper development toward their spiritual end perfects personality; "all shutting of oneself off from the fullness of life in communities means for the individual person atrophy and mutilation, a failure to realize one's being."[47] His primary and distinguishing gift of speech first evidences this necessity because that gift of rational communication cannot be expressed in isolation and the imitative dignity which flows from its communication of knowledge and love can be developed only toward and with other persons, given the free environment

47. Sturzo, "Totalitarianism and Man" in *Democracy, Should It Survive?* p. 48. Cf. Meyer, in *Proceedings of American Catholic Philosophical Association*, vol. XIV, p. 159; August Pieper, *Organische und mechanische Auffassung des Gemeinschaftslebens*, p. 21, (quoted in Rommen, *Natural Law*, p. 237).

for its actualization, coupled with the rational restraint which prohibits its abuse and indignity.[48]

His sociality is as natural an element of a person as his rationality, and the inevitable result of his rational powers and image-nature. Therefore only intelligently arranged and directed society is a natural help to his perfecting. While his rational activity must express itself and complete its natural perfected worth in community, he needs a society which manifests that it is a rational grouping with a rational and spiritually human sense of values, to provide him with aids to *human* perfection. This social perfecting he accomplishes in the love of friendship, the reception and bestowal of an evaluated knowledge of Creator, of image-creatures, and of lower creation, particularly of the person-images, the knowledge of whom is necessary for a perfected knowledge of one's own person and image and a greater knowing of the original. ". . . It is the last indissoluble essence of the concrete man's ego that there is no experience of the community through which individuality does not shine, and no experience of individuality not borne by the community and open to it."[49] It is evident then how futile it is and unnatural, to attempt to found and operate a civil community which refuses to be aware of these personal necessities for that rational, spirit development which must be if men are to satisfy their natures, and to be aware of the consequent role of the community itself in fostering men's true good. To try to set up an objective and follow a practice contrary to the inextinguishable drives in the human person is to whittle away his human dignity, to create a "fatal and rebellious dissonance" between human dignity which lies in his spirit, and in his spiritual powers only insofar as they imitate the manner of activity of the one they are created in the image of. To foster a society which obscures the only true and satisfying goals of man's nature is to act against the laws of nature and fight, however uselessly, against them; it is to so move contrary to the natural dignity of the rational person that sooner

48. II–II, q. 129, a. 6, ad 1.
49. Rommen, *op. cit.*, p. 77.

or later the personal frustration of his nature induced by such contrary and unspiritual forces, reasserts itself in personal revolution in order to move again toward its rational and divine goals. Man must make progress only in being more and more godlike, or his godlike nature breaks.[50]

For any efficient society, it is required that each member of the civil community be given opportunity to make his life fully *human*, that is a rational and divinely imitative contribution to the community and therefore to himself, and thus be constantly granted the rightful recognition of his personal and divine-like dignity.[51] For the evaluation of the aids to development of human personality and dignity, it is essential to realize that society is not a geographical location or a physical group only, or a localized accumulation of resources and machines possessed by men. It must, if it is to achieve any of its human purpose, be an ordered grouping of intelligent human persons working for goals which remain natural to spirit-natures. It must be an environment and a rational grouping whose aims and activities always foster first the independent and divinely imitative spirit perfection of human persons whose personal distinction and value lie in the fact that by insistent nature, they are dynamic images of divine intelligence and love. As things are, so they must act. "It is a matter of plain prudence on the part of a ruling state; human beings are endowed naturally with certain powers of initiative and action which nature obviously means them to use; it may be better *for men* that they should do a thing less well for themselves than have it done more perfectly for them; what society as a whole gains by work better done, it more than loses by citizens of diminished initiative and diminished power of action—the adding machine may make fewer errors than man, but the result of substituting all for

50. Smith, "Human Social Life," in *op. cit.*, pp. 288, 308; "Some American Freedoms," p. 111. The above statement may seem exaggerated when measured by normal and naive experience, but it stands true: disintegration of personality is in direct proportion to the contrary direction of irrational and materialistic living and the speed and constancy and persistence of it.

51. Duffy, *op. cit.*, p. 30.

men is a society of all correct additions, and men who have
lost the intelligent capacity to add."[52]

The whole point here is that while any society is doomed
to failure and upheaval if it persists in obstructing the rational and divinely inspired drives of men, yet the group and
the individuals are doomed if the group so takes over all initiative (even if fostering the true and spirit potentials of humans) that *self* perfection is smothered and the powers atrophy. Society is to be a help for man's personal development
and must let him actively develop himself although guiding
him against his own stupidities and incipient indignities, and
supplying proper opportunities and protective leadership for
his connatural and unimpeded *self* development of spirit. He
is more important than things and of more worth than the
temporal. The perfection of his immortal and image-dignity
is *due* him and is sooner or later always demanded by his
own nature, and societal relations are to foster his advance
toward this proper, satisfying and divinely imitative perfection of human personality or they are fighting not for but
against human persons and, since such demands are in the
laws of nature, they are impeding the natural law and the
God in whose image man is made.

HUMANITY. A word must be said upon the relation of the
individual to the created assembly which is the whole of humanity. This is inclusive of all living persons, and in a very
real and influential sense not only the presently living but
the dead of the past and the unborn of the future. There
exists among all these persons a looser bond than among
the immediate family or surrounding community, but never-
theless a real bond, a "brotherhood," of nature and dignity,
and above all the permanent tie of a common source and
goal in one Creator whom they are similar person-images of
and similarly imitative of in living. While the relations of
family and civil community life apply in some measure to
this world-relation, there is in this relation the implication
of fulfilling newness in its stimulus to perfection from these
further varieties of creature-images, which are seen in dif-

52. Sheed, *Communism and Man*, p. 113.

ferent races and different customs and places and times, all
of which are more unfamiliar than those of one's immediate
milieu, and yet still fragmentary images of the same God.

Taken both horizontally and vertically, in geographical
extension and in time, the total human society constitutes the
over-all environment for a man's development and destined
human full worth and is in its own way and measure a planned
stimulus to the perfection of his possible dignity. He is to
recognize his own worth, accomplished or destroyed, in the
acquired knowledge of men in history who had the same personal dignity as he. And if he is to realize his own present
potentials, he must recognize them in unfamiliar or different
others, and recognize the stimulating help possible from
others. He cannot boast of nor act upon his own rightful position of value without that intellectual, cultural and moral
development which recognizes the equal position of all other
persons of all times and races. And he cannot imitate Him in
whose image he lives, without imitating His attitudes toward
all other images; nor can he imitate and advance in similarity
toward absolute intelligence and love, without reacting in
godlike manner to the stimulus for knowing and loving offered him by all races of like *human* people. This broader field
for the development of personality and sharpening of the
image is perhaps often less tangible than the elements in
the immediately surrounding fields, but has its due and exclusive importance and without either the realization of this
relation or the activity consequent upon its stimulus, the individual person cannot fulfill his destined perfection as much
as might be expected of his potentials.

It is something belying the dignity of *this* human being to
unnaturally develop the attitude of mind which looks on the
indignities imposed upon equal and fellow images in another
state and climate, as impersonal things and no concern of
his, as it is contrary to his own rational development to black
out their possible contribution to his own perfectible knowledge and power of loving. If progress among men has to be,
because of every man's nature, a progress in imitation of the
Creator, any one individual's perfectibility here and now is

in some measure marked by the total progress or forced retrogression of his fellow-humans over the world. It is a limitation of his dignity and not an imitation of his original, which
looks upon other humans, who are foreign in appearance or
custom, as if they were not similar and equal person-images.
"To regard all past generations, as well as the present, as de-
void of intrinsic and personal value, is an outrageous affront
to those human persons who are ends also in themselves; it is
to invalidate the very ideal of progress."[53] There are certain
personality traits and perfections so developed by social custom as to become predominantly characteristic of this race
or that, which can be also surrounding perfective milieus for
others' development; they are not strange items to be looked
upon as unhuman traits so that any person of one particular
group must limit the ways of his realization of all his powers
by limiting his personal attitudes and rational activity to his
own local group. "In defining himself by the traits of his
ethnic group, a man travesties the true dignity of his own
human personality; ignoring his essence, he chooses to exist
in its accidents, and attempts to degrade his own person to
the rank of a non-human creature."[54] In its wide and true
sense, his "social personality," that expansion of personality
brought into being by social-personal relations, is completed
only by the recognition and use of the human relations constituted between humans everywhere, between *all* image-
creatures. It is not only a limiting of due development, but
at the same time a contradiction of true human nature either
to attempt a non-human domination of other races, or to impede and deny proper knowing and loving by refusal to exercise such human faculties upon humans who happen to
be accidentally different from one. There are world-wide relations natural and stimulating to human personality arising
from his world-family, and these opportunities are particularly important for him in a civilization which now gives him
ready access to them.

53. Sheen, *op. cit.*, p. 297.
54. Louis T. Achille, "What Color, Man?" in *Democracy, Should It Survive?* p. 109.

PERFECTING FUNCTIONAL RELATIONS

Throughout the different interdependent and interlocking relations caused by the organizational grouping of communal life, operating personalities exercise certain social rights and duties which create "functional ties" common to all the social relations, activities flowing from the nature of their social status and reciprocally influencing and perfecting the exercise of specifically *human* powers. Here it is a question of glancing at the activities of social relations consequent upon those relations, the social operations of mind and will among many related persons, the exercise of free choice in society, the rational process of education and the assertion of individual rights and authority, the perfective force of work, the directly perfective imitation of God and integrating social activity of worship.

FREEDOM. The fact of human freedom and the significance of it for human dignity has already been noted sufficiently, and in full understanding of that significance lies already the comprehension of its potentials for development to personal perfection in society. However, in view of the modern misconception of human civil liberty, it must be well remembered in the question of personal development and even emphasized, since freedom is of the spirit and yet man's free spirit is not a kind of gyrating thing without direction or rules of freedom, but is governed by rationality and further limited by his own limiting matter. Freedom is something to be developed, and never fully escapes the laws of reason or the bonds of matter. Personal dignity cannot be achieved in social living if human freedom is understood to be an irrational and ungoverned thing, because this is not true of man's nature from the beginning. "The famous phrase of Rousseau, 'Man is born free' is almost ludicrous in its untruth. No one who has ever seen a man recently born would be tempted to rhetoric about his freedom."[55] If this is not seen, if the necessary process of human development of its

---

55. Sheed, *Communism and Man*, p. 104. Cf. A. L. Rzadkiwicz, *The Philosophical Bases of Human Liberty*, Catholic University of America Press, 1949.

free spirit progressively from the bonds of the material and into the laws of reason is not realized as a necessary and rather lengthy process in living, then the true nature of man and the true perfective possibilities of his image-dignity will not be seen and personal dignity will be devalued through an arrogated license. There must be some limitation of each individual freedom by the demands of the free choices of others. But beyond this even, and before it, it must be realized that the determinism man must climb out of is caused by matter itself, the material side of his own composite and the surrounding material world. He must gradually perfect his spiritual dignity by freeing himself from the bonds of matter. This is no "theoretical truth" but one of immediate practical import in a present and very materialistic civilization. It is precisely a current immersion of spirit in the material and physical and corporal which has caused a modern personal tension and the devaluation of that human worth which rises from his spirit.

Another limit upon personal freedom which governs in some measure his own free perfecting of his spirit energies and spirit dignity flows from the previous exercise of his own free choices. He cannot start from zero each time he acts; and "yesterday's freedom weighs heavily upon today's." He becomes influenced more and more by his own developed inclinations. His development of his person is free only in that he can accommodate himself to his end and so imitate divine perfection, or he can deviate from his nature's goal. This tension, this developmental struggle, is each person's biography and the whole history of man, ". . . the story of how man has used his freedom and responded to his double vocation to use matter as a channel to the spiritual, and to perfect personality by progressive assimilation to eternal Life, eternal Truth, and eternal Will, Which is God" into whose image he develops.[56]

In freely perfecting himself then among other humans, man must remain himself; it is his own individuality he is perfecting. While he cannot be forced into a groove which iden-

56. Cf. Sheen, *op. cit.*, p. 362.

tifies him impersonally with a function as if he were only a statistic or a mechanical force, he cannot at the same time wildly imagine he will be "free" by such irresponsible and vague unrestraint as seems advocated by some modern philosophers who call such unreality "existential." That is a contradiction of the human person, an abandonment in final analysis, to anonymity and irresponsibility and indefiniteness of action. As Heidegger has said, "One must climb out of an indefinite pronoun world."[57] And as long as there is an "I" and a "thou," each one's freedom is both developed by and restrained by the other. It is those social ties in fact which give rise to the concept and natural reality of "right."

The question of man's realizing his personality and attaining his completion through the use of his power of free choice must be a question of intelligent use of that rational faculty. His value comes from his power of *self*-mastery and *self*-perfectibility, but the self is an image-intelligence and must be so directed. The initial dignity of the human person consists in his possession of the power of freedom of choice and action. But the perfection of the human personality is measured not just by that possession itself, which is inert as it were, but by the rational and ordered use among other free persons toward his proper image-perfection and theirs. His resemblance in the use of rational freedom to the absolute divine will measures his own worth, and in some degree determines others. So whether his free acts are performed in personal isolation, family life, or civil life, they are perfective of him only if they perfect the image he is and are modeled on God's intelligent activity which is supremely free because supremely intelligent in always accommodating a nature's action to that nature's end. Only in this direction does a man remain a true person and only in this kind of rational choice does he perfect his personality and proper hu-

57. Some injustice has been done to some of the statements and viewpoints of some thinkers still styled "existentialists," such as M. Heidegger, and above all, Soren Kierkegaard. When the latter's vocabulary is properly understood, no one has achieved a more devastating critique of modern collectivism and its anonymity, and managed so magnificent a defense of the individual person.

man dignity. He is "free" to obstruct his nature and frustrate it, to devaluate it and disintegrate it, or to expand it in the image of God. And because of this, he is "responsible" for what he does to his nature and his end by his freedom, and for what influence he thus exercises upon the development of perfected human worth in his fellowmen. Just in that lies his position of dignity and the possibilities for greater worth, that he alone in creation is *responsible*, because of his freedom, for his choices. He has no right to habituate himself to the control of material forces, nor to let another person so do to him, nor to do so to other human persons. Only the proper exercise of his freedom in imitation of God allows him to realize his potentials for being a more valuable image. The unrational use of that power upon himself or upon others pushes him and them closer to impersonality and nearer to control by impersonal forces, a human retrogression which is a denial of his person and a destruction of his due dignity before the Creator and other human creatures.

This is the conflict for each person and has been the history of all of them, and the error particularly of today, that the human person has been devaluated by thinking there is no direction to his freedom, nor rules for its use, and so abandoning himself to an irresponsibility and anti-rational operation which has smothered his personal satisfaction, disrupted consequently his social setup and the perfective possibilities of others and made it too often a practical impossibility for him to imitate anything rational and ideal, much less his model—God. For the whole erroneous attitude upon this and its tragical results for human worth, there is no better brief statement than one made by Wright: "The philosophy of responsibility in modern times has further suffered from the impersonal, collectivist theories of society and history which found favor during and since the last century. These linked human action more often to material forces and mass controls than to spiritual personality and individual responsibility. An earlier generation of God-fearing people had recognized the challenge of some environments and the limitations imposed by heredities, but they still acknowledged that the generality of men remain free to make conscious choice between life and death, good and evil. But the modern social theory followed new lines, along which it has attempted to lead legal theory and application. As against the old philosophy of responsibility, there has grown up the theory that . . . what the law calls 'crime' and conscience calls 'sin' (is) to be explained largely in terms of causes beyond the control of the 'sinner' and the 'criminal.' The philosophy of responsibility has been replaced by the philosophy of excuse . . . of ultimate irresponsibility. For more than a generation, it has undermined the moral and legal and individual social responsibilities upon which the stability of society must repose. . . . Social progress has not been accomplished by swinging along with impersonal 'destinies,' by riding the wave of the future, by the blind operation of uncontrolled, biological, economic, or social 'forces.' It has been achieved by the vision and determination, by the self-knowledge and self-discipline of single individuals, and of individuals in groups who have understood the meanings of the words: 'I know. I will. I do.' . . . Social stability and individual salvation still depend on the recognition of the central place of individual responsibility in whatever good may be accomplished or whatever evil must be suffered on the face of the earth over which God gave man dominion."[58]

Man must function as a free person or he does not function as a person. And the less he functions as a rational and god-like person, the more difficult he makes it for himself and also for other human persons to find personal satisfaction in life, or to achieve that free dignity of spirit proper to their perfected *human* powers. He must use freedom for the goal it is intended to achieve, or he does not realize and perfect his personality, but devaluates his own, and in some measure others'. In social functions, he must exercise it within the fabric of that personal grouping because from the relations of many persons exercising their freedoms, protecting each his own distinct person and independently operating per-

58. John J. Wright, "Philosophy of Responsibility," in public address. Cf. *Catholic University Bulletin*, Feb. 1949.

sonality, arises the natural protection of that individual freedom in what we call the individual right, that independence
from unwarranted invasion of his individual free operation
of his properly human powers in order to achieve his imitative perfection and divine end. It is upon this basis, and
measured by the manner of imitative operation of this power
that men found the validity of personal rights and personal
authority, and the social validity of justice and law. It is then
within such a framework that each person must freely work
out his completion in life, a perfection which is human and
personal and therefore rational, only when so attained within
the rational and natural limits which bound his worth and
dignity by the very fences of his nature, the boundaries of
reason itself and the rightful dignity of others who are operative as he and free as he and rational as he and images as he
and destined for the same perfection-goal as he. Man is not
"free" to be an unpredictable emotional power only, not
"free" to be only a physical animal or to treat others as animals and destroy therein the *human* dignity of both parties.
He is free to *rationally* perfect his image nature and to help
his fellow persons perfect theirs, not to impede himself or
them. He is free only to be like his intelligent God, and to
stimulate others who are equally images of that God, to the
imitative perfecting of their unique human dignity as God-
images.

SOCIAL ORDERLINESS. The first effect and functioning of
proper freedom is the creation and preservation of order
amongst persons. It is to the credit of man alone in creation
that he is freely able to achieve, and so be responsible for
the attainment in his world of free persons, of that ranked
and wise order which is rigidly imposed upon lower creation.
It is in this range that his self-development must take place,
within an order dictated by his own nature and necessary for
both the attainment of his end and his personal happiness. To
develop himself duly, the human person must be active in
that social orderliness he is part of. He is expected to complete in himself, and then contribute to in social relations,
that orderliness which the Creator has grooved into the rest

of action. But his natural thrust to rational and human per-
of creation and which in man's case alone He has entrusted
to man's power of personal freedom in order that the human
person might be credited with the divine dignity of creating
intelligent order by *imitating freely* the model order of
creation, and imitating the creativity and intelligence of
God by creating its parallel in a society of persons. The
ability to see this is participative of divine intelligence, and
the power to create such order is participative of divine will.
All this is not only inseparable from the nature of a human
person, but a due dignity of the causal creation, order, and
dominion accorded to him alone and therefore a due obligation set upon him so to imitate his God.[59] But man must imitate the rational order imposed upon his nature by the very
fact that he is the image of supreme intelligence. He is of
supreme worth in creation only by the fact of being such an
image, and so imitating, and the error of exaggerating his
autonomy and deifying it destroys the natural order, the real
ontological relations of being and truth and goodness. Such
an order imagines man may produce any "order." His freedom is only to coincide his intelligence and will with divine
intelligence and will, and so imitate in his personal and social
order the only order possible for reality. He must accommodate himself by intelligent and free recognition and imitation to the real order of things, not fantastically create a depersonalizing "order" in society which is contrary to divine
order and so contradictory of his own image. Only by such
proper exercise of freedom, within the limits of reason and in
the direction of his imposed end, can he create valid authority, right, and law.

PERSONAL RIGHTS. These real relations between human
destiny and powers and human social living, between free
person and free person and between spirit-persons and lower
creation, are what lead us to see the reality and validity of
human "rights." The image-nature of man, his obligation
to imitate his God-model, and his destiny of permanence,
give him a value and dominance over lower creation which is
not only lower in being but conspicuous by lack of freedom

59. Cf. Smith, *op. cit.*, p. 297.

fection, when faced with equal destinies and tendencies and obligations among other persons in society, bestows upon him the moral claim and power to exercise his faculties toward such self-perfection as is consonant with the objective and divinely ordained end in view, without any obstruction from other persons operating toward their own recognized and equal goals and destinies in equal dignity. The end is not of choice, but imposed upon nature and of obligation; the means to be used can be rationally chosen and independence preserved simply because man *is* independent. Such an absolute value before the bar of reason, such inviolability in the face of other persons, stems from his image-nature and imitative faculties which must attain their destined completion from within him, and freely. This is what makes him the subject of "rights," his inherent moral power to claim a God-given autonomy of operation. He is such an autonomous being by nature, as God is. Rights are not just corollaries of his possessions or trade or appearance or race or physical or even mental might,[60] but belong to him as a free person with an imposed goal in life. Rights are the projection of his personality into social living, the ordered relation of operation among persons. It is because the person is what he is, the sole image of absolute value and independence, and a permanent being above all secular and temporary values, that his supreme value and the operative perfecting of his image of absolute value is a right, a claim and privilege and autonomy not to be interfered with. Human persons must live a *human* life, and the doing of this among other independent persons makes it evident that each individual person is so imitative of the unimpeded activity of God and so "naturalized" to his destiny and perfection that he participates in that autonomy of God which is not to be obstructed or unduly impeded even by other human and free persons.[61]

Obviously, an excessively individualistic conception of or

60. Cf. McDonald, *op. cit.*, p. 130; Ryan, John A., *Living Wage*, pp. 50–51; Delos., *op. cit.*, p. 48.

61. Cf. Rommen, *op. cit.*, p. 58 ff.; Thom. P. Neill, *Weapons for Peace*, p. 155 ff., a good treatment of the natural law and the rights flowing from it; Ryan, *op. cit.*, p. 53; Kerby, *Social Mission of Charity*, chaps. on "Justice," "Equality."

arrogant seizure or exaggerated limiting of personal rights is some destruction of the very *rationale* of them, since they are validly such only in the face of other persons. Each person abides in his proper value not only as a self-sufficient being who is autonomous, but as a communal person, whose rights cannot be isolated or absolutely independent, but socially connected. A right has meaning only as a right to positively act with others, or negatively to be free from others' excessive action to one's detriment. Rights have their true meaning, and persons with them their true value, only *within* social order where they preserve a social system in counterbalance. They must take into account by very definition, the "necessary teleology of coexistence." Thus any right as opposed to another person, belongs as a duty of the other person to the former.[62] A distortion of this balance is to both sides an indignity which is subhuman.

Since rights flow from individual freedom and autonomy, and that is measured by intelligence, there will be a progressive difference in the magnitude and extension of rights between persons and an accompanying variation in individual worth and dignity. All are equal in the number of basic natural rights and all therein of equal human dignity. But not all will be equal in the developed extension or content of rights because individuals endowed with varying powers will possess personal rights commensurate with their own powers and position.[63] It is in this sense that each person has the power and immediate capacity and right to develop his personality to his own due perfection, and therefore to reach, in his own imitation of his God, a level of worth peculiar to himself, superior to some and inferior to others. But in all these varying degrees, each man still claims from his *personal* nature and goal all his necessary rights as anterior to the political rights of states which only proceed *from* persons and *for* personal development. The personal right *vim vi repellere* comes from the personal sphere, though exercised

62. Rommen, *op. cit.*, p. 193.
63. Ryan, *op. cit.*, treats this well, p. 45 ff.; also Smith, "Some American Freedoms," pp. 105–153.

only in community, and is man's first *suum* because he is an inviolable creature of supreme value in himself. This is the natural basis of his dignity and honor among men, a radiation of his person and active personality among others in the juridical and moral group. The honor and prestige is rooted *in him*, and the common juridical framework but guarantees it. Social sanction and social law are instruments for him, not man their instrument or tool.

LAW. Modern anti-intellectualism led us to a destructive application in law of positivism and relativism, which has meant a personal insecurity and position of indignity before the law resulting from the lack of a permanent standard and the overthrow of natural law as the basis of all legal justice.[64] But this is a contradiction of human nature and so of its source. The true relation of the human person makes of law a protective instrument for the development of human worth which should be public evidence of the superiority of the human person. Public law can only conform to the order outside it, and be applied with sanctions only to those beings for whose protection it is the instrument and for whose rights it is the guarantee. While persons are subjects of the law, they are so only for the social protection of their own superior dignity and permanent being, and the due development of public powers of their personality. Justice and its application, validly founded upon and measured by divine intelligence and authority, must recognize the image-dignity and fundamental *equality* of human persons, and therefore find its valid basis in that human person. The basis of ethics and justice is in the coincidence of the order of natures and ends and the social necessity of protecting equal persons from themselves, to preserve each one's proper autonomous dignity and divine image. It can only be the rational recognition of the objective ontological order which is identical with the divine will, and in humans, the law of their nature's

64. Holmes, the dominant influence in American jurisprudence and law gives the predominant evidence in himself and his philosophy of this destruction of law by legalists. Cf. *Collected Legal Papers*, especially the essay on Natural Law. Cf. LeBuffe-Hayes, *The American Philosophy of Law*, N. Y. Crusader Pr., 1947.

constitution and development. That order must be based on the immutable will of God and lead back to God, so that it can find its immediate basis only in the image-nature of humans and its imitative nature-laws of development in society. It is the nature of man which gives the frame for the law and the obligation of man then to preserve that law as such, as fitted to his divinely imitating nature. It is in his imitative office as *homo sapiens* that he participates in divine legislation by being the instructor of order. The *suum cuique* of law is not an empty formalism to be then filled up with content by the arbitrary whim of individual or state, but has itself a metaphysical content: the nature of man which comes to perfection through living in various necessary forms of society life. The metaphysical order is, under free will, identified with the moral order. Man's own perfection is the end of his being and of man-made laws, or they are not proper laws. In any one instance, both the author of a law and the subject of it are subject to the higher law upon which it must be modeled, the divine law, God's will evident in rational nature and known to that nature. So "both the validity of the authority and the dignity of the person-subject are preserved and even enhanced by the necessity and privilege of subjection to that divine law above them both." The *ordo juris* may change from time to time, but any expression of it is always measured by the *ordo justitiae* which is the law put by the Creator in human nature and is the representation there of the order and manner of expression of His own will.[65]

That is why, with this true picture of the superior dignity of the human person, and the instrumentality of laws based upon his nature and applied for his perfection, political authority can demand only reasonable obedience to its laws. Its commands must be justified before its own judge: personal reason. The person himself, though subject to it in this sense, is a value superior to law which derives its value from his. He can never be an instrument of law, but must keep law as an instrument for himself. Law is not really extrinsic to the human person, but only the external expression of his nature

65. Rommen, *op. cit.*, pp. 192, 198.

and goal and dignity, for his social operations toward developed completion within that order of human reason which is necessarily imposed upon him by his image-nature and imitative goal. Any creation of laws or application of them which is unreasonable is an abuse of reason and an invalid obstruction of the development of human persons to their due and proper perfective dignity. And on the person-subject's side, his development depends upon his reverent regard for an activity within the limits of laws which are only a reflection of that own divine-like and permanent worth residing in his image-intelligence upon which they are based. His respect for law, his obedience to it, is only his imitation of divine intelligence and his recognition of the final source of all order, legal and physical and moral, the ordered intelligence which is his own nature-model and responsible for his own supreme value in creation. Law is valuable only insofar as it coincides with human nature and helps perfect it. And human nature can progress in worth in society only insofar as persons imitate through laws divine perfection.

PERSONAL AUTHORITY. Since it is always the individual person who is of permanent value and whose perfecting is the supreme value in society, the exercise of *personal* authority by individuals is of supreme moment for individuals' active perfecting. In the first place, it must be noted that the individual differences arising from unequal endowments in rational ability not only give more value to one person than another, but naturally place a right of governing and a responsibility for governing and for its specific perfections, upon the more gifted person. In the more gifted person the divine image is obviously sharper and of more worth.[66] It is a perversion of human order as human, that among equals in development and age, the less gifted should freely dominate the more gifted. ". . . It belongs to the perfection of every nature to contain itself within that sphere and grade which the order of nature has assigned to it; namely, that the lower should be subject and obedient to the higher."[67] This uni-

66. Cf. II *Sent.*, d. 16, a. 3, solut.; I *Sent.*, d. 44, a. 1; *S.T.*, I, q. 113, a. 2, ad 3; *Prologue in Metaph.*; *Polit.*, I, cc. 3, 11, 13 (1254b); *C.G.*, III, c. 81.
67. Leo XIII, "Sapientiae Christianae," *op. cit.*, vol. 1, p. 146.

versal hierarchy we have spoken of before, and it applies in its measure and in a personalized way, among human persons. The one who holds authority, whether it be parental or public authority in civil community, is *by that* office, more an *imago Dei*, than the subject, and such authority perfects itself in exercise in the measure it directs its subjects in the proper rational human way to their proper goal. But when the authority is chosen from among equals, it is fitting that the person who is by greater talents more the image should assume the greater image-office.

In all cases the perfecting of the personality-image must be accomplished according to that power by which man is an image, according to reasonable will. Mere whim never makes a rule or command a just order, only its conformity with the purpose and personal dignity of the human person of both the authority and the subject. That man should serve another person in a way of an animal is destructive of the God-given image-nature of both the server and the served one, a deprivation of reason for the one and an abuse of it by the other. Initiative and self-direction cannot be destroyed without devaluating a man. And no authority, even parental, much less political, operates according to human image-nature and to divine will and intelligence, which assumes or attempts to enforce a total subjection beyond reason, or a subjection of all of another's person and powers and aims. The proper worth of man is consonant with his being subject to God completely in everything, but naturally subject to different human superiors only in limited ways determined by their participative office held under God. Human authorities are means of perfection for themselves, only within their relational limits in imitating divine reasonable willing and governing. And only then are they means of perfection for other persons by that directive, reasonable command-relation.[68] It is notable that all the political theories which praise power and unrestricted authority, violence and dictatorship, are fundamentally pessimistic because they misconceive the dignity of the human image-nature and misdirect human div-

68. II–II, q. 104, a. 5, ad 2.

inized persons, and so they soon meet discouragement in their non-human and imperfective process. The attempt to make authority irrationally autonomous and commanding, and to make therefore irrational and consequently impersonal means out of its subjects, is not only contrary to the superior image-being of human persons and their inviolable autonomy, but always unsuccessful and destructive, because such violence to nature is not received by nature, rational or irrational, for any abiding length of time. It is only when, in a complete and true picture, the human person is seen as the central value of all social activity that any person in authority can so exercise that divine-like office and power as to perfect his own nature in a due and personally satisfying way, and help perfect by direction the natures subject to him, both parties thus realizing their imitative purpose in life. To try to do otherwise is to doom oneself to failure. "No man may outrage with impunity that human dignity which God Himself treats with reverence, nor stand in the way of that higher life which is a preparation for eternal life . . . A man has no power over himself to consent to any treatment which is calculated to defeat the end and purpose of his being."[69] Only in Godlike action can anyone perfect in imitation his nature's implanted God-image. Therefore all offices and functions of authority, participating in a Godlike relation to human persons, increase the value and dignity of the person exercising that authority only so long as he exercises it in a manner so imitative of divine intelligence that his handling of it manifests a recognition of his own *derived* validity and the personal autonomy of the God-image subject to the right vested in him.

EDUCATION. This is no attempt to treat the specific objectives of education, much less its present defects of system or technics in our secularized civilization. Nor is it concerned with only the formal organized system of education, but with the relation of any manner of educative development and the perfectible value of human persons in those potentials which particularly make them persons, and *human*. This study is a

69. Leo XIII, "Rerum Novarum," in *op. cit.*, vol. 1, p. 190.

treatment of the divinely derived value of the human person and the consequent principles which must govern the individual and social activity of such a personal nature with such a divine destiny. Obviously, if the exact and complete truth about the human person, his nature, value and destiny are known, the applications of this are not difficult to understand, nor hard to find, even if the will to do so is impeded by other aberrations in men.

Since it is his rational power in intelligence and in intelligent willing which makes man a human and different from other creatures, which makes him *self*-perfectible, it is the whole process of education which is most specifically and intimately connected with his development of mind, and most influential perhaps upon his perfecting his will for choice actions. And taking human nature in its full implications as necessarily social, it is clear that elevation in knowledge and in knowing ability, and the perfecting of habitual tastes and strength of will, demand the opportunities of social surroundings, and the deliberate pointed help of others in instilling the requisite knowledge and habits of thought, the directions of will and the ideals necessary to continually stimulate a human person's movement according to his true nature, towards his destined and self-satisfying goal. Only the clear knowledge of the image-nature of man and the imitative character of his powers allows for a proper definition of education or the efficient carrying out of such a process. It has been shown that man is most like God in his intelligence, and most imitates God in the intelligent worship and imitation of his model. Then the process of the development of man's personality-powers must be governed above all by that standard alone which fits his nature and destiny and which will give him, in his individual measure, that imitative perfection which alone will complete his nature and satisfy that conscious and thinking person by the integrated fulfillment of his *natural* powers and tendencies. Whether at first an individual recognizes this or not, matters little. The adult analysis of the human person and the long experience of history prove what that nature is and what satisfies it deeply and permanently: so any process of education, informal in the home or community, or formal in school and class, which does not aim at nature's own goals and does not attempt to stimulate the total development of an undeveloped individual according to all nature's own imitative powers and coincidentally with all of that nature's drives and goals, is not only doomed to failure as a process in social efficiency, but devaluates the subject individual and fosters an historical disintegration in the community of persons themselves.

The relation between the person educating and the person being educated shows the distinctive development of each into the greater image of God. The educator is thereby not only developing his own image, and his imitative facility, but is by his influencing position participating in the authoritative and intelligently governing position and power of God. He holds a divine-like relation to the subject of instruction, and as such holds the responsibility in his conscious person, for an objective and a directive influence which identifies itself with the real order of being which is manifested in truth and goodness. Among the ranked values of nature and life, he must choose emphases parallel to those objective values and so instill them into the educatee. These statements are familiar, and yet they are so intimately bound up with the nature of the human person, and of such central import, and so commonly forgotten or misconceived, that they must be repeated constantly, particularly in relation to the treatment of the natural-worth of the human person. The process of education deals only with *human* beings, and must accommodate itself to that human nature as it really is. The inescapable consequence of this is that the process of education, however or wherever carried out, must know that nature and wherein consists its essential destiny and value, and must so direct that human person. This means that the measurement of all educating must be its efficiency in developing in a human person his *image*-nature and therefore must measure all its values, all its methods and all its content and aims, by their coincidence with the truth and goodness of the God in whose image each person is bound to grow. The development of the whole person evidently must be helped, but particular attention and therefore the most emphasis must be given to the development of those rational potentials which constitute most intimately the image of God. The educator must have evaluated his own values and then preserve that evaluation in the persons for whose development he is responsible. The educator is not progressing toward his own perfection and increasing his own image if he is not directing the human powers of other persons into a knowledge and a facility of national operation consonant with each one's Godlike nature. Therefore his directing must be theocentric or else it cannot be imitative of God as nature demands, either in himself or in the imitative creation of a growing divine image in the persons being educated.

For the person being educated, there lies in him a responsibility which is a necessity of natural powers to imitate the source and model of his nature and powers in the kind of knowledge acquired and the relating of that knowledge to God, and in the development of his Godlike powers into a perfected facility which is the readier imitation of the supreme immediacy of God's knowing and God's willing. The concern he may have for knowledge of material things and the mysteries of nature, the trouble he may take to protect the efficiency of the process by conducive surroundings and by the protection of the body-instrument through which his human faculties work, however rational that evaluation may be, must, if he is to evaluate truths and abilities according to their permanent and objective value in the order of being and in the created planning of God, never receive more value in his eyes, nor therefore more energy and time for him, than the spiritual values which are themselves closer to divine reality, and whose acquiring in imitation develops him into a closer image of the supreme value his initial nature has made him the dynamic image of. Otherwise, the very operation of his image-powers is able to blur the image he then is and obstruct the growth in that image to which his nature and God's plan hold him.

Upon these relations and this whole topic it is difficult to say anything without attempting to say everything. The implications of the little here said, for the current process and aims of education, are clear. The working out in detail of the dynamic relation for education between the divine image each person is, and the educational process which can have for its goal development of personalities only into that perfected image, is beyond the scope of this study. There is much written upon this and little of the right is followed in this civilization.[70] Yet everything has been said of the education of human persons when it is said that education is the social process of perfecting God's image in persons. Otherwise it is *not* education, not drawing out into operative and perfected habits the divine image implanted in each human person.

PROPERTY. It is perhaps not at first apparent what is the relation between the imitative development of personality to its true dignity, and the question of the possession and value of material property. But property owned is a kind of extension of the person, not "he" but "his," and therefore accredited to him. Its value for the perfecting of the person lies in the stability and security it gives him as an immediate environmental relation conducive to development, and as an external social sign of the independent position of the human person, a possession and a symbol which has deep psychological effects upon the possessor himself, in helping to make him conscious of his independent dignity, and stimulating him to attitudes and actions in accord with an ownership participative of God's.[71]

This question of independent ownership is intimately and ontologically connected with the human person and his development. There is such a nature in man as makes the permanent and exclusive dominion over some portion of the ma-

70. For treatments closest to this study in object, cf. Leen, *What Is Education*; Jordan, *Philosophy of Education*.

71. For some Thomistic viewpoints on this question, cf.: I–II, q. 47, a. 11; q. 50, a. 3; q. 84, a. 4; q. 105, a. 2; II–II, q. 57, a. 3; *C.G.*, III, c. 22; *De Reg. Princp.*, I, lect. 2; II, 3; Maritain, *Freedom and the Modern Man;* Berdyaev's *Destiny of Man;* Allers, "Ideas, Ideals, Idols" in *Conflict of Power in Modern Culture.*

182 THE DIGNITY OF THE HUMAN PERSON

terial universe a natural thing, a kind of limited participation in God's ownership and God's dominion, and indicative of the superiority of man over material creation. And since man's imaging of God is dynamic, since his nature is bound to development, expansion and perfection, he not only needs, for his more valuable spiritual development, the freedom of aim and movement accorded by possessions, but he expresses his own participation in divinity by his relation to his possessions and his rational use of them, and by that human working with them which effects an imprinting of his own personality upon them.[72] What is one's own is a kind of extension of his ego, and the possession of material goods follows from his make-up, from the body-spirit nature of man and from his position before the rest of creation, and his God-implanted imitative tendencies to achieve his perfected image of the Creator partly through his governing of matter. The very consciousness of self contains somehow the consciousness of property, and possessions are no arbitrary thing, but a natural impulse to extend personality, to imitate for oneself, and before other persons, the creative ownership of God and His governing dominion over what is His. This too is not a static thing, but an instrument for man's development, not just in the fact of possession which is a kind of underpinning for man's higher perfecting, but because ownership must imply use and the use of property in a rational and imitative manner after God is part of man's process of realiation of his image-nature and powers. "Die tiefste metaphysische Wurzel des Privateigentums liegt in der Gottebenbildlichkeit der menschlichen Geistperson, zu deren Wesen vernunftgemässe Disponierung und freie Verfügung über eine Sache gehört. Das 'ich' hat eine unmittelbar Beziehung zum 'es' in der Form des 'Mein.' "[73] Property is not only the

72. For a full development of this topic in its social implications, cf. McDonald, *Social Value of Property*. For his statement of this specific point, cf. p. 135 ff.
73. Meyer, Hans, *Thomas von Aquin*, p. 532. Cf. pp. 530–34. It is interesting to note that Meyer shows fairly clearly that Aquinas does not attempt to found the right of private property, as Maritain has claimed, upon the virtue of Art. Cf. p. 531.

essential guarantee of human dignity in promoting freedom of development and independence of action, but is itself part of the process of man's imitative perfecting of himself in the image of the creative and owning God.[74] Possession of material property is of major importance in giving man freedom from dependence upon matter itself, and freedom from a subhuman dependence upon other persons who do possess it. He is not only guaranteed his liberty by property, but through it exercises and *expresses* to his own satisfaction and for others' respect, his liberty and independence of both material creation and other persons. Rommen goes so far as to say that it is "morally impossible to exist as a free person without property. The sphere of freedom increases directly with the sphere of property or contrariwise . . ." the man who has no property easily becomes the property of another man and is therefore depersonalized himself and devaluated below his nature, beneath his proper personal dignity and due public respect.[75]

This whole philosophic contention that property is "part of a person" and necessary for his development to his image-perfection might well be contradicted today by anyone who is pointing out that this current civilization is full of persons who live freely without property. But that contention is subject to a great deal of debate, and we think it exceedingly difficult to show that human persons who possess no property in any sense are able to live what is actually a *human* life, and develop in a human manner toward a human goal with the readiness due to them and for which their native desires and powers are capable. In fact, the whole point of this study is that blindness to such truths as this has *caused* the modern tragedy of the depersonalization and devaluation of human beings, and by that destroyed or partially blurred in them the image of their God which is constitutive with their nature and whose development is not only a natural drive

74. Cf. Leclercq, Jacques, *Les droits et devoirs individuels*, p. 130 ff. for treatment of this point of property's guarantee to man to live in a *human* fashion.

75. Rommen, *op. cit.*, p. 189 ff.

within them, but due to them, and therefore not to be obstructed either by other persons or by themselves.

It needs little saying that the aid to personal development which is given by private ownership can become an impediment to the perfecting of personality-image. The mental attitude toward it can be founded upon a false sense of values, and the operative will in acquiring it, therefore, proceeds in a direction which is contrary to the purpose of that free spiritual choosing, in that it uses its own Godlike freedom to enchain itself again to the material creations it is intended to free itself of. In this respect, no error is modern, and the exaggerated evaluation of property is but one aspect of the tendency of humans to falsely evaluate both themselves and surrounding creation, and so let the irrational material dominate those who alone in creation are superior to matter, who are the dynamic images of spiritual intelligence itself. No one has stated the perennial error more simply than Augustine did long ago: "It pains them more to own a bad villa than a bad life, as if man's greatest good consisted in having everything good except himself."[76] This is the misuse of what is naturally good to man, because it is a misconception of object and a misdirection of energies in humans who reason against their spiritual nature in looking upon matter as an ultimate satisfaction, or who imagine that the secondary help and satisfaction of material possession can become primary and abiding by increase of quantity, when the question of value here is one of quality, when the value natural for the *human* and spiritual person must be *spirit*. It is precisely because of this aberration of values and devaluation therefore of man's goals and development, that a reconsideration of his nature and dignity is necessary. A sensist and utilitarian philosophy has made the measure of all human values a person's ability to increase material living standards, as if economic success were the proper and final measure for ethics or human perfection of spirit or consequent personal satisfaction. This has put property rights on a level above personal right and made an end out of an instrument, which immediately

76. Augustine, *De Civ. Dei*, III, 1; I, 100.

makes an instrument out of a human person who is the end. With such a contradictory attitude to all those eternal goals of spirit which made man so valuable before his Creator and in face of other persons, the very direct imitation of God in religious worship tends to become a kind of instrumental safeguard for the protection of property rights or an attempted psychotherapy to relieve the expected tension of their human and spiritual nature which cannot naturally find its satisfying perfection in such values or ends in any deep or abiding way. When the proper hierarchy of values in the rest of creation is falsified, then immediately the persons who falsify them have falsified the value of themselves and disturbed the internal and ontological order of their own nature; they thus create an inevitable tension between their natural tendencies and their natural and due ends. Property possession is natural to the human person and necessary for his proper development and his created level of free and commanding position of dignity over the rest of creation, but it is an adjunct of a person, an extension which is natural only as an instrumental means to be used in properly evaluated proportion as a help to the development of his *rational spirit* into the greater image of God, not to exaggerate his acquisitive instincts until he is an undignified slave to the material. It is rooted in human persons but not their root, and never the measure of their dignity except by their handling of it. Property is the assurance of their worth and the instrument of its free development only. It is only helpful as a ground is helpful for the development of seeds and as an external expression of a person's independence *from* matter and command over it, as indicative of his image relation to the owning Creator Himself. As such, and used as such, it is a kind of expansion of personality, and since he needs matter to free himself more and more from matter, since he needs matter even to express the creativity by which he imitates the pure spirit of his Creator, it is through his natural and personal right to private possessions and dominion that he derives the titles to the means of appropriation of possessions, occupation and work.

It is through the rightful use of material property that the human person can actively help develop his native thrust of communicative will, *to give*. It is in such use of property that he gives up himself in some way by giving what is *his* and by that mysterious spirit-process only "increases" himself, since the communication of goodness of being is always an increase of actualized being and realized goodness in the communicator. And by this same communicating, he aids in the perfecting of other persons, supplying them material means necessary for their free development of spirit. Such use of property increases the superiority of a person over matter and his free dominance of it, and the spirit-dignity of his rational person because it not only frees him from the binding claims of matter but is peculiarly imitative of the largesse of the Creator, infinitely communicating goodness and love, and so is perfective of the Creator-image in each human person. This is so much true that it is instinctively recognized by other persons and the public respect and admiration given is testimony to the inborn natural standards of human spirits and the Godlike dignity they respect and naturally want and in which alone they find permanent satisfaction of spirit.

WORK. "When man spends the industry of his mind and the strength of his body in procuring the fruits of nature, by that act he makes his own that portion of nature's field—that portion on which he leaves, as it were, the impress of his own personality."[77] In this viewpoint, the possession and right to use his own powers is transferred to the right to the products of his labor insofar as the product is considered to be "simply his energies transformed."[78] This viewpoint asserts the intimate relation between the human person who shares the creativity of God and the consequent relation he has, as does the Creator, between himself and the thing made. But the relation of particular interest at this point is the very ac-

77. Leo XIII, "Rerum Novarum" in *op. cit.*, vol. 1, p. 172. Cf. II–II, q. 180 ff.; I, q. 102, a. 3; II–II, q. 122; II *Sent.*, d. 17, q. 3; *C.G.*, III, c. 21; c. 25; III *Sent.*, d. 33, q. 2, a. 2, ad 2.

78. Killeen, S. M., *Philosophy of Labor in St. Thomas*, especially chapter on the "Dignity of Labor," pp. 52–70. Cf. McDonald, *The Social Value of Property*.

tivity of "work" as a personal and social aid in the development of man's personality and the perfection and manifestation of his human worth as the image of his God.[79]

Even the purely manual work of the human person is of a
value far beyond the effects achieved by natural forces, not
only because such work is done *by* a person and therefore
must be attributed *to* him, but also because the creative element in it, man's rational power to conceive a manufacturing
end in view and carry out his intention in actual production
by manipulation of matter, is not only an image-position of
the Creator's, but an activity which is imitative of His creative "work," and perfective of a working person. However,
it is that rational element which is perfective of the person
as person, insofar as it is intelligent and willing and aims at
good, and uses his physical powers sometimes as the fit instrument for the accomplishment of an intelligent end. Any work
man does with matter is similar, though of less value, to his
creative work in his cooperative creation of other humans by
physical generation, and is of value in the perfecting of the
person not only because he uses his powers which are God-
given and God-resembling, but because in him, the use of
all those powers is linked to and directed by intelligence, as
are God's. The intimacy of his actions with intelligence and
with an intelligent aim, and the proper rating of the action
or work according to its value for human personal perfection,
measures the value of the work.

Whether it is personal work in quasi-isolation or work in
social groups, the aim of man's labor, if it is to be an activity
instrumental in his development as a person-image of God,
must be intelligibly related to man's natural over-all purpose,
and therefore to those higher values which provide his most
human and abiding satisfaction, perfect his person, and most
reflect the supreme divine value. The more intelligence and
will for good is connected with any work in living, the more

79. This whole topic is admittedly extremely important today and a temp-
tation to lengthy discussion. We can do no more than indicate the bases of
solution and leads toward it. Certainly, since it is a *person* who works, the
solution to modern problems of work and wages lies in that person much more
than in the product or the wage.

valuable it is and the more of perfective value for the human person. If the immediate aim must be material, the more that aim and that work is kept within the frame of instrumentality, the more it retains its proper and secondary value. That such general statements of principles consonant with the image-nature of persons can be and are often mistaken, and that their mistake is realistically and intimately connected with man's progress in *human* completion and in resultant satisfactions to his person, is evident on every side. There is no argument with the necessity of sufficient work for man, who is a dynamic nature, nor with the necessity of limitation in amount of work, because he is not infinitely dynamic. Nor in society is there any argument with the necessity of recognition of that work as acquiring a value beyond the used material itself or any demand for it, by the very fact that it is a *person-product*. But the proper evaluation of work and its products, and the compensatory recognition of it in wage or profit value received, can be mistaken. Again, it is the human person *who* works, who is of value, and the work-activity is of value in the long run only because of persons, as instrumental means of their development toward God. Therefore the attitude which looks upon the worker as only an instrumental value equal to purely material and irrational instruments, is a false and devaluating attitude toward human persons. But the attitude of the worker himself which becomes apparently somewhat obsessed with the material compensation for his work-activity, is also losing sight of *human* values and is either a worker's looking upon himself as a function only or falsely thinking his perfection or even his immediate satisfaction can be found exclusively in the quantity of material pay for his personal expenditure of energies whose source is spiritual. It is not difficult to begin with an aim, for instance wages, which are a necessary social and personal instrument in a modern civilization for the free human living of persons, but so to continue striving for more and more of that material recognition that exclusive of any questions of justice, there is soon a more than remote danger that he forget the very basis of argument originally stressed in his climb from mechanical and unjust depersonalization to a position of justice and due respect for his dignity. Then personal concentration upon material pay begins *self-devaluating* the worker. He himself forgets the values most satisfying to his image-nature so what he fought for as an instrument becomes his own depersonalizing end in view.

It is again the aim and consciousness of creative activity in wholeness and intelligence and goodness and beauty which belongs to human persons and satisfies them. It is the awareness of his imitation of divine power and divine intelligence and divine creation and divine activity which is native to him most. It is pursuit of material production for this *human* reason and with this human restraint upon the valuation of matter, and with a human awareness of social helping of other persons toward their completion, toward their freedom for *human* realization, which most satisfies man because it is of his nature. Either the obstruction of human development of rational spirit by too little material recognition of his work, or that too concentrated focus of a person-worker upon material compensation, is a tampering with human nature and a false aim which cannot satisfy his native spirit nor help at all in his realization of *personal* completeness, which must be a completeness imitative of that model who is *spirit* and intelligence and will, who is goodness personified, and the very opposite of matter and quantity and temporality. It is the human person working who gives dignity to work. The labor performed further dignifies him only if it allows, and is evidence of, the active and proper imitative perfecting of his Godlike energies for a primary goal which is truly *human* and therefore divine. Values *for* man must be evaluated by the proper value *of* man, and man is valued as a person precisely because he is a *spirit*-image of all that is a contradiction of matter and the irrational. Therefore the human person is not developed in that image, nor therefore satisfied in his conscious nature, by any exclusive or exaggerated aiming at accumulation of material compensation. That this has to be reiterated is evident by a modern denial of human values, not only by those who manage both material productions and the human workers producing them, but a denial in some measure evidenced by human workers themselves, in their too great concern over accretion of material gain, a false and dissatisfying evaluation of their own human persons by humans themselves who imagine that increase of quantity of the material can satisfy a person who is so made that his primal thrusts of spirit must find satisfaction primarily in things of the spirit, and partially in material things only as instruments for his spirit. Such a proper evaluation is not a datum of revelation only, nor an ideal of social efficiency which need not be achieved. It is a simple recognition of an ontological order which cannot be denied without disintegration among things and frustration among persons. The "image of God" can be satisfied only by realities natural to God.

WORSHIP. In all relations and functions which are socio-personal, their value for human perfection arises from a human person's basic image relation to God who is supreme value. So the immediate and active relation of a human person to God in worship, as a *direct* recognition and movement toward God, both privately personal and social, is the primary and the integrating and most perfective human activity of all persons and every social grouping, a direct human-divine contact and activity so necessary to development and to the very preservation of humanness in human beings that persons and their social groups which neglect this most natural and necessary operation of their faculties and their most worthy, soon grow subhuman, or dissatisfied and frustrated, or disintegrate altogether. That is why this brief indication of the importance of using God as the standard measure of values and the model of perfection, and the importance of constant direct worship of Him privately and socially, is not a leap into theological considerations, but the most important and final conclusion coming from the study of the inescapable nature and powers of human persons and the energy-drives which can find their satisfaction only in activities and aims which fit their constituted natures.

If a human person's image-value is dynamic, and his importance must be progressively perfected in social living, his

most important functional relation and prime activity with
other persons must be his mutual activity with the original
whose image he is—with his God. No more realistic or practical statement can possibly be asserted about a human person: the image he is by nature, he cannot possibly divorce in
action from the original he is naturally intended to imitate.
Otherwise he can neither operate in the true sense of *human*
nor even understand his own image-nature in order to properly and happily act. Otherwise the puzzle he is to himself
is blacked out hopelessly from its only possible solution and
he is impeded from the exercise of any integrating and satisfying natural activity by his own lack of understanding of
the very nature which operates. He is, inescapably, an image,
and therefore his activity must imitate his original, must
recognize and in some measure understand, and then model
its actions upon that original. He is mystery enough, and
this most valuable, perfective social relation with another
person is the first necessity for his understanding of himself
and his perfecting of himself and for his daily actualization
according to his image-nature, in all his mutual activity with
other human images. Unless he first fosters his knowledge of
his Creator by the operation of his powers of mind and will,
he cannot know enough of his own make-up and the reasons
for it to act sensibly and humanly in any life activity or foster
any social improvement.

(The human person) ". . . bears in himself a mystery he will
never exhaust: an *ontological mystery,* since his own being can
never become transparent to himself save only by another, Who
is God; to see himself he must see himself in God; a *psychological
mystery,* which echoes the former, since the embodied spirit can
never apprehend himself save only through his body, the *I* only
through his *me*; and this interior tension, this ceaseless pursuit
that never ends in a capture, expresses the mystery of a spirit
too great for its matter—the mystery of a spiritual individual . . ."[80]

The mystery of a human person who is a person because he
is a rational image, is then at heart the mystery of God Him-

80. Mouroux, *op. cit.,* p. 118.

self, and man's first wisdom and first operation and prime obligation is his functional relation to that original, else the perfecting of his nature and powers and importance cannot be achieved at all but only ruined.

The same manner of bonds which tie human persons one to another, first bind a man to his Creator-original, the tie of image to original, of creature-image to Creator, of effect to cause, of dependent to his independent source. Man can efficiently operate only in imitation of Him whose image he is. Otherwise an unbearable tension will be developed in that operative nature and its disintegration only foster his own frustration and contribute to the deterioration of the natural perfections of other persons. His native prestige will be secured and his intelligence will be perfected and satisfied only if it first exercises itself upon intelligence itself, and thereafter, upon other image objects in imitation of the manner of that original intelligence's own evaluation of object. And his will, in its desires and loves, can exhibit and perfect its worth, and find natural satisfaction in an abiding manner only when all its secondary objects are measured by its first object of love and desire, its source love Himself. This does not constitute the best of many choices, but the first and necessary choice of operation for a human nature which is a derivative, participative, and dependent image-nature, without ability to chance objective values or without choice of final end in life. What is by nature an image, *must* relate itself first to its original model, must imitate it or cease being an image and destroy itself. Moreover, for this uniquely conscious creature, only such proper operation of his powers will effect satisfaction within his conscious awareness, only such will be "good" for him in any deep and stable measure and thus enable him to be perfective of other persons who are being imitative of him. Since he is constituted as an image of his God, his natural good and his personal satisfaction must arise from actions which perfect his imitative powers, in a manner of living which evidences in operation what he is in nature and which can be labeled as *godliness* in his personality, a label actually synonymous with what is truly *hu-*

man. Nothing else in his choice of standards or manner of action can substitute for what his own nature demands first and necessarily as the sum of his *human* living, and what the similar natures of other image persons demand *from* him in social living.[81] He must imitate or disintegrate and the measure of either process is the measure of his social efficiency and his human satisfaction. He must find his "good," his *person-satisfaction* in activity which measures up to his God-like dignity of nature and the God-attracted direction of his nature's deepest drives, must measure up to the level of his creation and the type of powers he has, which are rationally imitative of God and must therefore exercise themselves first upon God, and upon other creatures in imitation of God's intelligent manner. As he is first by image nature, he must be first in imitative action. He cannot perfect himself nor therefore find final satisfaction, in operations or upon objects sufficient for lower and completely material creatures, but so foreign to his rational powers as to be contradictory to them. He cannot escape from the supreme rank of dignity he holds in creation, nor the supreme value relation he alone has by his very nature to his Creator, a nature which operates under God, but above the manner and aims of other lower and irrational creatures. He alone was made to think and to love, as God does, and therefore to think of God first and love Him first, as God does Himself. In this light he must look upon himself and upon others, must measure social actions and reactions and social-personal influences, and must so direct his personal and social energies. Only in this way and in this direction and with this evaluation can a human person continue to enlarge his native dignity to the fullness of humanness which is the degree of full and destined likeness to God and the measure of his final worth and true human dignity.[82]

The human person cannot help himself. He is what he is, and his destiny and perfection must be achieved in his life's

81. Smith, "Human Social Life" in *New Scholasticism*, Oct. 1945, p. 290.
82. II–II, q. 19, a. 11, c. Cf. Rohner, "Natur und Person in der Ethik," *Divus Thomas*, 1933, p. 58; Pace, *op. cit.*, p. 214.

chosen and accelerating return to his first cause, to that ultimate reality which explains his existence and powers of
operation as any original does its image. Since in him alone
is mirrored the subsistent intelligence and love which is
God, his person must be directed to that source by the imitative operations of his rational powers of knowing and loving,
and his personality be continually actualized by the habitual
focus of those activities by which he alone can imitate, upon
that God and in the manner of that God in whose image
they find their power and end,[83] their very reason of being
and consequent value and personal satisfaction and dignity.

Although many activities are necessary to man, and all derive their relative value from him and for him, the *most human operation of a man* then is what is most divinely imitative, his direct and increasing thinking upon God Himself
and his resultant perfected rational desire for Him, which is
indirectly and progressively evidenced in all activity which
follows the pattern of choosing Him as the object and model
of activity. Primarily in the use of his rational powers will
the human person imitate his God, and in their use, imitate
supremely when they bend their energy upon the direct
knowing of Him, where their operation will most closely imitate Him who finds Himself the infinitely satisfying object
of intelligent activity and continually operates in knowing
Himself first, and then all else in and through Himself who
simultaneously operates in the direct loving of that self
whom He wholly and infinitely and continuously knows.
Man's nature demands that he so imitate by the direct study
of the nature and person of his God, and then by the concomitant choice of Him and His honor as the motivation for
and imitative mode of operation of all the actions instigated
by his will. And since man is at the same time a social person in that his activity is possible not only by relation to his
God, but even more, quantitatively and immediately, by relation to his fellow human images, all his actions toward them
and with them and for them must be motivated primarily,
if he is to imitate his original, by the knowing and honoring

83. Leo XIII, "Human Liberty," in *Social Wellsprings*, vol. 1, p. 122.

and loving of his God in and through them. He must measure by this standard all life's values for himself and others. He must by this direct imitation increase his value *for* others. This again is not the choice of many possibles, but the demand of his nature which is essentially imitative or else nonhuman. Man is, by created constitution, Godlike, and only those intelligent operations are truly human which are Godlike actions by manner and aim.

The inability of human beings to expand their person to its true human perfection, to actualize their powers into more complete personality and influence, a like development in other persons, without that divine end in view and a divinely imitative manner of operation, is empirically evident in current history. We have all too much objective and social proof of the failure of humans to remain truly and satisfyingly human when they cease recognition and worship and so cease to imitate what they were made to imitate. Once the importance of man and his very aim in living is set up supposedly without derivation from his God-value, without taking as a measure of every individual and social striving and as a standard of all human activity, the original and real upon which he is founded in image, humanity disappears in man, and he loses his value as a human person. This daily living as if human persons were not images but originals themselves, not imitators but self-sufficient creators, the attempted personal and social living of humans without their supra-human referent has visibly ended in that disorder which has best been labeled "Secularism," an attitude of mind and practice of life clearly contrary to the human image-nature and so doomed to achieve only that subhuman level of life and action which is destructive of all that makes this creature-nature human, and disruptive of all the proper operative aims of his powers which could cause in his imitative nature, his due and proper satisfaction. The pursuance of personally individual and socio-personal life upon such a basis has given experimental proof that it is not "good" for human nature, that it does not expand and complete *real persons*, that it fosters the disintegration of such personal living which alone is *human*, and causes the personal confusion and frustration and the social chaos which must result when he who is inescapably made to imitate, attempts to live without imitating.

What might have seemed a purely theoretical and perhaps grandiose viewpoint of man, that he is the peak of creation and the faint image of its God, has now been proved clearly and tragically factual, by the attempt in individual and social life to live as if that were not so. The inversion of created order and the lack of human imitation of the Creator in man's creator-like relation to the lower creation has caused man to be looked on too often as the instrument of things and, in a simultaneous contradiction, looked on as the self-sufficient god for whom things *and* other persons exist, without any further reference.[84] The "isms" of this day are only the symptoms of the universal underlying mistake of outlook and practice which misconceives the imitative make-up of human nature and the image-object of its destined perfection, and therefore of its own demanding way to personal happiness. The grossest possible indignity for man is that self-caused blindness to his image-nature which sets him up as his own original creator and standard. This false worth is so contrary to his nature that it not only misses the point of his creation and the secret of personal satisfaction, but degrades the human person into something grotesque and ultimately sad.

". . . (Our civilization's) *central* contradiction consists in the fact that our culture simultaneously is a culture of man's glorification and of man's degradation . . . an age which exalts man as the supreme end and, at the same time, vilifies man and his cultural values endlessly. . . . It is not strange that our culture has become homo-centric . . . man is its glorious center. It makes him the measure of all things. It exalts him as the hero and of the greatest value, not by virtue of his creation by God in God's own image, but *in his own right* . . . It substitutes the religion of humanity for the religion of superhuman deities. . . . Our culture and social edifice . . . has another—and more sinister face . . . the great degradation and de-humanization of man; the

84. Cf. Sheen, Fulton, *Philosophy of Religion*, p. 369.

debasement, distortion, desecration . . . of all cultural and social values. . . . Materialism identifies man and cultural values
with matter; for this reason it cannot help stripping man and his
values of any exceptional and unique position in the world."[85]

This revolt of man against his own nature and reason coincides obviously with that revolt against his Creator which
consists in the "prodigious egotism" that does not see the
need of that God either for a source of help or an object of
imitation. Revolt against one must destroy the dignity of the
other: perfection of effect is inextricably linked with perfection of cause. But current and previous history well proves
such an attitude and practice to be a rejection of civilization
itself and disintegrative of personal human nature and its
inborn dignity, because such a human "progress" always not
only falsifies what is truly valuable and satisfying to the
human person, but always ends in subjecting him to an enslavement to lower and less important realities, the profana-
tion of human purpose and values by some kind of obsessed
chaining to values beneath man which at the same time both
dehumanizes him and frustrates him with his own dehumani-
zation.[86] It is the old mistake and contradiction of nature
which is the synopsis of the errors of all men ontologically
and psychologically and religiously and socially: "vult te
Deus facere similem sui, et conaris tu Deum facere similem
tui."

So this insistence upon man's proper place and upon a
proper activity fitting his nature, personal and social, and the
insistence upon God being the conscious object of, and the
natural, sole standard and final measure for his actions and
the aim of his living and striving, is not something "idealistic"
and divorced from man, but irrefutably consequent upon

85. Sorokin, Pitrim, *The Crisis of Our Age,* pp. 242–244. At least Chap.
7 of this book should be read for the whole picture of man's devaluation. For
another sharply critical socio-philosophical picture of modern man, and some
tracing of the genesis of his present condition to former "purely theoretical"
philosophies, much interest and a great deal of truth will be found in Weaver,
Richard M., *Ideas Have Consequences* (Univ. of Chicago, 1948).

86. Smith, "Human Social Life," *op. cit.,* p. 300; St. Augustine, *Serm. IX,*
cap. 8, PL 38, 82. Cf. *C.G.,* III, c. 69.

any analysis of his nature and powers of operation. The original is the end and the model. Man is only the image and imitation. True, he is superior in that he is the only such image in creation, but he remains an image. To invert this order, as is commonly done, does not elevate a person creature, but is an unnatural apotheosis which debases a human person by destroying that in which his real dignity and consequent satisfaction must consist: in being an *image* of God and so acting in imitation of Him. He cannot be God. In assuming to oneself the prerogative of his original, history and philosophy show he not only fails and must fail, but destroys the image proper to him, and so descends to a subhuman level where there lies no dignity properly belonging to a rational animal, because the perfective completeness and conscious satisfaction of man and his operative powers, since he *is* a rational image, cannot lie in the non-rational corporeal order to which, so mysteriously, he always descends when he attempts to glorify himself as if divine. The superior in creation cannot find its perfection and happiness either in arrogating to itself the supreme, or in degrading itself to the inferior. Yet when *direct* worship of God, directly acquiring knowledge and practicing love, is lacking, such is always the final result.[87] The pursuit of supposed goals in life, and a manner of acting either as if there were only matter and men and no God, or as if he were himself God, is for any created human person a destruction of himself, because it is a contradiction of his image-nature and imitative powers wherein lies his value and dignity. He can neither abandon himself to complete "subjectivity" (as would a modern and rather fantastic movement in philosophy) nor completely to an "objectivity" which is immersion in matter, because he is neither God nor solely matter.[88] The realizations of the potential perfections of a human person must be accomplished according to and in

87. Cf. *S.T.*, I–II, q. 2, a. 5, c.; *Comp. Theol.*, II, c. 9; *C.G.*, III, c. 32. Cf. also Gilson, *Thomisme*, p. 493 (5th ed.).

88. Cf. Maritain, *Existence and the Existent*, p. 75 ff.; Pius X, "Casti Connubii," in *Social Wellsprings*, vol. 2, p. 159; Rommen, *The Natural Law*, p. 237; Pace, "Assimilari Deo," *New Scholasticism*, II, No. 4 (October 1928), p. 342.

harmony with a nature which is essentially an intelligent image of its maker, and therefore all the attitudes and actions of a human person must refer to and be modeled upon God's activity and follow God's divine created plan and order as the exemplar for any human order and happiness. Only with this reference to a common original can human image-persons themselves unite and achieve both completion of nature and satisfaction of spirit among themselves.

It is a historical fact that when social man ceases group worship of his God, he soon ceases private worship of Him and adherence to His law, and that the refusal to follow his socially imitative nature in socially worshipping the Creator, soon and always results in attitudes and actions which not only destroy the esteem due to that Creator, but the human dignity always and necessarily related to it. Man's very nature needs for the stimulus of practice and development what is its highest imitation and dignity, the direct worship of his model source. Such worship can no more be limited to private personal worship than man can develop his faculties in isolation. Moreover he is bound by social ties to other persons to help in their development, and their actualization demands from him the sensible stimulus of his own worshipping. His nature is such that he always shows a consequential connection between a deterioration of public worship and a resultant deterioration of private worship and private morals and personal satisfaction with life, and finally often a blindness altogether to his whole nature and purpose as an image in being and an imitation progressively perfect of his Creator in action. When he does not worship his Creator directly he soon does not recognize him indirectly in his temporal living and working and the result always is that he obscures the sight of his own true nature and the ranked values of his inner natural drives. Consequently, he has the same blurred picture of the natures and satisfactory aims of other persons, and his personal deterioration into the less human is bound to be influential in the person-deterioration of the humans who live around him. It is historically evident that human persons, for the continued direction of all man's social activity toward its proper and satisfying channels and goals, must preserve the end in view and the current *tone* of his personal and social atmosphere by direct social worship, else he cannot fulfill his obligation of fostering a perfective milieu of social grouping for other persons who are person-images of God who need for stability and perfecting possi-bility, the conscious and direct recognition of that God in their personal and social living.[89]

The public respect a human person receives is testimony to the divinely derived value he has. The preservation of his own recognition that he has only a derived dignity and the consequent perfecting of his personality as an image and not an imagined original, demands his constant and public recog-nition of the original. Only the human creature *knows,* and only he can *know* his Creator. Only men can worship their God. And however fantastic it may sound, it has been shown to be tragically true that in the measure humans quit wor-shipping divinity, in that measure they become inevitably even less than human. Man is so related to his God, and the social grouping of men so related to their God, that the preser-vation of personal and social values and the chance at per-fecting, not destroying, human personality depends upon the constancy and depth of man's worship of that God. God alone measures man's value and worth, measures man's dignity, which consists in his resemblance to divinity. And the com-pletion of that human dignity to its full perfection is pos-sible only when man's personal and social life includes and is even integrated by and governed by and stimulated by the persistent direct worship of his God which always preserves in the rest of social actions that human imitation of God that is so essential to, and so much the measure of, a true human dignity, that dignity of the human person derived from his image nature, a dignity which must be characterized, although with created limitations, as something divine.

89. R. J. Giguere, *The Social Value of Public Worship,* Catholic Univer-sity of America Press, 1950; V. J. Sheppard, *Religion and the Concept of Democracy,* Catholic University of America Press, 1949.

Conclusion

THE dignity of each human person is founded upon the fact that each one is an image of God. The aim of human life and the satisfaction of each person's deepest desires must be, inescapably, to grow into greater likeness of his God by active imitation of Him in intelligent living, according to *His* plan and *His* manner and so according to the image-intelligence of each person's nature. For this, men need thought and love within them and peace around them.[1] These are truisms. Yet the tragedy of our civilization is that they are true still in a time when no one seems to believe they have any practical significance. The very facts of human nature which constitute the unique superiority of a human person in creation, his intelligence and freedom and his permanence, are the facts least considered by current cultures.

Today more than ever before, there is wide use of the phrase, "the dignity of man." But there is less evidence than ever of any realization of the intelligent root of his dignity and the image quality of his nature. In such a situation, it is difficult to draw conclusions which are rational and philosophical and have practical application for social living and personal achievement, because the modern person, as a type, has so long discarded the proper use of intelligence that the remedy he needs first is some shocking stimulation of will to make him want to use his brains above his passing emotional states, and want to readjust his values.

Men have apparently forgotten what most must constitute

1. *C.G.*, III, c. 117: "Ad hoc quod homo divinis vacet, indiget tranquillitate et pace."

their own human satisfaction, the satisfaction of their own complete and true and unavoidable natures. When they fight for justice in economic fields, they fight only for material possessions, although such a diagnosis begins to need qualification lately. (Cf. the "Scanlon Plan," *Fortune*, Jan. 1949.) When they struggle for equality in geopolitical fields, they contend only for power; when they battle for individual freedom, they wage war only against any restraint upon their material comforts and their unrestrained physical desires. But none of these aims is the destiny of a human person nor feeds for long man's personal spirits. They are useless attempts to escape man's own nature and what is useless for creatures who are conscious and feeling and thinking creatures, always becomes sad and painful to them. The created person's worth comes from his rational, spiritual nature, because only that humanness is the image of the creating spirit. To remain *human* in the true sense, and attain the only happiness which can possibly satisfy a spirit for long, he must value the non-material *first* and aim his divinely imitative powers at the things his God aims at, *not first* possession of greater and greater quantities of matter or the quickly boring satisfactions of materials or of corporal comforts.

All we have shown in the preceding pages of the natural dignity of men and the type of human satisfactions which alone can fit their natures, all this history and personal experience have proved to be so. It is a truism. The only conclusion to be drawn is that our civilization today can *no longer afford* to forget that these things *are* true, permanently and unavoidably and painfully true. It is an explosion of truth we need. Man's personal nature is like his God's. In living his life, then, a man must imitate his God if he is to remain human and happy. It is all too evident always that when men forget their derived and participative and image nature enough to forget God, they do not act human. As they quit praying, they quit laughing. When they quit being an imitating image, they cannot be human—they must become sad misfits in nature.

The indestructible thinking and loving nature of human

persons must be lived up to. Not what a human person *has,* but what he *is,* alone constitutes his dignity and his happiness. Men must again be considered for what they truly are, and that means that the present chaos can be ordered again only by considering men's God, else no one can understand what men need nor wherein their worth lies, they whom alone in creation God made "into His own image and likeness." Men must look upon themselves and upon other persons as reflections of God upon earth and because of that, as wonderful creations. Men themselves, *in themselves,* are valuable and satisfying because men *contain the allure of God.* "Absolute, separate, simple, and everlasting . . . Beauty . . . which without diminution and without increase, or any change, is imparted to the ever-growing and ever-perishing beauties of all other things."[2] Because a human person is what he is, he is *the* prize of all creation. Because he is by image an intelligent creature, he can be appreciated only as such and can himself appreciate only the things related to such intelligent and wise living as imitates the living of God.

We must again see, if today we can still reach peace and happiness and any encouraging reason to look at any future, how little man is before his God, and how great he is in the face of land and oil and machines and arms, and even The Bomb. Human persons must again be seen as *human,* in meanings they have forgotten "human" had. And the human must be seen in a certain measure and manner, as *divine.* Men must not be approached as animals. We face each other as intelligent images of God. Our native rational appreciation of the God-model whose image we are, our native love of what is like us, and our natural recognition of the value and dignity of both our God and His divine images around us in men, must prompt us once more to approach our God, and almost also our fellow man—upon our knees.

2. Plato, *Symposium,* in *Dialogues of Plato,* Tr. B. Jowett, Random House (1937), p. 335.

Index